Aging from Birth to Death

Volume II: Sociotemporal Perspectives

AAAS Selected Symposia Series

Published by Westview Press, Inc.
5500 Central Avenue, Boulder, Colorado

for the

American Association for the Advancement of Science
1776 Massachusetts Avenue, N.W., Washington, D.C.

Aging from Birth to Death

Volume II: Sociotemporal Perspectives

Edited by Matilda White Riley,
Ronald P. Abeles, and
Michael S. Teitelbaum

AAAS Selected Symposium **79**

AAAS Selected Symposia Series

This book is based on a symposium which was held at the 1981 AAAS National
Annual Meeting in Toronto, Ontario, January 3-8. The symposium was sponsored
by AAAS Section K (Social, Economic, and Political Sciences) and was co-
sponsored by the Gerontological Society, the American Sociological Association,
the American Anthropological Association, the Society for the Study of Social
Biology, and AAAS Section H (Anthropology).

Copyright © 1982 by the American Association for the Advancement of Science

Published in 1982 in the United States of America by
     Westview Press, Inc.
     5500 Central Avenue
     Boulder, Colorado 80301
     Frederick A. Praeger, President and Publisher

Library of Congress Catalog Card Number 78-20320
ISBN 0-86531-382-2

Printed and bound in the United States of America

About the Book

The ways in which people age from birth to death over the life course depend upon where and when they live. Much evidence has been gathered to demonstrate that aging is not an immutable process; rather, aging varies as social structure varies and changes. But *how* does the life course vary? Under what conditions of place and time do particular individuals age in particular ways? This book, a companion to *Aging from Birth to Death: Interdisciplinary Perspectives* (edited by Matilda White Riley; AAAS Selected Symposium 30; Westview, 1979), addresses these questions from two perspectives. From the cross-cultural perspective, anthropologists and sociologists examine the cultural variability of aging as this variability reveals the nature and extent of social and cultural influences on the aging process, the lives of people of all ages, and the general significance of age norms and age-graded institutions in society. From the cross-temporal perspective, historians, sociologists, and demographers examine the impact of social change both on the process of growing up and growing old and on the place in society of people of all ages. The authors stress that the changing society is composed of people who are aging and who are not only shaped by, but are also continually shaping social institutions, values, and technologies. Thus, the book provides deeper understanding of the aging process, of the likely differences between the lives of past and future generations, and of the potential for optimizing these future lives.

About the Series

The *AAAS Selected Symposia Series* was begun in 1977 to provide a means for more permanently recording and more widely disseminating some of the valuable material which is discussed at the AAAS Annual National Meetings. The volumes in this *Series* are based on symposia held at the Meetings which address topics of current and continuing significance, both within and among the sciences, and in the areas in which science and technology impact on public policy. The *Series* format is designed to provide for rapid dissemination of information, so the papers are not typeset but are reproduced directly from the camera-copy submitted by the authors. The papers are organized and edited by the symposium arrangers who then become the editors of the various volumes. Most papers published in this *Series* are original contributions which have not been previously published, although in some cases additional papers from other sources have been added by an editor to provide a more comprehensive view of a particular topic. Symposia may be reports of new research or reviews of established work, particularly work of an interdisciplinary nature, since the AAAS Annual Meetings typically embrace the full range of the sciences and their societal implications.

WILLIAM D. CAREY
Executive Officer
American Association for
the Advancement of Science

Contents

About the Editors and Authors

Matilda White Riley *is associate director for behavioral sciences research at the National Institute on Aging and professor emeritus of sociology, Rutgers University and Bowdoin College. She has worked extensively in the fields of research methodology, mass communications, and the sociology of age and aging. Her publications include* Sociological Traditions from Generation to Generation *(with R. K. Merton; Ablex, 1980),* Aging from Birth to Death: Interdisciplinary Perspectives *(AAAS Selected Symposium 30; Westview, 1979), and* Aging and Society *(3 vols.; Russell Sage Foundation, 1968-1972).*

Ronald P. Abeles *is responsible for social-psychological studies of aging at the National Institute on Aging. Formerly on the staff of the Social Science Research Council's Committee on Life Course Perspectives on the Middle and Later Years and the Committee on Work and Personality in the Middle Years, he has done research on the interrelationships of work and personality and on the consequences of temporal patterning of life events for an individual's socioeconomic outcomes.*

Michael S. Teitelbaum, *a demographer by training, is senior associate at the Carnegie Endowment for International Peace. He has done research on the aging of populations, fertility and mortality trends in the developing world, the British fertility decline of the nineteenth century, and the social and biological bases of sex differences.*

Anne Foner, *professor of sociology at Rutgers University, has specialized in the sociology of age, social stratification, and social theory. She has published on age conflicts in political life, transitions over the life course, and work and retirement in a changing society. Her books include* Aging and Retirement *(with K. Schwab; Brooks/Cole, 1981) and* Aging and Society, Vol. 1: An Inventory of Research Findings *(with M. W. Riley) and* Aging and Society, Vol. 3: A Sociology of Age Stratification *(with M. W. Riley and M. Johnson; both volumes published by the Russell Sage Foundation, 1968 and 1972, respectively).*

Nancy Foner *is an associate professor of anthropology at the State University of New York, Purchase. She has done research on aging and on Caribbean populations and migration. She is the author of* Status and Power in Rural Jamaica: A Study of Educational and Political Change *(Teachers College Press, 1973),* Jamaica Farewell: Jamaican Migrants in London *(University of California Press, 1978), and* Old Age: A Comparative View of Inequality and Conflict *(in progress).*

Christine L. Fry *is an associate professor of anthropology at Loyola University of Chicago. She has studied the cultural dimensions of age, community formation among the elderly, and cross-cultural attributes of aging. She is the editor of* Dimensions: Aging, Culture and Health *and* Age in Culture and Society: Comparative Perspectives and Strategies *(Praeger, 1981 and 1980, respectively) and* New Methods for Old Age Research: Anthropological Alternatives *(with J. Keith; Center for Urban Policy, Loyola University of Chicago, 1980).*

Dennis P. Hogan *is assistant professor of sociology and faculty associate of the Population Research Center, University of Chicago. He has specialized in demography, social stratification, and life-cycle transitions, and he is the author of* Transitions and Social Change: The Early Lives of American Men *(Academic, 1981).*

Sally L. Hoover *is a statistical analyst at the Center for Demographic Studies, Bureau of the Census, Washington, D.C. A specialist in demography, human ecology, and gerontology, she has written on various problems facing the elderly, including criminal victimization and the effects of the energy crisis on older homeowners. She is coeditor of* Community Housing: Choices for Older Americans *(with M. P. Lawton; Springer, 1981).*

Denis F. Johnston *is a senior research scientist at the American Institutes for Research in Washington, D.C. A former senior advisor on social indicators for the Bureau of the Census's Center for Demographic Studies, he is the author of* Social Indicators III *(Washington, D.C.: U.S. Government Printing Office, 1981).*

Michael B. Katz, *professor of education and history at the University of Pennsylvania, has specialized in North American social history. He is the author of* The Social Organization of Early Industrial Capitalism *(with M. J. Doucet and M. J.*

Stern) and The People of Hamilton, Canada *(Harvard University Press, 1982 and 1975, respectively), and* Class, Bureaucracy, and Schools *(Praeger, 1975).*

Jennie Keith, *an associate professor of anthropology at Swarthmore College, has done research on the social significance of age, age groups, and community formation by old people. She is the author of* Old People as People: Social and Cultural Influences on Aging and Old Age *(Little, Brown, 1982) and* Old People, New Lives: Community Creation in a Retirement Residence *(University of Chicago, 1977; paperback ed., 1982).*

David I. Kertzer, *associate professor of anthropology at Bowdoin College, has done research and published extensively on life-course transitions, Italian household composition and life course, and African age-set societies.*

Albert Simkus, *assistant professor of sociology at the University of Michigan, Ann Arbor, has specialized in comparative social stratification. He has published on comparative social mobility and on residential segregation among socioeconomic groups.*

Barbara Boyle Torrey, *a fiscal economist at the Office of Management and Budget, is concerned with the impacts of an aging population on the federal budget, and especially with demographic shifts and their effects on pension systems and retirement-age policy.*

Maris A. Vinovskis *is professor of history and research scientist at the Center for Political Studies, University of Michigan, Ann Arbor. A member of the board of editors of the* Journal of Family History, *he has published numerous articles and books, including* Studies in American Historical Demography *(Academic, 1979) and* Family and Population in Nineteenth-Century America *(with T. K. Hareven; Princeton University Press, 1978).*

_____ *Matilda White Riley, Ronald P. Abeles*

Introduction:
Life-Course Perspectives

Three years ago the stage was set for this book by the AAAS Selected Symposium entitled Aging from Birth to Death: Interdisciplinary Perspectives.[1] Three years ago we took a radical approach--an approach that embraces the entire life course and that relates it to the changing society. The approach was so fruitful that it is continued in this second volume.[2]

Contributors to the earlier symposium sought new understandings of the aging process as the product of hitherto unexplored complex interconnections among phenomena examined in widely disparate fields of study. They spoke for sociology, lifespan and experimental psychology, economics, history, demography, biomedical sciences, and even that elusive field--futurology. Despite the difficulties of interdisciplinary communication, their several contributions gave support to four central principles of the life-course perspective, each principle in itself in some way radical:

1. Aging is influenced by the society in which people live.

> Aging is not a completely immutable process; it varies as society varies and changes. Human beings do not grow up and grow old in laboratories, but in highly diverse and changing social environments. Thus, within a single society, rich and poor, black and white, male

---

[1]Matilda White Riley (ed.), AAAS Selected Symposium 30. Boulder, Colorado: Westview Press. 1979.

[2]This Introduction benefits from suggestions and criticisms from Anne Foner, authors of the other chapters, and John W. Riley, Jr. The volume as a whole benefits from the skillful clerical assistance of Kathleen Gordon.

and female age in different ways. Moreover, in differing societies, and at differing historical periods, patterns of aging vary. Aging is anything but fixed for all time and for every individual. Yet this is a radical view, countering the intuitive sense that our own life experiences constitute the aging process.

2. The ways in which people age are continually re-shaping society.

Not only does society influence people's lives, but these lives in turn, when so influenced, bring about changes in society. As people are socialized to changing norms, adopt new beliefs and behaviors, live longer, such changes in their lives create social changes. Again this is a radical view that departs from conventional treatments of aging and of social change.

3. Aging is a lifelong process of growing up and growing older.

Aging does not begin, as common parlance implies, at some arbitrary point in mid-life. Rather, it begins with birth and ends with death. According to this principle, no single stage in the aging process (childhood, adolescence, adulthood, senescence) can be understood apart from its antecedents and consequences; nor can people of one age be understood apart from those people of all other ages who co-exist in the same society.

4. Aging is a complex process, composed of interdependent biological, psychological, and social sub-processes.

Aging is not, as commonly believed, a single, biologically determined process. Without exception, to be sure, every human being is born and every human being dies. Yet the uncommon sense is that, as people's bodies change during the life course, their minds are also subtly changing, and they are also moving through a continually changing society. The ways in which they experience social roles, interact with others, and accumulate wisdom and experience exert profound influence on how they live and how well and how long they live.

During the years intervening since publication of the first volume, the evidence in support of these principles continues to mount. Yet the principles remain global and

abstract. Much further exploration and testing are needed to
specify the conditions under which these principles hold true
and to uncover the mechanisms through which they operate.
This second volume, devoted to sociotemporal perspectives,
begins to address this need. Still remaining for future
symposia are elaborations of other aspects of the life-course
approach, including the biosocial perspective which is a
topic for the 1982 annual meeting of the AAAS. Taken
together, these efforts reach toward deeper understanding of
the aging process, of the differences between the lives of
past and future generations, and of the potential for
optimizing these future lives.

Synopsis of the Book

This volume on sociotemporal perspectives is guided by
the first two of these principles set out three years ago:
(1) that aging is influenced by the society in which people
live and (2) that the ways in which people age are continually re-shaping society. It is already clear that people's
lives—the ways people age over the life course from birth to
death—depend upon where and when they live. But, if aging
is not a completely immutable process, how does it vary as
social structure varies and changes? Under what conditions
of place and time do particular individuals age in particular
ways? What mechanisms provide for mutability of aging?

Contributors to the symposium[1]/ from anthropology,
sociology, history, economics, and demography were asked to
consider such questions, treating from their own disciplinary
framework topics of their own selection. Their diverse
approaches are both cross-cultural and cross-temporal. Some
chapters consider how age is built into the norms and
structures of society. They examine the sociocultural
variability of aging as this variability reveals the nature
and extent of sociocultural influences on the aging process,
the lives of people of all ages, and the general significance
of age norms and age-graded institutions. Other chapters are
concerned with the relation of aging to the past and to the
future. They examine the influence of social changes both on
the process of growing up and growing old and on the place in
society of people of all ages.

---

[1]/In addition to the AAAS (Sections K and H), this
symposium was sponsored by the American Sociological
Association, the American Anthropological Association, the
Gerontological Society of America, and the Society for the
Study of Social Biology.

Since the chapters were not planned to form a comprehensive whole, there are overemphases and omissions. In particular, far more attention is paid to the later than to the earlier years of life--undoubtedly because of the revolution in longevity. The world is now confronted not only with vast numbers of older people, but also with older people who remain competent far beyond the age of retirement. Comparatively little attention is paid to genetic dispositions or to early life experiences as these may interact with the aging process as precursors to later life. There is little reference, for example, to such important cross-cultural studies as those on the later-life implications of intimate bodily contact between infant and parent, or those on age grading that brings little children more into contact with peers than with adults. There is little reference to such striking parallels as that between discoveries of the untapped potential reserves both in the neonate and in the octogenerarian. These and many other omissions underscore the aim of the book--to stimulate continuing conceptualization and specification of the life-course perspective.

The opening chapter by Matilda Riley, "Aging and Social Change," provides background for several major themes that run through the book. Epitomizing the volume's innovative approach, this chapter contends that there is a dynamic interplay between people growing older and society undergoing change. First, it reviews evidence that there is such an interplay. It illustrates how the changing society is composed of people who are aging and who are not only shaped by, but are also continually shaping, social institutions, values, and technologies. Second, the chapter provides emerging clues to the mechanisms linking together aging and social change. Such linking mechanisms are explained as: the flow through the society of successive cohorts, each cohort composed of people born at the same unique historical period, so that members of different cohorts cannot age in precisely the same ways; life-long socialization, which is not restricted to the early years, as often believed, but continues throughout life, thus allowing individuals to adjust to social change; and the tensions and potential conflict among young, middle-aged, and old people in society, who differ both in experience and in access to material benefits and positions of power and prestige.

Aging in Society

Among the major themes from the opening chapter that can be discerned in subsequent chapters is the view of society as an age-stratified system affecting the aging of its members.

Basic to this theme is the need for a clear distinction between "generation" and "age" as two important and distinct elements of social stratification that can influence aging. In his chapter on "Generation and Age in Cross-Cultural Perspective," David Kertzer notes that throughout history in most human societies, generation in the kinship sense has provided a major basis of social structure. Yet, if this concept of generation is used to order relations beyond the nuclear family, a tension often results from the conflict between people's social position (their status, roles, etc.) as determined by their generational location and their social position as linked to age. Kertzer cites several anomolous situations as examples of such conflict. Thus where generational categories govern the selection of marriage partners, a girl may be regarded as the "grandmother" of a neighboring boy who is two to three years older than she. Or the early death of a senior kinsman can mean that a youth must settle down to social elderhood and become a homestead head, even if according to age he should be "living it up" as a member of a bachelor set. Stressing the importance to aging of both generation and age as structural features of society, Kertzer provides a thorough exegesis of the literature on "generation." He points to the conceptual confusion emanating from multiple usages of the term that refer both to descent relationships and to age groupings. He concludes with the plea, which we underscore, to reserve "generation" for the kinship context, while using "cohort" as a set of people of similar age born at approximately the same period.

The chapter by Christine Fry and Jennie Keith, "The Life Course as a Cultural Unit," though using different terms and a gerontological emphasis, also focuses on the general notion of aging within an age-stratified society. The life course is examined as a culturally shaped unit, which organizes the timing and the meaning of the span between birth and death, and which provides a basis for stratification and allocation of roles in society. Based on a search through the anthropological literature, these authors set out several postulates requiring further research. For example, separate housing and sleeping arrangements, organized by age, appear to be common in many societies, possibly tending to reduce conflict across age lines. Cross-age alliances, or alternate generation alliances between grandparents and grandchildren, may be useful in counterbalancing the power or authority of those in the middle. Egalitarian relationships between age-mates occur most frequently among those "out of power," namely, pre-adults and the very old. Age stratification or differentiation appears to be complementary, rather than subsidiary to, other types of social stratification.

Also reporting on a comparative analysis of age inequalities and age relations, Nancy Foner's chapter on "Some Consequences of Age Inequality in Nonindustrial Societies" views age systems as systems of social inequality. Members of different age strata (i.e., socially recognized divisions based on age) not only differ in age or life stage but they also have unequal access to highly valued roles and social rewards. Such social inequality means that the potential for discord and strain is always present. Those at the top of the age hierarchy, who are often the elderly in nonindustrial society, may be resented by those below. Moreover, as many older people become downwardly mobile because of their age, losing rewards and privileges, they may resent the more successful young and become bitter over their own declines. By analyzing certain trouble spots between young and old, Nancy Foner dispels the notion of old age as idyllic in nonindustrial societies. Her analysis shows that, whether or not the old are given a privileged status, and how great the tensions may be among people of different ages, depend upon the nature of the age stratification system of the entire society.

Moving from the level of the social system to the level of the aging individual, Dennis Hogan investigates the role of social structure in influencing the timing and sequencing of age-graded transitions through which American males move from youth to adulthood. While many millions of individual decisions are involved, these decisions appear to be channeled by normative expectations about the appropriate age ranges for completing school, beginning a first job, or entering first marriage, as well as by normative expectations prescribing an appropriate sequence of these transitions. For example, most persons agree that it is desirable to delay marriage until after schooling is completed. However, such normative expectations are presumed to vary with the young man's position in society as, for example, those of higher social status are more likely than other men to stay in school longer, to start work later, and to marry before completion of schooling. Using a sophisticated quantitative analysis of a large sample of young men, Hogan's chapter on "Subgroup Variations in Early Life Transitions" investigates the joint effects on transition timing and sequencing of three aspects of societal position: social class, size of community of residence, and ethnic ancestry. Moreover, though mentioned but not reported in this chapter, Hogan's analysis foreshadows the theme of subsequent chapters by noting that both timing and sequencing of early life transitions varies substantially by cohorts as well as by position in society: men born in more recent cohorts, like higher status men generally, are more likely than men in earlier cohorts to stay in school longer, to start work later, and to marry before finishing school.

History and Aging

A second major theme introduced in Chapter 1, that aging is responsive not only to social structures but also to historical changes that affect these structures, is developed in several other chapters in the volume.

Two chapters on pre-industrial America written by historians, Maris Vinovskis and Michael Katz respectively, show how aging can be affected by longterm changes in the economy, the spiritual and intellectual climate of society, and the family. Vinovskis selects for attention "'Aged Servants of the Lord': Changes in the Status and Treatment of Elderly Ministers in Colonial America." He uses Puritan ministers in New England as a prototype for understanding the lives of older people in the 17th and 18th centuries. Controverting the widespread static view of the status and care of the elderly as constant and unchanging in pre-industrial America, he documents dramatic differences in the aging process among three cohorts of ministers. The first cohort migrated from England in the 1630s and 1640s under a unique set of circumstances which insured most of them respect, admiration, and power as they aged in the New World. The second cohort came to the colonies in the 1660s and 1670s, at a time when the high population growth and economic prosperity experienced by their predecessors had dwindled. This cohort faced not only poor economic conditions but also a waning of the spiritual ardor of their congregations. Thus, as the members of this cohort grew old, they did not receive the same respect and veneration from their parishioners as the earlier cohort. The third, most recent cohort, composed of ministers graduating from Harvard or Yale in the first half of the 18th century, fared even less well. They were confronted with inflation, the Great Awakening (which precipitated disputes between ministers and their congregations), and the inability to send even one son to Yale or Harvard. Thus in old age this cohort, and especially their widows, suffered--not because of age per se--but because of economic and religious circumstances that were unfavorable. The details of the analysis give cogency to the author's call for a dynamic perspective "which places the aging process within its proper historical context."

In Katz' view, aging individuals as members of families make myriad choices among the limited opportunities afforded by the impact of social change upon domestic life. In his chapter on "Families and Early Industrialization: Cycle,

Structure, and Economy," the family appears as an "institution in process," moving through a series of relatively well-demarcated stages in its own cycle, and also reflecting the pressures and inequalities of the social order of which it is a part. While all families possess a cycle, a structure, and a domestic economy, these three attributes assume different forms in response to historical changes. Major changes in the organization of family life, changes familiar to students of the 20th century, are analyzed here as they occurred during early industrialization (in 19th century New York and Ontario): the nuclearization of the household, the separation of home and work, and the decline in marital fertility. In explicating the nature of these historical processes, Katz emphasizes the relation of the family to the class structure and the economy of the larger society. Moreover, reflecting the dialectic in Chapter 1 between individual aging and social change, Katz shows how the process of family change is not evolutionary but dialectical. For example, the family formations responsive to the historical shifts toward industrial capitalism unleashed newly dependent and exploited strata among women and young people, which in turn produced such social changes as the increased authority over the family of the state through schools, courts, and welfare systems. Thus, as Katz concludes, "family forms partly generate the contradictions which lead to their supercession."

The theme of the influence of history on aging is carried one step further by Albert Simkus who examines this influence both on patterns of aging within given cohorts and on differences in patterns of aging among cohorts. The chapter by Simkus is entitled "Socio-economic Careers in the Context of Radical Social Change: Evidence from Hungary." Focusing on the relationship between socio-economic careers of individuals and radical historical changes in socio-economic structures, Simkus uses as his crucible the historical changes in Hungary during the last 50 years. The extent of these changes has been awesome, involving a rapid transition from agriculture to industry and a high degree of state intervention. Moreover, there exists for Hungary an unusually rich collection of data describing many of these changes as they affect both the nation as a whole and the careers of individuals. Through skillful analysis, Simkus demonstrates how radical social changes can bring substantial alterations in the aging process through within-career shifts. However, in regard to the higher social positions requiring above average education and training, he finds that cross-cohort differences are likely to be the greatest source of change; and that those within-career shifts which do occcur tend to take place during relatively young ages. If

such patterns are apparent even in the case of a country
experiencing such rapid transformations of its labor force as
Hungary, Simkus postulates that these patterns should be even
clearer in societies going through more gradual changes.
Thus he formulates an important question for further
research: under what conditions are changes in the social
order likely to have greatest effect primarily on those
persons just beginning their careers during the critical
period?

Toward Understanding the Future

A third theme, running through the remaining chapters,
concerns the utility of the life-course perspective in
anticipating the future. Many people who will be alive in
the years 2000 or 2020 belong to cohorts whose earlier lives
are already in place and can be traced into the future. Many
policy questions of current concern can be most judiciously
deliberated against the background of the possible
consequences for cohorts already born.

A case in point is the chapter by Barbara Torrey on "The
Lengthening of Retirement," which defines this vexatious
issue in life-course terms. For example, when Bismarck first
established a public retirement system in 1885, setting the
age of retirement at 70 years, life expectancy at birth was
approximately 42 years. Today a retirement age that bears
the same proportionate relationship to life expectancy (now
73 for the United States) would be 122 years of age! The
20th century's revolution in extension of life means not only
that the numbers of old people are increasing, but that more
and more individuals can look forward to living out their
lives to the full. As life expectancy has been extended, the
proportion of the adult life that might be spent in retirement has also increased. In the United States, when the
Social Security Act was passed in 1935, the average 20-year-
old adult could plan to spend almost four years at the end of
life in retirement—about 7% of adult life. Today, the
average 20-year-old can plan to spend nearly 13 years in
retirement—or 23% of adult life. By calling attention to
this striking increase in the share of adult life devoted to
retirement, Torrey points to perhaps the largest historical
change in the benefits from Social Security, but one rarely
recognized in this form. It is against this background, with
the implications for how people can benefit from these added
years, that Torrey redefines the question of how and to what
extent society can support the added years.

In a similar vein, Denis Johnston and Sally Hoover in
"Social Indicators of Aging" point to many ways in which

"being old" in the past will differ from "becoming old" in the future. The data are interpreted to show that the older population of the United States is growing older, healthier, better educated, and more independent with respect to marital status and living arrangements. It is also becoming less poor and less active economically. The chapter concludes with the question of quality of life: are older people becoming increasingly happy and satisfied with their lot?

The concluding chapter by Anne Foner, "Perspectives on Changing Age Systems," provides its own integration of the diverse materials in this book. Attitudes towards old and young, and the relations among age strata, have changed over the last several centuries and will predictably continue to change in the future. As the age structure changes, so does the process of aging over the life course. Such structural changes cannot adequately be explained, as is commonly attempted, simply through external processes such as the processes of modernization or other historical changes outside the age stratification system of society. For there are also processes at work within the age system itself which inevitably lead to change. Since age systems are systems of social inequality, conflicts between the advantaged and the disadvantaged can generate change. And because age systems must accommodate to the continuous succession of new cohorts of personnel, tensions and imbalances within the system are bound to create pressures for change. Thus a comprehensive approach to changes in the aging process must consider how the age system is influenced by internal forces interacting with external social, economic, demographic, and epidemiological trends.

As to the future, Anne Foner concludes with a cautionary note. In dealing with societal changes, new cohorts will help fashion future age systems, and some of the outcomes can be anticipated. But by no means all of the outcomes can. For the operation of processes internal to the age system interact with large-scale political, economic, and social trends--and the direction of these trends is uncertain. "People may not make history as they please," as she restates Marx, "but they do make history, often with unintended consequences."

1. Aging and Social Change

Research on aging stands at the frontiers of science.* As sociologists, we have formulated two general principles that are generating new insights into the aging process and its relation to the changing society. We have come a long way toward demonstrating the first of these principles: that aging is not a completely fixed or immutable process, but is influenced by social structure and social change. We know that some people lead long, healthy, effective, fulfilling lives; while other people succumb early to ill health, unhappiness, loneliness, withdrawal from affairs. We know that aging is not fully programmed by genetic dispositions or early childhood experiences, but is continually subject to social modification and change. We are beginning to understand <u>how</u> society influences the aging process; how the economic, cultural, and social aspects of society affect people's lives; how major changes in society (wars, depressions, inflation, energy shortages) influence the ways in which individuals grow up and grow old. Less well understood is the second principle: that the changing ways in which people age are continually reshaping society.

This chapter focuses on these two principles and the dialectical relationship between them. Its central theme is that there is a <u>dynamic interplay between people growing older and society undergoing change</u>. People age in different ways because society changes; and in turn the ways in which people age are continually shaping society. To repeat: aging is variable--it is influenced by social change; and reciprocally, aging influences social change.

---

*An earlier version of this paper was delivered at the AAAS session on "New Frontiers in Science," San Francisco, 1980.

At this frontier of science, these principles and their dialectical relationship are informed by new conceptual developments in the sociology of age and aging.[1] This emerging conceptual scheme, as in the series of volumes that my colleagues and I have published over the last dozen years (cf. Riley, 1976), connects individual aging with social change. The scheme focuses on the <u>individual</u> who is aging, changing biologically and psychologically, performing a sequence of social roles over the life course, interacting with other people, forming a social self. It focuses on the flow of <u>cohorts</u> of individuals, who fit together to produce age <u>strata</u> of the young, the middle aged, the old. It focuses on change in the total <u>society</u>, as roles and institutions change; historical events occur; science, beliefs, and values are transformed; and the age structure of the population alters.

In this conceptual scheme, these processes are not isolated. They are interdependent. Thus, as in the central theme of this chapter, aging is not fixed but varies with the society in which we live; and, at the same time, the ways in which we age are continually molding society.

This sociological view is a radical one. It is sharply opposed to widely accepted beliefs both about social change and about the aging process. It rejects the usual notions that social change springs exclusively from <u>societal</u> alterations in institutions, values, or technologies--without regard for the changing behavior of the people involved. We do not accept this one-sided notion. Instead, our sociological view brings the people in. It stresses the fact that the changing society is composed of <u>people</u>--of ourselves--who are aging and who are not only shaped by, but are also continually shaping, social institutions, values, and technologies.

This view also rejects widely publicized and widely believed notions of set stages in the aging process: for example, children must read by age seven, men must experience a mid-life crisis by age 45, old people must become decrepit by age 75 (e.g. Levinson, 1978; Sheehy, 1976). Our new perspective rejects this notion of fixed stages. Rather, it is providing mounting scientific evidence that aging cannot be viewed as an immutable process, fixed for all generations by biological programming or by universal features of the

---

[1]   Developed in association with Anne Foner, Marilyn Johnson, John Riley, Joan Waring, and many others.

social environment. Nor can aging be viewed apart from the
many and powerful influences of the changing society.
Indeed, at the sociological frontier, aging must be seen as a
series of continually changing--and mostly changeable--
experiences involving and often transforming individuals and
society, sometimes for better and sometimes for worse.

This chapter discusses three aspects of the dynamic
interplay between people growing older and society undergoing
change, as the power of this new scientific perspective is
attracting scholars from several disciplines. The chapter
deals first with the compelling evidence that aging and
social change _are_ interrelated; second, with some clues as to
how the two processes--aging and social change--influence
each other, suggesting certain mechanisms that link the two
together; and third, with some implications for public policy
and professional practice--with the fact, and the
responsibility posed by the fact, that we ourselves are
participating in these processes and helping to form them.

Interplay between Aging and Social Change: The Evidence

First, there is much evidence of this critical, but
little understood, interplay between aging and social change.
I shall give three examples: from education, retirement, and
family relationships. In each example I shall emphasize the
interplay:

- The effect on aging: The life-course patterns of
  individuals are _affected by_ social and environmental
  changes to which they are exposed.

- And the reverse effect on social change: When many
  individuals in the same cohort (born at the same time)
  are affected by social change in similar ways, the
  change in their collective lives can in turn _produce_
  further social change.

As in a feedback system, new patterns of aging are not only
caused by, they also cause, social change. Many familiar
phenomena take on fresh meaning when viewed as processes
within this interplay.

Consider the first example of _education_. _Because_ of
social changes in 19th and 20th century United States
(industrialization, educational ideologies, increasing value
attached to children), there have been long-term increases in
educational attainment. That is, successive cohorts of
children spent increasing portions of their lives in school
(the effect on aging over the life course). For example, 6%

of the cohort born in 1880 graduated from high school, in
contrast to 82% of the cohort born 1945-49. Such cohort
differences in education have incalculable consequences, not
only for the early lives, but also for the entire life course
of the individuals affected. Consider the consequences of
education for the life course of women: for experience in
marrying and having children, for participation in the work
force, for ranges of interests and friendships, for the sense
of personal control.

Meantime the feedback system is continually operating.
As more and more girls in each successive cohort achieve
increasingly high levels of education and lead their lives in
new ways, social norms and social institutions in turn
undergo still further changes (the effect on social change).
Consider how recent cohorts of women have been recreating
their place in society--at home, at work, in the professions,
in athletics, in the arts, in science (Riley, 1980). Thus a
social change (rising education) has left its mark on the
lives of women in successive cohorts, who, in turn, have
helped to restructure the institutions in which they
participate.

Take another example of the interplay. At the other end
of the life course, similar feedback processes are at work in
respect to retirement for men (for women, retirement is not
yet a massive phenomenon). Long-term social changes (the
changing character of occupations, the expansion of pension
plans, and so on) have resulted in earlier and earlier ages
of retirement. Of the cohort of men reaching age 65 in 1900,
e.g., approximately 2/3 were still in the workforce; but this
proportion had dropped to 1/3 by 1960, and to only 1/5 today
(Rosenfeld and Brown, 1979). Combined with increases in
longevity, these cohort differences in work mean increasing
numbers of years of life after retirement (as Torrey notes in
this volume). And these added retirement years have marked
consequences for the aging process in terms, for example, of
income, social involvement, leisure activities, health, and
effective functioning.

In turn, as fewer and fewer older men in each successive
cohort remain in the work force, many social norms and social
institutions are affected and are undergoing still further
changes. Laws and contracts are changing. In the 1930s, age
65 was arbitrarily built into the Social Security
legislation; now the appropriate age for Social Security is
in question, and the age for mandatory retirement has been
raised to 70 or omitted entirely. Earlier emphases on the
Protestant ethic and norms of achievement are shifting.
Leisure activities are being shaped by the growing numbers of

retirees. Meantime, added demands to pay taxes are imposed upon the younger people still in the labor force, and--what with inflation and energy shortages--the situation for retirees in the future will predictably be still different. New age norms and new life-course patterns are bound to emerge (Foner and Schwab, 1981).

Other noteworthy evidences of this continuing interplay between social change and aging derive from studies of the structure of kinship relationships. Several social changes are involved: the demands of industrialization and post-industrialization, the dissolution of parental authority, the secular decline (save for the World War II baby boom) in birth rates (Teitelbaum, 1979), and--most striking of all--the dramatic decline in mortality over many decades. The declines in mortality (or increases in longevity) mean that increasing proportions of successive cohorts outlive the ills of infancy and risks of young adulthood, and thus reach higher limits of the life span. In the United States, a person born in the middle of the last century could look forward to no more than four decades of life. Today, by contrast, a male at birth can expect to live to age 70, a female to age 77. Even at age 65 life expectancy has risen since 1900 from 12 to 18 years for white females and from 12 to 14 years for white males (Brotman, 1981, p. 25). This increased longevity, swelling the numbers at the oldest ages, is something new under the sun. It has transformed the kinship structure. It means that in many families four, even five, generations can now be alive at the same time.[1] Never before in human history could the kinship structure assume this multi-generational form.

Consider the impact of these social changes on the aging patterns of family members:

● Children co-exist with their parents longer now than they used to. In earlier cohorts many children were infants when their parents died. In recent cohorts, a daughter lives into her late 50's, on the average, before her mother dies (estimated by Winsborough, 1979). Thus it is surprising to realize that the relation between mother and daughter is concentrated, not in the daughter's childhood, but in her adult years. Indeed, there are now large numbers of

---

[1] Michael Teitelbaum notes out that the effect of increasing longevity has been to some extent offset by the later ages at which members of recent cohorts bear the first child.

65-year-old daughters interacting with their still surviving aged mothers.

● Married couples today live together much longer before separation by death than did their earlier counterparts. The average married couple today has some 13 years together after the last child leaves home and before one of the spouses dies--very different from the mere one or two years of joint survival experienced by couples in earlier cohorts (Glick, 1977). This post-children period now constitutes nearly 1/3 of the couples' married life-time--and it typically brings comparative affluence, freedom for outside pursuits, diminished preoccupation with child rearing.

● Widowhood has been postponed to the later years, usually striking in old age when the risks of ill health are greatest.

All such transformations in the lives of family members, rooted in social change, in their turn have many consequences for further social change. Important among these consequences, the norm of independence is reenforced. Increasing proportions of people, in particular older widows, live entirely alone (most widowed persons are women, since women live so much longer than men). Adequate support for the frail elderly has become a problem. And many older people die alone, apart from relatives or friends.

Ironically, this reenforced norm of independence has other consequences for social institutions that, according to recent studies, may further enlarge the kin network and perhaps also the potential for strengthened family bonds. To be sure, divorce rates in this country, which have been rising over the last 50 years, are now so high as to dissolve an estimated 1/3 of all first marriages. But most divorced people (3/4 of women and 5/6 of men) remarry (Glick and Norton, 1977). Thus sequential marriage has become not only a possibility but a realistic alternative to permanent conjugal commitment (Furstenberg, forthcoming).

Such a social change toward remarriage, for which few norms or guidelines have yet been institutionalized, adds complexity to the aging process for each individual involved. It has been estimated that over 1/3 of all children today spend a portion of their childhood during which their mothers are between marriages (Bumpass and Rindfuss, 1979). Most of these children will eventually be part of a second marriage--with the average time spent "between marriages" an

estimated 4-1/2 years, much longer still for a substantial
minority of children. How will these children weather
parental divorce, and age into adulthood? How will they
relate to step-parents? To half-brothers and half-sisters?
How will laws of custody be affected? Research is just
beginning to address such questions.

For spouses, too, new roles as step-parents must be
learned. How will they negotiate relationships with
step-children and with own children in the same family?

Older people will also be affected. Will their opportunities for social support be enhanced or diminished by the
proliferation of in-laws, step-children, step-grand children?

In sum, these three examples provide illustrative
evidence of the interplay between particular aspects of aging
and of social change. Through such re-analyses of existing
information we can infer that changes in society produce
changes in the aging process which, in turn, produce further
changes in society. And so on and on in an endless chain.
This means that neither aging nor social change is immutable.
Each provides wide margins of plasticity for the other.

Connections between Aging and Social Change

This brings me to the second aspect of my theme, to the
mechanisms connecting aging and social change. Clearly it is
not sufficient merely to describe the many such correlational
evidences that aging and social change influence each other;
that neither is entirely fixed; that each derives flexibility
through interaction with the other. The causal connections,
though they often seem plausible enough, must be teased out,
specified, and tested. We need to know how these mutual
influences work. How and under what conditions individuals
alter their lives in response to changes in their social
environs. How alterations in individual lives affect social
institutions or norms. What kinds of mechanisms are at work.
Clearly the interconnections are intricate, the research
tools clumsy. Yet I believe we are at the edge of certain
important and exciting understandings. Scattered ideas and
findings from several strands of current inquiry are
beginning to suggest some of the interconnections. I shall
take note of just three such interconnections: the flow of
cohorts, life-long socialization of individuals, and the
interdependence among age strata in the population.

Cohort Flow

The most direct link between aging and social change is
cohort flow, the endless succession through society of

cohorts of people. Indeed, it is now beginning to appear
that cohort flow may be a universal source of change for both
individual and society (as Anne Foner notes in this volume).
To be sure, since people within each cohort are born at the
same time and age together, there is an apparently inflexible
rhythm: children become youths, youths are transformed into
adults, and adults become old men and women. Yet this rhythm
is continually disturbed by the uniqueness of each new cohort
and by societal alterations in the roles to be filled.

Each cohort has several unique characteristics. It has
a distinctive size and composition (as by race or social
class background). It has its own average longevity. And
its members, because they were all "plugged into" the same
era of social change, share a unique slice of history.
Members of a particular cohort were all the same age when
they experienced, for example, the Great Depression, or
Kennedy's assassination, or the moon landing, or the Iranian
capture of hostages. No other cohort experienced the same
events at the same age. Research has focused, e.g., on how
the cohort who were children during the Great Depression
"grew up faster" than children in other cohorts, attached
special value to home-making and child-rearing as they
approached middle age (Elder, 1974); or on how the cohort who
were youths during the Viet Nam war rebelled against society
in ways very different from the cohorts who, like their own
parents, were youths during earlier wars.

In all such ways each new cohort differs from its
predecessors. A weighty pronouncement. With two weighty
corollaries. First, the members of successive cohorts cannot
age in precisely the same fashion (Ryder, 1964). Because of
cohort flow, aging must be variable. Even biological aging
(e.g., the age of menarche) varies (Tanner, 1972). Second,
the members of the same cohort, as they respond to shared
historical experiences, gradually and subtly develop common
patterns of response, common definitions, common norms. Thus
in its own way each cohort exerts a collective force,
pressing for adjustments in social roles and social values
(Riley, 1978).

What happens as all these differing cohorts succeed each
other? It seems obvious--though we are only beginning to
study it--that there can never be a perfect balance between
the cohorts of people who are aging and the changing roles
available for them in society. Instead there is an intrinsic
imbalance between people and roles. For example, differences
in cohort size provide one source of imbalance (Waring, 1975;
Easterlin, 1978). It is well known how the large numbers of
people in the baby boom cohort confronted too few places in

school, too few entry jobs, too few homes to live in. Yet a
little later on many new places created in response to this
spiralling demand could not be filled by the subsequent
smaller cohorts. Consequently there is a current surplus of
teachers, for example, and schools and colleges are having to
be closed. Equally disturbing to the balance between people
and roles can be cohort differences in <u>longevity</u>. Tremendous
dislocations have arisen from the persistent increase in
longevity of successive cohorts over this century, as older
people have outlived their traditional roles both in the
workforce and in the family, and new roles have not yet
replaced them. The plight of many older people in
contemporary society needs no reminder.

Consider the implications of such imbalances between
cohorts of people who are aging and the age roles available
in society. The result can be strains and pressures for
change for both individual and society. Individuals who are
underemployed, or unable to find work, or unsuccessful in
finding marriage partners can feel frustrated and depressed,
demand remedial action, resort to deviance. And social
institutions and norms can be disturbed when there are not
enough places in the workforce for young people, not enough
trained soldiers in case of war, not enough people motivated
to provide caring services for infants or for the elderly,
not enough jobs for highly educated women wanting to join the
labor force in midlife.

These strains on both individuals and society produce
societal changes. And, in turn, these social changes
differentiate the life-course patterns of successive cohorts.
The interplay again. Yet now it appears that these strains
are inevitable. We can see how they are intrinsic to the
imbalance between individual needs and societal requirements,
as we note how the changing social structure must accommodate
the perpetual flow of one cohort after another, and how
individuals must try to adapt to new roles and new
intergenerational relationships.

Thus the concept of cohort flow provides one type of
explanatory link between the process of aging and social
change.

Life-long Socialization

Cohorts cannot be understood, of course, without
reference to the individuals who are aging within them. Thus
another explanatory link can be sought in aging <u>individuals</u>,
and in the means whereby they respond in particular ways to
particular changes in society. For each cohort, society

affords a sequence of roles through which individuals move
from birth to death. These roles, and the situations they
present--in kindergarten, battleground, family, workplace,
nursing home--reflect the customs and institutions of
particular moments in history. In the aging process, age
roles set one boundary of the possible, just as biology sets
the other boundary. Yet within these boundaries, individuals
are far from passive: They define situations for themselves,
make decisions, take initiatives. Though aging is channelled
by history, there are wide latitudes within which individuals
shape their own lives.

One key mechanism connecting individual aging with
social change, though widely misapprehended, is life-long
socialization. A person's beliefs, values, competencies are
not indelibly imprinted in childhood. For every role
provides more than opportunity to express genetic makeup and
capacities acquired in early life. Every role also provides
opportunity for maintaining or altering current performances
and for learning new ones. Thus socialization is not
restricted to the early years, as is often believed, but
continues throughout life. The research findings now coming
in are exciting indeed (Riley and Bond, forthcoming). Even
in very old age socialization is shown to be effective in
modifying attitudes and behavior. E.g., elderly nursing home
residents, for many months unable to feed themselves, are
being successfully taught to regain this skill--to become
independent again (Baltes and Zerbe, 1976). And learning
abilities, once thought to peak in the early 20s and then
decline, are now being shown to persist into late life
(Schaie, 1979) and to respond to challenge in work and in
other social settings (Kohn and Schooler, 1979).

Full recognition of lifelong socialization calls
attention to another neglected idea--to expectations as the
driving force in adjusting to social change. Students of
childhood socialization often emphasize imitation of parents
as models. But how, in a changing society, can parents
reared in earlier cohorts serve as appropriate models for the
future cohorts to which their offspring belong? Indeed, if
each generation were to imitate its parents precisely, there
could be no social change. How, then, can parents teach
norms of the future? How can they encourage their offspring
to transcend the limits of their own education, their
occupational failures, the constraints imposed on their early
lives by rigid sex-role stereotypes? Here our own earlier
studies have pointed to the answer (Johnson, 1976; Riley,
Johnson, and Boocock, 1963). Even in the face of dramatic
cohort differences, parents can still influence their offspring in important ways by expecting them to keep pace with
social change.

Expectations can have power at all ages, of course, a power that often goes unrecognized. And expectations can have diverse consequences. Because of misdirected expectations, nursing home residents have been taught utter dependency, disadvantaged children have been discouraged from school achievement, young unemployed workers have become unemployable, doctors have failed to treat reversible illnesses simply by assuming "senility" in elderly patients. Yet expectations carefully directed are now being shown to have many beneficial effects on the aging process. For example, experiments with mass communications have demonstrated that people will correct life-time habits of eating, exercise, or smoking, if they expect thereby to escape heart attack or stroke in later life (Maccoby and Farquhar, 1977).

Thus studies are showing the great power of continuing socialization, for good or for ill, at every age. Life-long socialization can keep individuals abreast of social change. Life-long socialization, as another link between aging and social change, has untold implications for professional practice, for public policy, and for our own personal lives.

Interdependence Among Age Strata

In addition to cohort flow and lifelong socialization, I shall mention one other mechanism connecting aging and social change: the interdependence among age strata. At one level, cohort flow is an aggregate of individual biographies; at another level, it constitutes the age-stratified population moving through society. The several co-existing cohorts form the age strata of young, middle-aged, and old. And, different as these strata are in age and cohort experience, they are continually interacting in the same society. They are interdependent. Thus a change in one age stratum can have consequences for the other strata--again contributing to potential changes in social structure and in the aging of individuals.

Consider the radical shift in ideology in the youth stratum of the 1960s. That youth revolt at first aroused the wrath of the older strata, who countered violence with violence in open conflict. What followed was a questioning of the overall goals of society that permeated the age strata--a challenge so sharp that at the time it was likened to a "revolution of consciousness" comparable in scope to the Protestant Reformation or the Industrial Revolution. Emanating from one age stratum, the disturbances had a lasting impact on other strata as well, affecting a range of life styles from dress to sexual behavior.

Or consider the baby boom cohort again, that Juggernaut which by 1990 will be moving into the age strata from 25 to 44. During the coming decades the workers in this cohort will produce a huge bulge in the labor force, vacating for the reduced numbers of younger workers a plethora of entry-level jobs, but exerting unprecedented competitive pressure on workers in the mature strata. What will ensue from such drastic change in the age structure of the labor force? Will the mature workers who hold the superior jobs continue to claim their entrenched positions? Or will they retreat in increasing numbers into retirement?

Or consider the spectacular long-term shift from a preponderance of pre-adults in the economically dependent population to a preponderance of retired persons. According to some estimates as much as 40% of the federal budget will be going to care of the aged by the year 2030. Can such a shift fail to disturb those in the intermediate age strata who are active in the labor force and bearing the brunt of the taxes? Will such disturbances be compounded by predictable future difficulties as economic growth slows?

Such interdependencies among the age strata, though they often produce relations of harmony and exchange, can also produce tensions, cleavages and conflict. And tensions, cleavages, and conflict are still another source of potential alteration in the basic structure of society and in the nature of the aging process.

Implications

We are at the threshold, then, of identifying some of the interconnections between aging and social change. We are beginning to examine these interconnections, to scrutinize their operation.

With incipient understanding comes the need for greater deliberation, discrimination, and precision in the interventions we make. This is the third and final aspect of my theme: <u>our own power of control over aging and social change</u>, and the responsibility entailed.

For, like it or not, we <u>are</u> continually intervening. In our personal decisions, each of us daily affects the ways we age. And the ways we age—our sickness or health, happiness or despair, industry or sloth—affect the lives of our family members and friends, the ways they age. Each of us is continually developing age stereotypes—as to how much and how fast new-born infants can learn, whether old people still enjoy sex, whether a mid-life crisis is inevitable, whether teen-age pregnancy produces special risks, whether confusion in an elderly patient is sufficient cause for a doctor to discuss the case, etc. Such stereotypes, whether or not they accord with realities, can have power as self-fulfilling prophecies. They can become expectations about what is appropriate or right, influencing how people are socialized. They can control people's lives.

Moreover, many of us participate in public policy formation or in professional practice that will change the social structure, and will thus have broad consequences for the process of aging. Think of some of the structural changes currently under debate:

- Whether to provide tax credits for home care of older people?

- How and in what direction to change laws governing custody of children?

- Whether and under what conditions to encourage uninterested students to leave high school early?

- Whether to spread work more evenly over the life course, by providing longer vacations, flexible work hours, incentives for mid-life switching to new careers?

- Whether to reduce the heavy transfer payments by the middle-aged and to require that both the old and the young become more nearly self-supporting?

- What age is appropriate for retirement, given the increases in life expectancy?

- How to restructure the health establishment to meet the special needs of geriatric patients?

- How to design communities, housing, shopping centers, roadways to meet the human needs that are changing over the life course?

Many such decisions confront us. We must continue, as in the past, to make such decisions and to act upon them. But with a difference. For now we can be more aware that the resultant changes affect not only social structures but also the aging process--the lives, present and future, of the cohorts involved. We are rapidly amassing scientific evidence on the continuing interplay between social change and aging. We can use this new knowledge to make decisions that are both more precise and more humane. We can use it to make informed assessments of the consequences of alternative decisions. We can use it to focus efforts and expenditures of scarce resources. We can use it to move toward the goal of optimizing the aging process and enhancing the life course from birth to death.

References

Baltes, Margret M. and Melissa B. Zerbe, 1976. "Independence Training in Nursing-Home Residence." The Gerontologist (26): 428-432.

Brotman, Herman B., May 1981. "Every Ninth American." In "Development in Aging 1980." Annual Report of the Senate Special Committee on Aging.

Bumpass, Larry and Ronald R. Rindfuss, 1979. "Children's Experience of Marital Disruption." American Journal of Sociology (85): 49-65

Easterlin, Richard A., 1978. "What Will 1984 be Like?" Demography (15): 397-432

Elder, Glen H., Jr., 1974. Children of the Great Depression, Chicago: University of Chicago Press.

Foner, Anne and Karen Schwab, 1981. Aging and Retirement, Monterey, California: Brooks/Cole Publishing Company.

Furstenberg, Frank F., forthcoming. "Remarriage and Intergenerational Relationships." In Robert W. Fogel, Elaine Hatfield, Sara B. Kiesler, James G. March (eds.), Stability and Change in the Family. New York: Academic Press.

Glick, Paul C., 1977. "Updating the Life Cycle of the Family." Journal of Marriage and the Family (39): 5-13.

Glick, Paul C. and Author J. Norton, 1977. "Marrying Divorcing, and Living Together in the U.S. Today." Population Bulletin 32, Population Reference Bureau, Inc., Washington, D.C.

Johnson, Marilyn, 1976. "The Role of Perceived Parental Models, Expectations and Socializing Behaviors in the Self-expectations of Adolescent, from the U.S. and West Germany." Unpublished dissertation, Rutgers University, New Brunswick, New Jersey.

Kohn, Melvin L. and Carmi Schooler, 1979. "The Reciprocal Effects of the Substantive Complexity of Work and Intellectual Flexibility: A Longitudinal Assessment." In Matilda White Riley (ed.), Aging from Birth to Death I: Interdisciplinary Perspectives, AAAS Selected Symposium 30. Boulder, Colorado: Westview Press, 47-76.

Levinson, Daniel J. et al., 1978. The Seasons of Man's Life. New York: Knopf.

Maccoby, N., et al., 1977. "Reducing the Risk of Cardiovascular Disease: Effects of a Community-Based Campaign on Knowledge and Behavior." Journal of Community Health 3(2): 100-114.

Riley, Matilda White, 1976. "Age Strata in Social Systems." In Robert H. Binstock and Ethel Shanas (eds.), Handbook of Aging in the Social Sciences. New York: Van Nostrand Reinhold Company, 189-217.

Riley, Matilda White, 1978. "Aging, Social Change, and the Power of Ideas." Daedalus 107 (4): 39-52.

Riley, Matilda White, in press. "Implications for the Middle and Later Years." Research Conference on Women: A Developmental Perspective. National Institutes of Health, November 20-21, 1980.

Riley, Matilda White and Kathleen Bond, forthcoming. "Beyond Ageism: Postponing the Onset of Disability." In Beth B. Hess and Kathleen Bond (eds.), Leading Edges, Washington, D.C.: U.S. Government Printing Office.

Riley, Matilda White, Marilyn Johnson, and Sarane S. Boocock, 1963. "Women's Changing Occupational Role: A Research Report." American Behavioral Scientist (6): 33-37.

Rosenfeld, Carl and Scott Kampel Brown, 1979. "The Labor Force Status of Older Workers." Monthly Labor Review (102): 12-18.

Ryder, Norman B., 1964. "Notes on the Concept of a Population." American Journal of Sociology (69): 447-463.

Schaie, K. Warner, "The Primarily Mental Abilities in Adulthood." In Paul B. Baltes and Orville G. Brim, Jr., (eds.), Life Span Development and Behavior (2). New York: Academic Press: 68-117.

Sheehy, Gail, 1976. Passages. New York: Dutton.

Tanner, J. M., 1973. "Growing Up." <u>Scientific American</u>: 17–28.

Teitelbaum, Michael S., 1979. "As Societies Age." In Britannica Book of the Years, <u>Encyclopedia Britannica</u>, Chicago: 138–143.

Waring, Joan M., 1975. "Social Replenishment and Social Change: The Problem of Disordered Cohort Flow." In Anne Foner (ed.), <u>Age in Society</u>. <u>American Behavioral Scientists</u> (19): 237–256.

Winsborough, Halliman H., 1979. "A Demographic Approach to the Life Cycle." Center for Demography and Ecology working paper no. 79–110, University of Wisconsin, mimeographed.

2. Generation and Age in Cross-Cultural Perspective

Few key terms of sociological discourse have been so consistently muddled in their definition and application as that of 'generation'. The source of this conceptual malady lies in the absorption into the social scientific lexicon of a polysemous folk concept. The resultant confounding of the different meanings of 'generation' continues to impair our theoretical understanding of the life course and of age stratification. To provide greater theoretical clarity and to allow us to raise a number of new theoretical issues, 'generation' should be reserved for its only defensible conceptual meaning, that bound to reproductive or descent relationships.[1/]

In the first portion of this chapter I will identify the conceptual confusion found in many current social scientific discussions of generation. That Ryder's (1965) cogent analysis of many of the bases of this confusion has had limited effect will be made clear through a brief review of the generational literature published since his article appeared. After making the case for a more precise and limited definition of generation, the importance of generation for understanding the life course and age stratification systems will be discussed, largely by reference to anthropological cross-cultural studies. While anthropologists have long been concerned with generation in the sense I am advocating, to date there has been little systematic attempt to relate this concern to questions of the life course and age stratification. Finally, the persistent (and ill-advised) attempts by Western scholars to link generation to age groupings will be

---

1/Preparation of this chapter was begun while the author was a participant in the Summer Institute on Life-Span Human Development at the Center for Advanced Study in the Behavioral Sciences, 1980.

shown to be symptomatic of a cultural trait found in many
societies, the linking of generation to age.

Generation: Sources of Confusion

Karl Mannheim has been the most influential scholar in
the development of generational studies in this century. His
work epitomizes the confusion which results from confounding
a genealogical principle with a mode of age grouping. Unlike
later standard bearers of this approach, however, Mannheim
was writing before the conceptual apparatus of the sociology
of age had been developed, and his work must be judged in
this historical context.

Mannheim wrote that the "sociological phenomenon of
generations is ultimately based on the biological rhythm of
birth and death" (1952:290). He was careful to point out
that while the sociological phenomenon is based on biological
facts, these only become significant through cultural
reflection and elaboration. Mannheim clearly had in mind an
image of generation that is not genealogical in nature but
which groups people born in the same period of history. The
significance of this for Mannheim stems from his view that
over time a succession of waves of new individuals reach
adulthood in a society, coming anew into contact with its
culture and remodeling what is found. This constitutes
Mannheim's famous concept of "fresh contact" (1952:293).

By trying to link together people born at the same time
in history on the basis of their distinct worldview and
experience, Mannheim ran into the obvious problems of social
stratification and cultural diversity. Not all people born
in the same period share similar experiences or outlooks. To
resolve these problems, Mannheim distinguished between a
generation and a 'generation unit':

> The generation unit represents a much more con-
> crete bond than the actual generation as such.
> Youth experiencing the same concrete historical
> problems may be said to be part of the same
> actual generation: while those groups within
> the same actual generation which work up the
> material of their common experiences in different
> specific ways, constitute separate generation units
> (1952:304).

The precarious ontological basis on which Mannheim's formulation rests becomes clear as he elaborates on this generation vs. generation-unit distinction:

> Whereas mere common 'location' in a generation
> is of only potential significance, a generation
> as an actuality is constituted when similarly
> 'located' contemporaries participate in a common
> destiny and in the ideas and concepts which are
> in some way bound up with its unfolding. Within
> this community of people with a common destiny
> there can then arise particular generation-units
> (1952:306).[2]

Mannheim in fact is on weak epistemological ground in
his generation concept. He argues that "/t/he biological
fact of the existence of generations merely provides the
possibility that generation entelechies may emerge at all--
if there were no different generations succeeding each other,
we should never encounter the phenomenon of generation styles"
(1952:311). It is a far cry from saying that biological processes of birth and death make generations possible to saying
that the existence of generations is a biological fact.[3]

It is ironic that insofar as Mannheim sought to provide
ideological content for his notion of the generational unit
he produced a social category which has little necessary link
to age at all. Unless we are willing to believe that past
the age of 25 people's lives and consciousness cannot be
fundamentally altered by new historical events and influences,
there is no reason why people who participate in a common
view of the world need to be of the same or similar age.
What begins as a concept based on the biological universals
of birth and death ends up being severed from any demographic
foundation at all.

A similar conception of generation has been articulated
by Ortega y Gasset and his disciples. Like Mannheim, Ortega
y Gasset conceived of generations as units of people born in
the same historical period and therefore sharing a common
vision of life. Indeed, he argued that the generation "is
the most important conception in history." Even those contemporaries who saw themselves as having utterly different
points of view were in fact to be understood as having much

2/That Mannheim is prone to reification in formulating his
generation concept may also be illustrated by his contention
that "it depends on...social and cultural factors whether
the impulses of a generation shall achieve a distinctive
unity of style, or whether they shall remain latent" (1952:
311).

3/Curiously, earlier in the same essay, Mannheim seems to
warn of the danger of biological reductionism of the generation concept (1952:290-1).

in common. Hence, the "reactionary and the revolutionary of
the nineteenth century are much nearer to one another than
either is to any man of our own age" (1933:15). Generations,
though, represented more than aggregates of people who happened to be contemporaries, for Ortega y Gasset argued that
each generation has its "special mission," even though, like
individuals, generations may "leave their mission unachieved"
(1933:19). Ortega y Gasset's conception of generation, then,
is plagued by reification.

Julian Marias, a follower of Ortega y Gasset, was
charged with discussing the general concept for the International Encyclopedia of the Social Sciences (1968). Marias
attacked those who have attempted "to formulate a sociological theory of generations in the biological sense of kinship
descent" as being on the wrong track. The reason offered for
this position is that "the temporal continuity of births
makes impossible any determination of social generations so
long as 'generations' is understood in a purely biological
sense." In harmony with Mannheim he concluded that "It is
therefore necessary to arrive at a strictly social and historical interpretation of the generation concept in order
for it to acquire relevance in the field of the social
sciences" (1968:88).

Marias is guilty of confusing what is a cultural principle of classification, i.e., the tracing of kinship descent,
with the biological continuum of births. Moreover, while the
one phenomenon has its point of reference in an individual
family or kinship grouping, the other has as its reference an
entire population. When Marias goes on to lament that "the
studies of generations have left in obscurity the questions
of what generations are, why they exist, how long they last,
what their scope is, and how they are determined " (1968:89),
we have reason to believe that the epistemological weaknesses
of Mannheim are afflicting a new 'generation'.

Troll (1970:199-200) has distinguished five different
meanings currently in use for the term 'generation': "1. Generation as ranked descent; 2. Generation as age-homogeneous
group; 3. Generation as developmental state; 4. Generation
as time span; and 5. Generation as Zeitgeist." These different meanings are not simply associated with different
scholars, or with different disciplines, for some analysts
utilize two or more of them. In fact, Troll and her colleagues have distinguished among the different meanings of
'generation' in order to then employ generation in all of
these different senses. I would argue that it is only useful
to use 'generation' in the first sense listed above (i.e.,
descent), and that more precise terms exist with which to
deal with the other concepts associated with the term.

In its sense of ranked descent, generation refers to the relationship between parents and their children, these children and their children, and so on. Of the five listed meanings, this is the only one to have clear boundaries provided by biological properties (assuming incest prohibitions).[4] Moreover, used this way, generation is a purely relational term, rooted in the parent-child relationship, and not applicable to societal-level groupings. The study of generation then involves the study of parent-child relations, grandparent-grandchildren relations, and relations among people differentially positioned within a sibling group. Troll and Bengtson (1979:128) have extended this concept by speaking collectively of individuals who are "first generation" or "second generation", denoting by this whether the individual has living parents, or living grandparents. In this vein they maintain that a "second-generation member may be anywhere from two seconds to 72 years old." I do not believe that this extension is analytically warranted, for it creates the illusion of a group (e.g., 'member') where in fact no meaningful grouping exists.

In its second sense, as an age-homogeneous group, generation is defined by Troll (1970:201) as follows:

> Where the ranked-descent meaning of generation derives from the family system, the generation concept we are now considering has relevance primarily to the social system. It cuts across family lines and verges on subculture status. An age-homogeneous group, as used here, includes all people of the same age who share a common set of culture characteristics, who perceive themselves as belonging together, and who are recognized as belonging together by the rest of society.

The formulation obviously follows from Mannheim and Ortega y Gasset. It has two analytical components: a birth cohort (i.e., people born in the same period of time) and cultural homogeneity. Presumably, using this definition, some societies have no generations, for they do not culturally define birth cohorts in this discontinuous way. Other societies presumably have numerous generations all of the same birth cohort, for there are competing cultural groupings to which people of the same birth cohort subscribe. Or there may be some birth cohorts enveloped in one or more generations, while other birth cohorts of the same society could not be said to belong to any generation.

4/Of course, this underlying biological process is subject to complex cultural elaboration and reformulation.

In a more recent formulation, joined by Bengtson, Troll has expressed this formulation a bit differently:

> /This/ process of generations has its base neither
> in the family nor in the individual, but rather in
> wider social systems (Riley, Johnson and Foner,
> 1972). It cuts across developmental and family
> statuses, simultaneously influencing both. Such
> an age and culture-homogeneous group includes all
> people born at the same time who have been raised
> under comparable historical and cultural circum-
> stances and were thus subject to similar sociali-
> zation. Members of such an age cohort may share
> many attitudes and values, perceive themselves as
> belonging together, and be recognized as belonging
> together by others. This is the kind of generation
> implied by the terms "youth culture," "the establish-
> ment," and "the aged" (1979:128).

Here Troll and Bengtson seem to be making cultural recognition of the generational grouping optional. Yet in doing
so we are left with a conflict between the criteria advanced
for a generation and the examples given. For example, what
people recognized in American society as the "youth culture"
certainly did not include all people of a given birth cohort
reared in similar historical and cultural circumstances.
The same could be said for the "establishment." As for the
"aged", this is a purely age-identified category with no
necessary cultural content.

The reference in the above quote to Riley, Johnson and
Foner is open to misinterpretation, for in fact Riley et al.
opposed use of the 'generation' concept in the sense employed
by Troll and Bengtson and confined its usage to "its kinship
reference to the parent-child relationship." They specifically called on social scientists to use the term 'cohort' in
referring to people born at the same time (1972:5).

While in its second sense generation is used to refer
to birth cohorts (with a variable cultural content), in its
third-listed sense it is used to refer to an age grade or
stratum. The use of 'generation' as an all-purpose analytical workhorse is thus reinforced. Troll and Bengtson (1979:
128) explain this usage of the term:

> In the course of their life span, individuals move
> through a developmental progression that can be
> heuristically divided into segments or stages.
> These segments are sometimes informally referred
> to as "generations." For example, adolescence

has been termed a different generation from childhood, youth from adolescence, adulthood from youth,
and old age from adulthood.

It is difficult to see why this usage of 'generation'
should be defended or propagated. We have the clear concept
of age strata in sociology, while in psychology concepts
such as developmental stages are employed. To say, for
example, that "There is always an adolescent generation in
existence" (Troll 1970:203) not only is fallacious by reason
of reification, but it inevitably leads to confusion among
the various definitions of generation which are being
advocated.

Even Eisenstadt, who is responsible for one of the most
provocative studies of age relations, contributed to this
confusion by identifying generations with developmental
stages or age strata in his book, <u>From Generation to Genera-
tion</u>. He writes of the "elder generations" (1956:277), of
the "younger generation" and the "adult generation" (1956:
33), viewing them as synonomous with age strata. This
weakens his otherwise useful discussion of the relationship
between the problems of intergenerational dynamics within a
family and the societal mechanisms through which the individual is weaned from the family.[5]

The concept of generation has also been used to characterize a historical period, as the work of Mannheim and
Ortega y Gasset set out to do.[6]   The claim has been made
that historical periods change every thirty years or so,
and that this ties into the length of a generation. This
argument is illogical because at the societal level births
are continuous. Yet we also find scholars who argue that
when social change becomes more rapid, generations change
every twenty or even fewer years. Once the time span is
down to three or four years, even the hardiest defenders
of multi-definitions of generation balk at applying the
generational label (see Troll 1970:203; Troll and Bengtson
1979:129).[7]

Berger (1959) asks a similar question in the title of

5/In this regard a similar criticism could be leveled at
Abrams (1970) who has in effect blended Mannheim's and
Eisenstadt's perspectives.

6/The antiquity of this usage is made evident by the Old
Testament, in which historical periods are referred to by
reference to individuals along a descent line.

his article, "How long is a generation?" He concludes that
certain distinctions must be made:

> There are, in short, literary generations, political
> generations, musical generations, etc.; the length
> of each fluctuates, and the age-range which consti-
> tutes the 'younger' generation in one may be consid-
> erably older (or younger) than the age-range con-
> stituting the 'younger' generation in another, to say
> nothing of the internal differentiation which may
> fragment a single cultural generation however defined
> (1959:16).

Here we have metaphor replacing scientific terminology.

Probably the major issue to which the foregoing concepts
of generation have been applied over the past decade has been
that of social change. Yet, rather than help clarify the
processes of social change, the concept of generation,
employed in this multi-purposed way, has obscured the
dynamics of social change and led to a conceptual quagmire.
The price the analyst pays for an eclectic approach to 'generations' is evident in Troll's discussion of "the issue of
change":

> Sometimes we get the impression of generational
> change, when we are really witnessing historical
> change. Or, to be inclusive of all our generational
> definitions, some change can be of the generation
> of all the people living at one time rather than
> of a youth group generation in transition to
> adulthood...(1970:211).

Laufer and Bengtson, in attempting to justify and to defend
their use of the concept of generation from Ryder's criticism, maintain that "generational analysis, as distinct
from cohort, lineage, or maturational analysis, is concerned
with age groups as agents of social change..."(1974:186).
Following Mannheim, Laufer and Bengtson "define a generation
unit as: those self consciously active age based groups within a specific social strata /sic7 which are creating competing and/or complementary styles of life and thought"
(1974:195).

7/Troll uses the term "age cohort" to refer to this 3-4 year
span, while Troll and Bengtson refer to "a new age group"
emerging every 4-5 years. How historical periods can be identified with limited birth cohorts is less than clear.

Bengtson, Furlong and Laufer have heralded a new era in generational interpretation, in which "A growing number of scholars have begun to apply tools and perspectives of empirical sociology and psychology to the classic problem of generations and succession and social change" (1974:2-3). But the problem is that the 'classic' problem of generations, as set forth by Mannheim, is a confusion of two problems, one concerning the relationship between cohort succession and social change, and the other concerning the relationship between parents and children through the life course. Bengtson, Furlong, and Laufer bounce from the one problem to the other, obscuring the crucial distinction by the double-barrelled use of the term 'generation'. We have reached the point where a statement such as Lambert's (1972:23)--"The thesis is basically that the process of generations succeeding each other is one of the most important mechanisms in sociocultural change"--is not clear without further elaboration.

The same problems in the use of the generation concept found in sociology, psychology and gerontology have made their way into political science as well. Rintala, writing on political generations to complement the sociological piece by Marias in the International Encyclopedia of Social Sciences, defines a political generation as "a group of individuals who have undergone the same basic historical experience during their formative /17-25/ years. Such a generation would find political communication with earlier and later generations difficult, if not impossible" (1968: 93). Rintala's estimate of the time span of a political generation in twentieth-century Western societies is ten to fifteen years (1968:94). Yet when political analysts attempt to apply this generational concept they often employ generational categories which have no comparability in time span. When Cutler and Bengtson (1974:165) write of "current youth and the current adult generation," they not only are employing diverse ranges of birth cohorts for their categories, they are also confusing a developmental stage with a life-long birth cohort identification. When they attempt to make generational categories comparable in terms of age span they end up with five eight-year birth cohorts which are simply that, birth cohorts; labelling them generations adds nothing but confusion.

While Ryder's (1965) critique of the fallacy of these uses of generation still remains the most concise statement on the subject, other sociologists and historians have addressed the problem. Vinovskis (1977) criticized the well-known studies by Greven (1970) on the colonial settlers of

Andover, Massachusetts, and by Reuben Hill and associates
(1970) on three generations of family life in America,
on the grounds that genealogical generation and birth cohorts
must be analytically distinguished. Elder (1978:41) has
criticized Bengtson and Lovejoy's (1973) study on similar
grounds.

Anthropology and Generation

In contrast with the broad use made of the generation
concept by sociologists, psychologists and political scientists, anthropologists have primarily utilized generation in
its genealogical, kinship-related sense. This is largely a
product of the attention paid by anthropologists to the
analysis of non-Western kinship systems and, particularly, to
the study of kinship terminology. Indeed, generation has
been a more fully articulated concept in anthropology than
has age. To give but one (though perhaps extreme) example,
in Fox's (1967) standard work, Kinship and Marriage, 'age'
is not listed in the index, while for the 'generation' list-
ing a total of sixty-four pages are cited. It is revealing,
too, that when generation is discussed in anthropology text-
books, it is almost always brought up in connection with
kinship terminology systems.[8]

Anthropologists have been sensitive to the fact that
other usages of the generation concept may lead to confusion.
Legesse refers to the mingling of the concepts of age and
generation as "one of the most enduring fallacies in Western
culture and, by extension, in the social sciences" (1973:51).
Rodney Needham, while recognizing the same confusion, has
curiously abandoned the descent-linked meaning of the term
generation:

> It is necessary to distinguish between a 'generation'
> as commonly understood in English, i.e., as a body
> of individuals born about the same period and also
> the time covered by the lives of these (S.O.E.D.),
> and a 'generation' as constituted by those individuals
> who fall into one level in a genealogy. We shall
> call the latter means of definition a 'genealogical
> level'...(1974:75).

8/Not all such usages are informative or useful. Greenwood
and Stini (1977:332) for example, provide the following
definition for the beginning anthropology student: "Generation refers to the fact that most kinship systems recognize
generational differences and have different terms for members
of different generations."

In his own work Needham focuses on the relationship between 'genealogical level' and relative age.

One other reason why anthropologists have been careful to avoid confusing the genealogical and the birth cohort senses of generation is that they have worked in societies having great age differences between spouses and where polygyny is often the norm. The identification of age with genealogical generation is facilitated in our own culture both by age homogeneity between spouses and by monogamy. In societies where men not uncommonly have junior wives who are younger than their older children, the analytical diffi-culties which result from the dual use of the generation con-cept become evident. This same problem becomes evident in American society in cases of remarriage, where a child from a man's previous marriage is the same age as his second wife, producing age-related role conflict in the relations between the new wife and her step-daughter.

In the remainder of this paper, I would like to sketch out some of the valuable sociological questions which can be addressed by disentangling generation from its popular connotations as an age stratum or a birth cohort, and by examining the relationship between generation (in its genea-logical sense) and age.

The Relationship Between
Generation and Age

Both age and generation are important elements of social stratification systems. The fact that these two distinct societal elements have been so often confused means that the relationship between them in social systems has not been well studied. The value of such study for theoretical devel-opment in the field of age stratification and life course studies becomes all the more important when the issue is placed in cross-cultural perspective. This is the case be-cause in most human societies throughout history kinship has provided a major basis of social structure. In such soci-eties the principle of generational relations, bound to a genealogical organizaaion of people's social worlds, often plays an important part. Yet, as we shall see, a tension inevitably develops once people employ the concept of gener-ation to order relations beyond the nuclear family, a tension stemming from the conflict between generational position and relative age.

Rodney Needham, in a provocative essay which is little known outside social antrhopology, contends that the conflict

between generation and age is a general social problem to
which different societies provide "very different cultural
answers" (1974:93). Needham asks what are the societal cor-
relates of an emphasis on categorization by generation as
opposed to categorization based on relative age. While
relative age appears to be a universal principle influencing
social relations, relative generational standing beyond the
nuclear family is not. Yet in some societies relative generational standing becomes more important in governing certain
social relations than is relative age. For example, Needham
discusses the case of the Kodi, a cultivating and herding
people of eastern Indonesia, who have a bilineal descent
system. Among people who are considered to be close kinsmen,
the nature of the social relationship between two individuals
is "strictly determined" by relative generational standing,
"to the extent that a youth will be accorded formal deference by a far older man if the latter belongs to a junior
category" (1974:89). A similar principle, relating the
salience of generational considerations to the proximity of
kinship connection, was noted four decades ago by Fortes in
his study of Tallensi of West Africa. Each Tallensi lineage
is ruled by a head, defined as its "senior male member."
Seniority is figured on the basis of generation for lineages
which trace their ancestry just four generations or fewer
back. However, in lineages of greater depth, "age is the
criterion, since generation seniority is no longer determin-
able" (1940:251). Seniority in this society is a crucial
principle of social organization, yet it is based on two
alternative, and potentially conflicting, principles--age
and generation.

One of the most common ways in which generational categories are employed in social organization is found in
prescriptions governing the selection of marriage partners.
In some societies there is a rule prescribing marriage
within one's own generation and proscribing marriage with
individuals considered to be of one's father's or child's
generation. In many societies marriage partners are supposed
to be selected from prescribed kinship categories, and hence
determination of relative generation is facilitated. Yet
just because principles of relative age and relative generation increasingly come into conflict the further back generational relations are traced genealogically, societies
having generation-based marriage rules run into conflict
with age-linked norms about marriage. Needham, for example,
mentions a case from the Penan, north-central Borneo forest
nomads, which is relevant here. In the local group is a boy
who is 2-3 years older than a neighboring girl, yet the girl
is genealogically considered to be his 'grandmother.'

In small-scale societies in which generational relations among the population are recognized, but in which generation-based marriage prescriptions are not found, the computation of generational relations between any two people can become murky indeed.[9] This leads Needham to conclude that marriage restrictions are necessary in systems in which relative generational standing is to serve as a principle of social organization beyond the nuclear family.

The tension between generation and age enters into the understanding of kinship-based societies in another way as well. Anthropologists have long noted how people in such societies categorize their social universe in genealogical categories: 'brothers', 'sisters', 'in-laws', etc. This social categorization, however, does not necessarily correspond with a biological model of genealogy, for people manipulate placement of individuals into categories based on social and political factors. Whether one is considered to be a 'brother' or not, for example, may have little to do with his genealogical position and much to do with his past record of mutual aid or hostility. What has been less frequently noted by anthropologists is that genealogical computations people make in such societies are influenced by another non-genealogical factor as well, namely age. As the disparity between individuals' relative generational standing and their relative age becomes great, tension may result. One solution commonly found is to alter an individual's genealogical placement to better conform to his relative age vis-a-vis his kinsmen (Needham 1974:105-6).

Just as _intergenerational_ status relations are an important element of social organization in many societies, _intragenerational_ status relations are also important features of many societies. Intragenerational status distinctions are based on birth order, and, most commonly, individuals are expected to show deference to those born before them. Here it would seem that we have a generational principle which is entirely in harmony with relative age principles. Yet this is not always the case. Jackson (1978: 351) points out that in a number of societies intragenerational seniority is "relative to a person's position in the descent system rather than a direct expression of relative age." This is commonly the case in Polynesian societies where, according to Firth (1970:274):

Within an elementary family it is the birth order

9/For example, when an uncle marries a niece, the generational status of the offspring is ambiguous.

of siblings that supplies the index to their ranking
but outside the elementary family, or in the
application of sibling terms to the cousin field,
it is usually the birth order of their parents or
remoter forbears who formed the original sibling
set which is taken as the relevant factor. Since
actual age may be thus ignored, the seniority factor
is then a social factor of differentiation, not
simply a demographic factor.

A similar conflict between age and status position
within a generation is found in many polygynous societies.
Where intragenerational standing is based on the order of
marriage of a person's mother, the younger child of a first
wife may be considered to be senior to the older child of a
second or third wife. Needless to say, this tension between
the two principles often leads to conflict.

The relationship between age and generation is not only
of importance for understanding aspects of social organization, but also for more fully understanding processes of
the individual life course. The intragenerational issue of
birth order, for example, discussed above in organizational
terms, also has implications for the study of the individual
through time. While in American society one's birth order
in the sibling group has some impact on the individual, in
other societies this influence is considerably greater. For
example, the age a man marries and sets up an independent
household is linked in many societies to whether he is the
first born son or not. The likelihood that an individual
will undergo the impact of migration may also be linked to
birth order. Where, for example, primogeniture is the norm,
second and third sons may have to leave the parental homestead to seek their fortunes elsewhere.

In addition, intergenerational relations may be influenced by one's intragenerational position, and vice versa.
In the case of primogeniture, a man's relation with his
first-born son may be emotionally quite different from his
relation with his other children (see Jackson 1978:343).
Thus, a person's relationship with his or her parent may not
simply be linked to the ages of parent and offspring, but
also to the individual's birth order position. Both age and
generational location must be considered.

The individual's life course is also influenced by
events occurring in the lives of people of more senior and
more junior generations. The roles a person assumes may
depend not so much on his or her age as on whether he or
she represents the senior generation of the family (however

this may be culturally defined). The death of one or both
parents can provide 'adult' roles to the relatively young
individual, while in many societies middle-aged individuals
whose own parents are alive are not considered fully adult,
for they must rely on their parents to give them the pre-
requisites (e.g., land, livestock) of social adulthood.

Nor is this process necessarily linked to the death of
individuals of the elder generation, for retirement may have
the same effect. This works both ways, for not only may the
life course stage of the individual depend on his or her
parent's retirement, but the member of the elder generation
may determine the timing of his or her own retirement based
on the presence of suitable descendants. In societies
characterized by high mortality, this may be a major factor
in bringing about inter-individual variation in life course
timing (Goody 1976:118-19). Even in societies having formalized age-set grouping, as in East Africa, an individual may
abandon the appropriate age-set-linked social roles if his
senior kinsmen die and he becomes responsible for the herds
of the kin group. In such a case, Baxter and Almagor (1978:
13) tell us, he "must settle down to the social elderhood
and become a homestead head, even if by age, temperment and
age-set rules he should be living it up as a member of a
bachelor set."

Not only are a person's economic and marital roles
linked to events occurring in the generation senior to him,
his taking on of ritual roles may also be affected. A good
case of this is provided by Fortes for the Tallensi. The
spirits of ancestors are believed to have an important influence on the lives of the living, and rituals directed at them
are an important part of life.   But a man only acquires
full rights to perform such ceremonies once his own father
has died (Fortes 1974:83-4).   Hence, generation rather than
age defines the individual's life course in the ritual
sphere.

One's life course is, as already mentioned, not simply
affected by the events bearing on the senior generation, but
also by the existence of generations junior to the individual. In many societies, for example, an individual's transition to social adulthood is linked to the birth of his or
her children. Similarly, the birth of grandchildren may
have an impact on one's life course. Plath (1980:9-10), for
example, tells of a Japanese woman in her mid-fifties whose
child had a baby, making her a grandmother. The woman
resisted being identified as a grandmother, feeling that she
was too young for the role. Despite her protestations, however, she was forced by others to act like a grandmother.

Generation as a Principle
of Social Grouping

My argument to this point has had two main components:
1) that conceptual confusion continues to surround the use
of the concept of generation, and that generation should be
reserved to refer to relations of descent; and 2) there are
a number of issues of life course and age stratification
analysis that involve the relationship between generation
and age. One other point, directly related to the first
two, remains to be discussed: The tendency of Western social
analysts to generalize from the process of generational succession along a descent line (i.e., from parent to child,
etc.) to the identification of age-based groupings conceived
in generational terms is itself a cultural phenomenon found
in many societies.

Many cultures group people into generationally-conceived categories, categories which use the idiom of generational succession but which are linked to notions of age
homogeneity. In short, the same conceptual confusion found
in Mannheim and his followers is incorporated as an aspect
of culture and social organization in many non-Western
societies as well. Because the generational principle of
descent and the principle of age homogeneous groupings are
in conflict, societies having such generationally-conceived
social units must have mechanisms for dealing with the conflicts that are generated.

The most highly institutionalized development of
generations as social groupings is to be found among a number of East African societies. In these societies, every
male is a member of a named generation group, and the
specific named group to which he belongs is determined in
relation to that of his father. In the simplest system a
man joins the generation group immediately following that of
his father. Such is the case, for example, of the Jie
(Gulliver 1953). Each generation group is theoretically
open for recruitment for a period of 20-30 years, with age
of formal induction being in the boy's late teens. A new
generation group is initiated when all the sons of the
members of the generation group two senior to the new group
have had their sons initiated. As a result, there are normally just two generation groups in existence at any one
time: the senior generation group and the generation group
of its sons which remains open for recruitment (see discussion in Stewart 1977:42-5).

Not all East African generation group systems are so
simple, however. Before discussing the significance of

these systems for our subject, a brief outline of a more complex generation system is in order. The Galla peoples of Ethiopia are noted for a combined generation- and age-system known as the Gada system (see Legesse 1973). In this system, each male at birth joins the fifth generation group following that of his father. As a new generation group is initiated each eight years, this means that a forty-year cycle is established between the generation group of a man and that of his son. Moreover, to simplify a bit, every eight years a transition takes place such that members of each generation group move up one step in the generation stratification ladder, giving up roles associated with the previous step and taking on new roles associated with their new stage in Gada system. These generation group-linked roles include political, economic, and ritual activities and responsibilities.

These systems of formalized generation-based groupings which unite people within a society on the basis of common generation membership are related to age-group systems, also prevalent in East Africa, in which people join named association of age similars with whom they collectively pass through the transitions of the life course (see Foner and Kertzer 1978; Kertzer 1978; Baxter and Almagor 1978). Indeed, in many cases the two systems are intertwined in the same society. Yet the sociological puzzle presented by generation-group societies is that social roles are allocated on the basis of descent-linked, society-wide groupings which tend to conflict with age-based role allocation.

Where roles in a society are allocated on the basis of an individual's generational identity and this generational location is traced over many generations and standardized among all different descent lines, over time the members of generation groups will become progressively more age hetero-geneous and there will be progressively greater age overlap between the generation groups.[10] This raises the question of why generational principles are used to group individuals outside of a family or kin-group context. Baxter and Almagor (1978:6) portray this process as an attempt "to tame time by chopping it up into manageable slices." Yet by generaliz-ing an idealized societal image of one generation begetting the next, and creating social groupings based on that cog-nitive image, conflict between generation and age is built into the system:

generation implies begetting, replacement and

10/This point is demonstrated by Stewart (1977) and Legesse (1973).

> continuity. When a man's placement within a
> system is determined by that of his father's
> an underlying assumption is that fathers will
> beget sons within a limited time span, and that
> therefore there will be approximate accord between
> age and generation. In social reality this
> assumption is false so that a continuing dilemma
> in all such systems is the reconciliation of age,
> generation and the steady flow of time. The bio-
> logical facts of birth and death must slide out of
> alignment with the social order with which they
> should conform (1978:5).

In short, according to Baxter and Almagor, we have a classic
case of the "conflict between biological and sociological
categories, or nature and culture" (1978:8). Indeed, the
extreme example of this, found in a number of societies
having generation group systems, is provided by the boy who
is born into a generation group which has already retired
(Bischofberger 1972:30; Legesse 1973). This happens when,
generation after generation, men have children relatively
late in their lives: it is the plight of the youngest son
of a youngest son.[11/] For the same reason, in societies in
which allocation of the most prestigious political or ritual
roles is dependent on being a member of the most senior
generation group in a society, most people will be consigned
at birth to never reaching that most privileged stratum.
Such is the case among the Dassanetch, where the age range
found in any generation grouping is great, and the age overlap among generation groups is large. Since a given generation group can only make the transition to the highest level
in the system once the last members of the generation group
senior to it have died or become disabled, the considerable
portion of a generation group that overlaps in age with
the generation group senior to it cannot hope to ever make
the transition (Almagor 1980).

When unfettered by specific age restriction, the use of
the generational principle leads to age-heterogeneous groupings and can result in the solidarity of age dissimilars.
As generation-group systems have often been explained as
having evolved from age-group systems, this observation
seems paradoxical. Some have dealt with this paradox by
claiming that generation-group systems are in fact not

11/In a number of generation-group societies mechanisms
exist for dealing with such cases, normally by initiating
the boy into a generation group junior to that dictated by
his father's generational group membership (e.g., Dyson-
Hudson 1966:175).

related to age-group systems, but are a form of descent group system (Lowenthal 1974). Yet we should not be so quick to dismiss the link between the two, apparently contradictory principles of social organization. What we see, from the pastoralists of Etheopia to the professors of Europe and the United States, is a tendency to abstract from the process of birth within a family to a wider, societal process of social replenishment. This can be understood in both psychological and sociological terms. Psychologically, Radcliffe-Brown and numerous others have demonstrated the tendency of people to generalize out from their nuclear family experiences in categorizing socially significant others. One of the elements of nuclear family organization which is incorporated into this process is the generational relationship, and this is commonly incorporated into kinship terminology. Just as the kinship idiom orders the social world for many nonliterate peoples, elements of this family-based generalizing process may be found outside a kinship framework. The preoccupation in the 1960s in the United States with the 'generation gap' can be seen as a reflection of people's cognitive tendency to simplify their social universe by creating elementary categories based on a family model.

While there may be certain psychological or cognitive universals which can help us explain the widespread human tendency to conceive of extra-familial social groupings in generational terms, the social organizational factors involved in this process are more variable, linked to specific social structural factors which differ by society. In the case of generation-group societies such as the Galla, Legesse suggests that the generation system may serve to defuse the tension between father and son. In a polygynous society, particularly one in which the family of the man must accumulate bridewealth payment to enable him to marry, the father may become a direct competitor of his son for a wife. It may be in the interest of the elder to delay the social adulthood of his sons in order to permit himself to acquire additional wives. The son may be older than his father's younger wives, further confusing the generational separation associated with family life. By providing everyone in the society with a generation-group category, and having rules forbidding sexual contact with women associated with one's father's or one's son's generation group, these familial tensions may be reduced (Legesse 1973:111). Furthermore, by providing the young man with an extra-familial group membership, he is afforded a measure of independence from his father.[12]

12/This argument, it should be noted, parallels that made a quarter century ago by Eisenstadt (1956).

Generational groupings reflect familial process in another way as well, for the phenomenon of the solidarity of alternate generations--the classic case of the grand-child's warm relationship with his or her grandparent--is commonly found institutionalized in generation group systems. Among the Karimojong, for example, Dyson-Hudson (1966:158) writes: "The correspondence of alternate generation-sets is deliberate and explicit, and embodies a fundamental principle of the age system. Karimojong say of generation-sets that 'they re-enter the place of their grandfathers'."[13] Correlated with this is the more formal and more conflict-prone relationship between adjacent generations, reflecting the parent-child relationship. Among the Kuria:

> These rules preserve the nature of the relationship
> between adjacent generations as one of distance,
> respect and mutual reserve, while allowing the
> relationship between alternate generations to be
> one of equality and familiarity, as between people
> of the same generation (Ruel 1958:5).

Again, we find the social organization of the family becoming a model for the larger social organization of soci-ety. It has even been suggested that, in this way, the tendency of the middle 'generation' to be dominant in society may be countered by a coalition of the young and the old. Speaking of African societies in general, Legesse (1973:116) makes the observation that:

> Again and again we learn that the father and son
> are in opposite camps and that grandfather and grand-
> child are allies. This strategy transforms an
> inherently asymmetric and authoritarian relation-
> ship into a much more egalitarian system. The
> pattern tends to minimize the inherent inequalities
> between the generations.

Yet, as we have seen, developing generational groupings at a societal (rather than a familial) level produces its own problems, for in the absence of strict norms governing the period in which a person may sire offspring, the generation groupings fail to be homogeneous and non-overlapping.

Conclusion

We have examined the analytical confusion which charac-

---

[13]/It is worth noting that this alternate generation prin-ciple is not universally found in such societies. For a con-trary case see Laughlin and Laughlin (1974:273).

terizes much of the literature dealing with generations and
have found that this reflects a widespread cultural phenomenon: the tendency to utilize the model of generational succession found within the family to categorize the larger
social universe. In this light, the broad use of the generational concept exemplified by Mannheim is better considered
as a ethnographic datum for study, alongside that of the
Borana Galla and the Jie, rather than as an appropriate
conceptual tool for social analysis.

By defining the concept of generation precisely and
unambiguously some interesting questions for the sociological
study of age and the life course can be raised, for we can
ask what is the relationship between generation and age?
In these pages I have tried to identify a few aspects of
this question, but many remain. Clearly we have a long way
to go before the implications of this relationship are fully
understood.

References

Abrams, Philip. 1970. "Rites de passage: The conflict of
generations in industrial society." The Journal of
Contemporary History 5:1:175-90.

Almagor, Uri. 1980. Coevals and Competitors: Features of
the Dassanetch Generation-Set System. Manuscript.

Baxter, Paul T. W. and Uri Almagor. 1978. "Introduction,"
pp. 1-35 in Paul T. W. Baxter and Uri Almagor (eds.),
Age, Generation and Time. New York: St. Martin's
Press.

Bengtson, Vern L., Michael J. Furlong, and Robert S. Laufer.
1974. "Time, aging, and the continuity of social
structure: Themes and issues in generational analysis."
Journal of Social Issues 30:2:1-30.

Berger, Bennett M. 1959. "How long is a generation?"
British Journal of Sociology 10:10-23.

Bischofberger, Otto. 1972. The Generation Classes of the
Zanaki (Tanzania). Studia Ethnographica Friburgensia,
Vol. I. Fribourg: University Press.

Cutler, Neal E. and Vern L. Bengtson. 1974. "Age and
political alienation: Maturation, generation and period
effects," The Annals of the American Academy of Political and Social Science 415:160-75.

Dyson-Hudson, Neville. 1966. Karimojong Politics. London: Oxford University Press.

Eisenstadt, S. N. 1956. From Generation to Generation. Glencoe: Free Press.

Elder, Glen H., Jr. 1978. "Approaches to social change and the family." American Journal of Sociology 84:S1-S38.

Firth, Raymond. 1970. "Sibling terms in Polynesia." Journal of Polynesian Society 79:3:272-87.

Foner, Anne and David I. Kertzer. 1978. "Transitions over the life course: lessons from age-set societies." American Journal of Sociology 83:5:1081-1104.

Fortes, Meyer. 1940. "The political system of the Tallensi of the Northern Territories of the Gold Coast," pp.239-71 in Meyer Fortes and E. E. Evans-Pritchard (eds.), African Political Systems. London: Oxford University Press.

_____. 1974. "The first born." Journal of Child Psychology and Psychiatry 15:81-104.

Fox, Robin. 1967. Kinship and Marriage. Baltimore: Penguin.

Goody, Jack. 1976. "Aging in nonindustrial societies," pp. 117-29 in Robert H. Binstock and Ethel Shanas (eds.), Handbook on Aging and the Social Sciences. New York: Van Nostrand.

Greenwood, Davydd J. and William A. Stini. 1977. Nature, Culture, and Human History. New York: Harper and Row.

Greven, Philip J., Jr. 1970. Four Generations: Population, Land, and Family in Colonial Andover, Massachusetts. Ithaca: Cornell University Press.

Gulliver, P. H. 1953. "The age set organization of the Jie tribe." Journal of the Royal Anthropological Institute 83:147-168.

Hill, Reuben. 1970. Family Development in Three Generations. Cambridge: Schenkman.

Jackson, Michael. 1978. "Ambivalence and the last-born: birth-order position in convention and myth." Man 13:3: 341-61

Kertzer, David I. 1978. "Theoretical developments in the study of age-group systems." American Ethnologist 5:2:368-74.

Lambert, T. Allen. 1972. "Generations and change: Toward a theory of generations as a force in historical process." Youth and Society 4:1:21-45.

Laufer, Robert S. and Vern L. Bengtson. 1974. "Generations, aging, and social stratification: on the development of generational units." Journal of Social Issues 30:3: 181-205.

Laughlin, Charles D., Jr. and Elizabeth R. Laughlin. 1974. "Age Generations and Political Process in So." Africa. 44:266-79.

Legesse, Asmarom. 1973. Gada New York: Free Press.

Lowenthal, Richard A. 1974. Tharaka Age-Organization and the Theory of Age-Set Systems. Ann Arbor: University Microfilms.

Mannheim, Karl. 1952. "The problem of generation," pp.276-320 in Essays on the Sociology of Knowledge. New York: Oxford University Press.

Marias, Julián. 1968. "Generations: the concept," International Encyclopedia of the Social Science 6: 88-92.

Needham, Rodney. 1974. (1966) "Age, category, and descent," pp. 72-100 in Rodney Needham, Remarks and Inventions. London: Tavistock. Reprinted from Bijdragen tot de Taal-, Land- en Volkenkuunde 122:1-33 (1966).

Ortega y Gasset, José. 1933. The Modern Theme. New York: Norton.

Plath, David W. 1980. Long Engagements: Maturity in Modern Japan. Stanford: Stanford University Press.

Riley, Matilda White, Marilyn Johnson and Anne Foner. 1972. Aging and Society. Volume Three: A Sociology of Age Stratification. New York: Russell Sage Foundation.

Rintala, Marvin. 1968. "Political generation." International Encyclopedia of the Social Sciences 6:92-96.

Ruel, M. J. 1958. "Kuria generation sets." Proceedings of
    Conference held at the East African Institute of Social
    Research, Makerere College.

Ryder, Norman B. 1965. "The cohort as a concept in the
    study of social change." American Sociological Review
    30:843-61.

Stewart, Frank H. 1977. Fundamentals of Age-Group Systems.
    New York: Academic Press.

Troll, Lillian E. 1970. "Issues in the study of genera-
    tions." Aging and Human Development 1:3:199-218.

Troll, Lillian E. and Vern Bengtson. 1979. "Generations
    in the family," pp. 127-61 in Wesley R. Burr, et al.
    (eds.), Contemporary Theories about the Family Volume 1.
    New York: Free Press.

Vinovskis, Maris A. 1977. "From household size to the life
    course: some observations on recent trends in family
    history." American Behavioral Scientist 21:2:263-87.

3. The Life Course as a Cultural Unit

Lives as lived through time are the raw material for soccial science research on aging. Gerontologists who initially focused on the later years alone have recently returned old age to a life course context. Anthropologists, although they have seldom focused on the aged, see and describe life courses in a wide variety of cultural settings. This paper combines these two perspectives to consider the life course as a variable cultural unit and as a perspective for cross-cultural research. Central to our view of the life course is a notion of time and the way in which the universal journey through the life course is culturally charted. We first examine variation in these cultural conceptualizations of the life course and secondly, we explore the culturally shaped uses of the life course in social differentiation and in the allocation of roles.

Culture And Time

In a sociotemporal consideration of aging, one of the most important variables to explore is time. Our understanding of aging is predicated upon a concept of temporal flow and changes in a temporal dimension. Yet, with few exceptions (Hendricks and Hendricks 1976), time remains only implicitly conceived. It is implicit because the scientists investigating the phenomenon are products of similar cultures (ie. Western or Euro-American). Hence, the conceptualization of time is taken for granted, assumed as obvious. Time is not obvious, but elusive. As social and cultural creatures we create time by defining the intervals of social life. As linguistic beings, we condition these definitions further by the structures of our languages.

In Western cultures, definitions of time are rooted in discoveries of the physical sciences, especially astronomy. Our units of measure derive from the well-known cycles of ce-

lestial mechanics: the orbit of the earth around the sun and
the rotation of the earth. Although these cycles do have profound effects upon the environments in which people live (eg.
the seasons, night/day), they are extra-cultural and extra-
social. Time thus is perceived as objective and external to
the individual. Our images of time are predominately geometric metaphors (Leach 1961a). Most commonly, we refer to
time as a non-repetitive straight line stretching from a near
infinite past to a near infinite future.

This model of time has both advantages and pitfalls as
we use it to investigate aging. First, it is extremely attractive in that it is readily operationalized and produces
accurate measurement. Exactitude in measurement is a pre-
condition for good science but no guarantee of it: regardless of exactness, measurement must mean something. This is
precisely the lament in gerontology over reliance upon chronological age as the measurement of aging. As our research pro-
gresses we are increasingly aware of variability in physical,
psychological, and social circumstances of individuals who
have lived the same number of years (Butler 1968). The Western model of time, in spite of its extra-cultural referents,
is definitely culture-specific. Time itself has no geometric
qualities; these images are clearly cultural in origin. Ob-
servers have also noted our preoccupation with time and the
tyranny of the clock (Woodcock 1944). We personify time (eg.
Father Time with his scythe); we feel the pressure of time;
and we perceive the stream of time. Time is a commodity to
be bought; to be sold; to be invested; to be spent; to be
wasted; to be filled; to be lost or to be used to the best
advantage. Anthropologists with their lessons from cross-
cultural studies are quick to remind us that such notions are
by no means universal (Bock 1966; Bohannan 1953; Evans-
Pritchard 1940; Maxwell 1972; Smith et al. 1961). Scheduling
by the clock and calendar is only one way of doing it. Schedules are important to social life, but schedules may be more
relative and flexible and may be reckoned without reference
to exact units of time.[1]

On a cross-cultural basis, time and schedules are ripe
territory for misunderstandings. Rather than permit these to
permeate our study of aging or to further digress into a phil-
osophical essay on the nature of time, we must return to a

---

1. Exactness in schedules (ie. calendars for agricultural
cycles and clocks for work schedules) are products of and
requirements for larger scale cultures which must coordinate
larger numbers of people and greater quantities or resources.

realization that we create time. The question is, How? We recognize repetition and define it with beginnings and ends. The repetitions are repeated reversals between polar opposites (Leach 1961a). They are oscillations between such opposites as night and day, winter and summer, life and death. The oscillations are the intervals which punctuate time and which we select and integrate into a cultural model of time. Time, however, involves more than intervals. It also requires a recognition of change and a notion of speed or rate of change (Leach 1961b). Time is culturally defined as intervals (oscillations in nature or in human affairs) with changes occurring at a recognized rate between the beginning and the end of the interval. A culture may emphasize exactness by selecting such oscillations as stellar cycles upon which to base temporal intervals. On the other hand, a culture may predicate intervals on a rough approximation of natural cycles and emphasize cultural oscillations such as entrance and exit from parental roles.

Wide variation occurs both in definitions of the entire life -- oscillation between birth and death -- and of its internal structure. It is interesting to note that in Western gerontology the term "life course" has increasingly supplanted "life cycle". The life course signifies a linear, irreversible progression between the beginning and end points. Its focus is on individuals, their expectations, alternatives, and actual experiences as they pass through the biological, psychological, social, and cultural markers of aging. Life cycle, on the other hand, refers to a societal process of generational succession: the entrance and exit of people to and from the social system (much like cohort flow). Cyclical age grade systems, in which the long-lived may actually be "re-cycled" as their grade is joined by the youngest age sets, and belief in reincarnation are two ways that life and death may be linked in a circle or spiral rather than a line.

A metaphoric oscillation between birth and death appears on a micro level, within one life, when we consider the discontinuities with which cultures punctuate the life span. As documented in the early part of this century (Van Gennep 1960, original 1909) rites of passage demarcate the stages of the life course. As rites, they are ceremonies which strip individuals of earlier statuses and move them into the statuses of the next stage. Rites of passage are replete with explicit symbolism which universally falls into stages of a symbolic death, a liminal or marginal state, and a rebirth. Time does not march forward continuously throughout the life course as an even procession of minutes, hours, days or years. Time moves in halts and starts through uneven intervals as rites of passage transform and pass an individual onto the

next life stage. The life stages, the intervals and their
boundaries are culturally defined and are culture-specific.

Life Courses In A
Comparative Perspective

The challenge of all cross-cultural research is how to
encompass the tremendous variability of human societies.
Methodologically, anthropologists have been most ingenious in
their solutions (Naroll and Cohen 1973) with strategies ranging from the sampling and coding of cultural data found in
the Human Relations Area Files to integrated and coordinated
field research in several cultures (e.g., Whiting and Whiting
1975). Although a life course perspective could focus comparative ethnographic reporting, the life course has not been
given a full systematic anthropological "treatment". This is
not because anthropologists are lacking in a vocabulary with
which to dissect the life course analytically. Indeed, as
documented by Cain (1964) many of our basic concepts derive
from the work of anthropologists and cross-cultural research.
For instance, such concepts as rites of passage (Van Gennep
1960, original 1909), cultural discontinuities (Benedict
1938), age grades (Radcliffe-Brown 1929), age status and age
and sex categories (Linton 1940, 1942), age homogeneous
groups (Esenstadt 1956), age class, age sets (Prins 1953),
and age differentiation (Gulliver 1968) are only a few of
those developed by earlier researchers. Their work provided
foundations for and has been incorporated into the perspectives directing current research: 1) Social-psychological
as represented by the work of Bernice Neugarten (1968), and
2) Age Stratification as represented by the work of Matilda
White Riley and her associates (1972). In spite of differing
emphasis (Neugarten and Datan 1973), the life course continues to be seen as a complex of roles and statuses which
are culturally structured and for the individual change
through time. Roles and statuses are successive and are se-
quenced. As members of a society age, they occupy these sequential statues which are made predictable through normative
expectations of a societal age status system.

Anthropologists continue to contribute to our understanding of the human life course. A major thrust in or research
has been the documentation of diversity and the development
of hypotheses through ethnographic case studies. Notable a-
mong our discoveries is that the life course is a variable
cultural unit, but at the same time that the variability is
not infinite. Our initial question is how does it vary, followed by a query whether in all this diversity we find any
uniformities? The life course is variable: 1) in the per-
ceptions of life as a unit; 2) in definitions of its internal

structure; 3) in the possibility of individual variations and multiple pathways; and 4) in the criteria used to evaluate and the exactness with which careers are monitored (Keith 1980). Each of these points of variation will be discussed separately.

The life course may or may not be perceived, planned for and evaluated as an integrated unit. Lives may have definite trajectories, or be an amalgamation of distinct threads in multiple domains (i.e., reproduction, occupations, politics, spirituality or they may be continued round of seasonal tasks. Certainly, for the Tiwi of Australia (Hart and Pilling 1960), a man's life course has a definite trajectory as charted through marriage negotiations: his own, his daughters', and his widowed mother's. In this marital gerontocracy, a successful older man is one who acquires several wives (usually many years his junior), receives betrothals of infant brides; builds alliances with other successful males by betrothing his wife's daughters; and because of this aggregated womanpower, is free from subsistence activities to attend to ceremonial and political affairs. In India, the Hindu Asram system with its "four stages of life"[2] codifies an ideal life plan for earthly existence and eventual rebirth (Vatuk 1980). One prepares oneself for and then takes over the management of the family wealth, followed by a withdrawal from worldly affairs and a contemplation of spiritual matters in preparation for death and rebirth. The Quechua Indians of the Peruvian Andes view their life course as a cycle of first an unfolding of vigor and then a decline and loss. Human existence evolves vigorously until the middle or "twelve o'clock years" followed by the second stage "the midnight" when the decline sets in. Here in the Andes, the metaphor for vitality is earth or soil. As a people walk and climb through life they leave behind particles of their "earth supply" resulting in age and finally in death (Holmberg in Smith et al. 1961). The life course of the Abkhasians, the long-living people of the Caucasus, as reported by Benet (1973), is filled with moderation, continuity and gradual change toward a positive and extremely old age. Gradualness of change and continuity are also reported for the working class of industrialized smaller towns of Germany (Weatherford 1981). In the Arctic, the harshness of the seasons reinforces a theme of productivity in Eskimo life. Life is work and work is largely dictated by the sea-

---

2. The stages are 1) Celibrate Student (Brahnacharya), 2) Married Householder (Girhasta), 3) Retired Life of the Forest (Vanaprastha), and 4) Complete Renouncement of Worldly Attachments (Sannyasa). It is unclear to what extent this ideal was actualized in Indian life.

son. There is no peak to life, only a gradual curve of increasing respect with age (Hughes, in Smith et al. 1965).
Eskimo elders, however, are noted for delaying old age by com-
pensating for their declining productivity and by "renewal"
activities which ally an older person with those who are
younger. For men this is accomplished by marriage to a younger woman; for older women the strategy is the adoption of
children (Guemple 1969). Regardless of the enormous range of
cultural variation in the conceptions of the life course, one
point of variation remains invariant: men and women are likely to perceive their life courses differently.

    The life course may or may not be monolithic and thor-
oughly explored path. For instance, Robert Levy (cited in
LeVine 1978a) found that Tahitians have no sense of alternatives to a single life paradigm rooted in their local culture in which they view themselves as fully autonomous beings
very early in life. Nepalese, on the other hand, view the
life course as filled with many branching paths for individual choice, development and exploration even into late life.
These differences may represent the life course as it is
understood in a small scale, undifferentiated society, in
contrast to one that is a product of a complex, highly differentiated and urban culture. In the latter, choice is the
rule rather than the exception. This is reinforced by life
course studies in our own society (Neugarten and Hagestad
1976), and by the research of Alexander Moore in Guatemala
(1973). The life course for Indians in Atchatlan is clearly
defined with little or no room for variation and experimenta-
tion. However, the mestizos of the same village who are linked to the Guatemalan national social structure have diverse
careers dependent upon their contacts, skills, education, opportunities and goals.

    More obvious but significant variation appears in the
criteria used to calculate performance and in the preciseness
used to reckon age itself. Most urban societies, such as the
United States, use chronological years to calibrate life. Although this is also used by a few traditional societies such
as the Fulani of West Africa, among most non-literate peoples
chronological age is unknown. Age is calculated roughly,
approximately, relatively, functionally, not absolutely. The
criteria for the calculation of individual performance are
culture-specific, being dependent upon the institutional ave-
nues and awareness of acceptable life careers. Robert LeVine
(1978a) hypothesizes that a contrast between agricultural and
foraging peoples is reflected in the Gusii farmers' attention
to the monitoring and evaluation of fertility histories and
the comparative lack of concern over "reproductive careers"
among the !Kung San (Bushman) hunter-gatherers. These dif-

ferences are rooted in significant contrasts in strategies of
resource accumulation and the way social groups are articulated with resources.

   These and other hypotheses are ripe for evaluation in
the anthropological test ground as we sift through diversity
in the search for universals. For comparisons to be made and
generalizations to be found which probe beyond the tantaliz-
ing ethnographic descriptions, the data must be collected in
a way that will ensure comparability. Similar analytic techniques must also be used to guarantee comparability in the
interpretation of results. Far too little of this has been
undertaken in anthropology, not to mention the downright scarcity of comparative studies of the life course. Major exceptions are two studies: one done in Kenya among the Masai,
a pastoral society with age sets (Kirk and Burton 1977), and
the other conducted in the United States among adult Americans in Indiana (Fry 1980b). Although each anthropologist
focused on considerably different problems (among the Masai
it was on personality descriptors, while in Indiana it was
age classification), both researchers utilized elicitation
procedures developed within cognitive anthropology. These
procedures rely upon the judgments of similarities/differen-
ces or on judgments of cultural appropriateness by informants
(see Fry 1980a for a more detailed discussion of this methodology). Among the Masai, these techniques involved a triad
test, while in America a card sort was used. The Masai triad
test asked informants to choose the two out of three adjec-
tives that were the most appropriate to describe a male or
female of a particular age set. i.e.. adult female or male
warrior. American informants were asked to examine a deck
of cards describing people and then to group the cards into
age categories. Informants' judgments constitute the data
for these two studies: Masai made judgments about personality descriptions for age sets; Americans made judgments about
age appropriateness of configurations of social statuses.
To further the comparability of these two studies, both used
age as a point of reference (Masai used age sets; the Americans sorted according to judgments of age similarity) and
both used multidimensional scaling to analyze the resulting
data. The results do reflect cultural differences. The
Masai "picture of age" is a zig-zag with marked sexual differentiation, while the United States picture is one of a
horseshoe shaped curve with little sexual differentiation
(see Fry 1980b for a more detailed discussion of these differences). Marked similarities surface in the dimensions
underlying these pictures of the life course. Both researchers identified responsibility as one underlying dimension
and both identified a domestic criterion in the second dimension: marriage for the Masai and reproductive cycles for

the Americans. These similarities, with further comparative
research, may indicate that despite all the diversity within
the ethnographic record, the human life course, at a deeper
level, may not be as variable as we think it is. It may be
constrained by the bounds of responsibility for production
and reproduction.

Cultural Uses
Of The Life Course

Social Differentiation

Basic to the study of social organization is the inves-
tigation of role differentiation. Roles lay down the rules
of conduct: how we interact, we exchange and we are interdependent. Role differentiation, however, is more complicated
than a simple cross-classification of how roles are differentiated. An appropriate image is one of borders or boundaries
between people, over which, around which and through which
they negotiate. Social borders are one of the things anthropologists study. Old age is not new to anthropology, but age,
per se, is a border we are only beginning to "attack". Certain borders appear more "natural" than others and consequently we tend to minimize their cultural definitions. Age
and sex have not received the attention of anthropologists
equal to apparently more "cultural" borders, such as kinship
or ethnicity (LaFontaine 1978). Cultural variation in gender
roles has recently blossomed as a sub-area of anthropology.
Age differentiation, its degrees, kinds and consequences have
not been explored across cultures or across the life course.
When all the results on sex and age are in, they may appear
as culturally elaborated as the other naturally derived cate-
gorizations of kinship and ethnicity.

Differentiation of the life course into age grades is a
clue to the age borders in a society. Age grades are categories slicing the life course into indexed or ranked states.
Categories are cognitive indicators of the important boundaries and significant identities. Differentiation of the
life course has not totally escaped ethnographers in their
cross-cultural studies. Most of our comprehensive ethnographies include descriptive summaries of a typical life
course in a particular culture. The age-explicit (age-set
or generation-set) societies of East Africa, Latin America
and the Great Plains of the United States have served as
ideal case studies. However, the questions asked have not
been those eliciting data on the categories and the criteria
used to differentiate the life course.

This question involves a real-life sorting by infor-

mants who are thoroughly immersed in their specific cultural
context. In the United States, a sample of American adults
did just that as they sorted through a card deck placing hy-
pothetical people or social persona into the age categories
they habitually used (Fry 1976). The results indicate variability in numbers of categories, but notable consensus on
boundaries. These informants distinquished between 2 and 15
age categories (mean is 5.16 and standard deviation is 1.88)
and provided over 200 age terms to describe their age grades.
This variability is indicative of the ambiquity in age grading in the United States, a calendar-conscious society. Why
do some people distinquish so many age categories and other
people so few? The data from this study suggest that the
number of age distinctions is related to the age heterogeneity of one's social network, especially one's kin network.
This is not a simple linear relationship of increasing age
heterogeneity in the actual social network with a corresponding expansion in cognitive age distinctions. Instead, the
rhythm of the domestic cycle is mirrored in the number of
age distinctions. First there is an increase in both heterogeneity and age distinctions with the expansion of the family
of procreation, followed by a contraction with the empty
nest, and finally another expansion with the appearance of
grandchildren. What boundaries gradate the life course for
this American sample? A cluster analysis in which the number
of age distinctions is controlled for, reveals the boundaries
most commonly encountered are: The presence/absence of
children; career advancements (promotions); pre-post high
school children; grandparenthood; and retirement (Fry 1979).
This is one study. For comparability and to answer broader
questions, we need more like it. Will we find that age
grades are less variable in small scaled, traditional societies? Will we find that the boundaries between age grades
are distinquished by different or variants of similar criteria: will we find that the number of distinctions made by
any one informant is attributable to the age heterogeneity
of their social networks or by their position in the age
hierarchy? Stratification studies suggest that those in the
lower ranks or out of power will make more distinctions as
they look upward in comparison to those looking downward. In
some societies this will be the young, in others the old,
and in still others, both looking "up" to the middle.

The significance of age distinctions is also a virtual
unknown other than as general guideposts for behavior. Two
comparative studies suggest that age categories affect intergenerational tensions and have consequences which are most
pertinent for older people. In a controlled comparison of
African societies, Nadel (1960) found that a greater number
of age categories was positively associated with the corres-

pondence between social age and physical ability. For example, among the Korongo who have a larger number of age
classes, social age and ability are more congruent, transitions are more gradual and accepted, and the old men are less
resentful of the young. In a sample of 60 societies drawn
from the Human Relations Area Files, Glascock and Feinman
(1981) discovered that over a third of the cultures in the
sample had more than one category of older person: young-
old or intact old in contrast to the old-old or decrepit
old.[3] The latter category emerged from such references as
the "overaged", "the sleeping period", "the age grade of the
dying", and the "already dead". The consequence of classification in this case is life or death. All the societies in
which old people were subjected to non-supportive or death-
hastening treatment make the intact-decrepit distinction.
These same societies also support and hold their elders in
great esteem. This two-faced finding is not contradictory.
The two kinds of behavior are directed to the respective
classes of old: life and respect to those who can participate adequately, and death to those who can't. An important
caveat about this relationship is that reports of death or
non-supportive treament are rare in world-wide terms, and are
found in societies with certain characteristics: egalitarian
and located in harsh climates that have no agriculture or
only shifting gardens (Glascock and Piennam 1980).

Timetables And
The Allocation of Roles

Age grades are the mileposts; age norms set the speed
limits. Some people "exceed" the speed limits; others "poke"
along (both are off time), but know the "proper" (on-time)
speed and monitor their own passage through life (Neugarten
and Hagestad 1976). Most societies have a notion of social
time or a "social clock". These clocks are variable in the
institutional pathways; in life events; in the attention
given to the age at which they should occur; and in the a-
wareness of age norms. On a comparative basis, we know very
little about timetables and transitions. Most of our exploration has been conducted within our own society and has
been directed toward social psychological and developmental
issues (Goulet and Baltes 1970; Baltes and Schaie 1973); the
development of life course models (Perun and Del Vento Bielby
(1980); historical changes (Hareven 1978, 1980; Fischer 1977;

---

3. This is an approximate, but not exact parallel of
Neugarten's distinction between young-old and old-old (1974).
The meanings and the implications are very different for peo-
ple in industrial societies.

Elder 1979); the complex unraveling of expectations vs. individual and cohort performance (Uhlenberg 1978) and the measurement of life events and the age in life events (Nydegger 1980).

Age norms are not divorced from roles. Age norms are the standard allocation of roles across the life course. Our view is complicated by the realization that seldom, in any society, do we find a pure, pristine age role. Age is an attribute of the actors performing their roles in the institutional sectors of a society. Age norms set the bounds for entrance to and exit from these roles. Life course research in the United States and other industrial societies has found occupational careers and family cycles to be the most central with a lesser saliency in political and community roles (Clausen 1972; Neugarten and Moore 1968). The Gusii farmers, on the other hand, have three careers: reproductive, economic, and ritual (LeVine 1978b). Variation in timing is reported for different classes in the United States with the working classes arriving at the older age grades earlier than the middle class (Neugarten and Peterson 1957). The rules on the timing of transitions are guidelines, often negotiated. In a study of 21 age-set societies, the researchers discovered that even in these formal systems, transitions are not rigidly fixed but are sometimes recognitions of gradually accumulating individual transitions, sometimes foci of conflict between pressing young and resistant old (Foner and Kertzer 1978, 1979). Awareness of age norms varies across the life course, but our current evidence from two industrial societies points to some parallels across cultures. In Japan (Plath and Ikeda 1975), awareness of age norms by Japanese informants mirrors the age-awareness of those Americans who participated in Neugarten's Chicago study (Neugarten, Moore and Lowie 1965). Awareness of age norms increased with age; impressions of the normative expectations held by others and by self merge with increased age; the later the event in the life course, the greater the salience of age in judging it; as men age they are more aware of age norms than women, and norms are more salient to the actions of men than women.

Life courses, life histories, life careers, are all elegant concepts until they encounter life as it is lived by individuals. Lives are filled with idiosyncracies, compromises, and events beyond the control of the person. A seemingly simple domestic cycle can be very complicated when we consider alternate timing patterns (i.e., Hill and Associates 1970). Methodologically, in the search for patterns in the variability in age transitions, anthropologists have suggested the use of graphs: life graphs (Nydegger 1980); aging graphs (Fry, in press). Through graphic representation, the temporal aspects (age) may be plotted along the Y or horizontal axis and the role and institutional dimensions along the vertical axis. Thus, horizontal lines would represent continuity in the occupation of a role and the vertical lines would represent status change (entrance or exit). Such a graph could be used as a survey instrument or could be used to compare societies not only for age norms, but also for age-salient roles, the critical institutional sectors and even the calibration of the temporal dimension.

The Social Significance
Of Age

The life course is a cultural framework people like to use to organize their world and to chart their way through it. The life course is not a truly bounded unit. Its only bounds are the institutions of a society through which its path or pathways lead. By cross-cutting and permeating other social borders found in a society, the life course presents yet another window through which to explore cultural diversity. Age becomes the focal variable as we examine the conditions and consequences of culturally defined views and uses of the life course.

Preliminary results of a search, still underway, through anthropological literature suggest general patterns of age differentiation, some of which counter common notions about the social significance of age.[4]

1. Age differentiation is complementary to other forms of social differentiation. As societal differentiation increases, age differentiation also increases. This challenges our assumed "naturalness" of age. When other criteria, the more cultural criteria, are used to differentiate a society, they cross-cut and blur the more basic, primary feature such as age (van den Berghe 1973; Foner 1974). These preliminary results, on the contrary, indicate that age is not residual. As societies become more differentiated, age and its cultural definition are likely to do the differentiating.

2. Spatial separation of age groups, at some point in the life course, is not unusual. In almost half of the so-

---

4. Two sources of data were used: 1) A probability sample of 60 traditional societies in the Human Relations Area Files designed to minimize such methodological problems as contacts between cultures; to guarantee inclusion of a variety of subsistence types and culture areas; and to include those cultures where ethnogrphic reporting is of high quality; 2) Ethnographic monographs chosen for quantity and quality age data.

cieties in the sample, residential separation by age is the
norm. This is contrary to the common view that age-segrega-
ted housing is an unusual and recent development. Residential age segregation have yet to be sorted out, a task which
will be easier with the realization that it occurs frequently
in a wide variety of cultural contexts.

3. Cross-age alliances involve a principle of alternat-
ing "generations". Alternation of generations is a familiar
principle to anthropologists, sometimes being extended into a
division into two separate streams. The core feature is a
counter balance to those in the middle and to relationships
marked by authority or competition. The alternate generation
alliance is similar to our ideal grandparent-grandchild relation. Grandparents, having no authority over grandchildren,
have an affective, warm and indulgent relationship. This
complementarity of affect and authority between grandparents
and grandchildren has been documented cross-culturally (Apple
1965). Cross-generational aid in the purchase of age societies among the Hidatsa (Bowers 1965) involves the alliance
of non-adjacent age sets. Adjacent sets are competitors who
are busy buying a society from their immediate seniors and
selling a society to their immediate juniors. Many African
age systems conceive of alternate generations as two opposing streams in the social organzation (Spencer 1965). Alliance between alternate age groups, the young and the old
against the middle has been suggested for our own culture
(Kalish 1969), and is in fact a central part of Gray Panther
ideology.

4. Age criteria and age grouping occur most frequently
among those life states that are "out of power". The relationships between these age-mates are egalitarian. An enduring equality of age-mates has been a central assumption
in almost all studies of age systems (i.e., Evans-Prichard
1940, Spencer 1965) and peer groups. The preliminary results
challenge this assumption. Evidence from age-explicit societies indicates age is most salient prior to social maturity. For instance, among the Akwe-Shavante of Brazil, the
bonds of age set membership are compelling up until adulthood when an individual's ties to their clans and factions
take priority (Maybury-Lewis 1967). Among the Dassanetch
of Ethiopia, the ethos of equality actually reinforces inequality with the onset of social maturity (Almagor 1978).
In our own culture, it is among the young preparing for and
the old retired from social maturity that we would expect to
find high salience of age and equality among peers.

These hypotheses are questions to entice us as scientists to take another look at our assumptions and some of

our propositions about aging. The life course window sharp-
ens our focus. To answer these questions, we need to take
them to the anthropological laboratory. We need to work in
different industrial contexts, varying cultures, rural, urban
and suburban communities, different ethnic groups, and in old
and newer settlements.

Conclusions

The life course is a cultural framework people use to
organize both timing and meaning of the span between
birth and death. A cross-cultural perspective on the life
course reveals how much variation -- in both time and meaning -- exists between, or cycles around, those two fixed
poles. The exploration of that diversity should be high on
our research agenda: The laboratory is the 3000+ human cultures in the world. The prize is the possible discovery of
definitions of time and meaning that promote more satisfying
passages through the course of life.

References

Almagor, Uri. "The Ethos of Equality among Dassanetch Age-
    Peers", In Age, Generation And Time: Some Features of East
    African Organizations, edited by P.T.W Baxter and Uri
    Almagor. New York: St. Martins' Press, 1978.

Apple, D. "The Social Structure of Grandparenthood". American
    Anthropologist 58 (1956): 656 - 63.

Baltes, Paul B. and Schaie, K. Warner. Eds. Life-Span Deve-
    lopmental Psychology: Personality and Socialization. New
    York: Academic Press, 1973.

Benedict, Ruth. "Continuities and Discontinuities in Cultural
    Conditioning". Psychiatry I (1938): 161 - 67.

Benet, Sula. Abkhasians: The Long-Living People of the Cau-
    casus. New York: Holt, Rinehart and Winston, 1974.

Bock, Philip K. "Social Time and Institutional Conflict".
    Human Organization 25 (1966): 96 - 102.

Bohannan, Paul J. "Concepts of Time Among Tiv of Nigeria".
    Southwestern Journal of Anthropology 9 (1953): 251 - 262.

Bowers, A.W. Hidatsa Social and Ceremonial Organization.
    Washington, D.C.: Smithsonian Institution, Bureau of
    American Ethnology Bulletin 194, 1975.

Butler, R.N. "The Facade of Chronological Age". In Middle Age and Aging. Edited by Bernice L. Neugarten. Chicago: University of Chicago Press, 1968.

Cain, Leonard D. "Life Course and Social Structure". In Handbook of Modern Sociology. Edited by R.L. Faris. Chicago: Rand McNally, 1964.

Clausen, John A. "The Life Course of Individuals". In Aging and Society, Vol. 3: A Sociology of Age Stratification. Edited by Matilda White Riley et. al. New York: Russell Sage Foundation, 1972.

Durkheim, Emile. Elementary Forms of the Religious Life, trans. J.W. Swain. New York: The Macmillan Co., 1915.

Eisenstadt, S.N. From Generation to Generation: Age Groups and Social Structure. New York: Free Press, 1956.

Elder, G.H. "Age Differentiation and the Life Course". Annual Review of Sociology, Vol. I. Palo Alto, Calif: Annual Reviews, 1975.

_____. "Historical Change in Life Patterns and Personality". In Life-Span Development and Behavior. Edited by Paul B. Baltes and Orville G. Brim, Jr. New York: Academic Press, 1979.

Evans-Prichard, E.E. The Nuer. Oxford: Clarendon, 1940.

Fabrega, Horacio, Jr. and Zucker, Martinez "Comparison of Illiness Episodes in a Pluralistic Setting". Psychosomatic Medicine (1977) 325 - 43.

Fischer, David H. Growing Old in America. New York: Oxford University Press, 1978.

Foner, Anne, "Age Stratification and Age Conflict in Political Life". American Sociological Review, 39 (1974): 187-96.

Foner, Anne and David Kertzer, "Transitions over the Life Course: Lessons from Age-Set Societies". American Journal of Sociology 83 (1978): 1081 - 1104.

_____. "Intrinsic and Extrinsic Sources of Change in Life-Course Transitions". In Aging from Birth to Death: Interdisciplinary Perspectives. Edited by Matilda White Riley. AAAS Selected Symposium #30. Boulder: Westview Press, 1979.

Fry, Christine L. "The Ages of Adulthood: A Question of Numbers". Journal of <u>Gerontology</u> 31 (1976): 170 - 71.

_____. "Attributes of Age". Paper Presented at the 78th Annual Meeting of the American Anthropological Association, Cincinnati, Ohio, 1979.

_____. "Cognitive Anthropology and Age Differentiation". In <u>New Methods for Old Age Research</u>. Edited by Christine L. Fry and Jennie Keith. Chicago: Center for Urban Policy, Loyola University of Chicago, 1980a.

_____. "Cultural Dimensions of Age: A Multidimensional Scaling Analysis". In <u>Aging in Culture and Society</u>: Comparative Viewpoints and Strategies. Edited by Christine L. Fry New York: Praeger (a J.F. Bergin Book), 1980b.

_____. "Temporal and Status Dimensions of the Life Course". <u>International Journal of Aging and Human Development</u>. In Press.

Fry, Christine L. and Jennie Keith, Eds. <u>New Methods for Old Age Research</u>. Chicago: Center for Urban Policy, Loyola University of Chicago, 1980.

Glascock, Anthony P. and Susan L. Feinman. "Toward a Comparative Framework: Propositions Concerning the Treatment of the Aged in Non-Industrial Societies". In <u>New Methods for Old Age Research</u>. Edited by Christine L. Fry and Jennie Keith. Chicago: Center for Urban Policy, Loyola University of Chicago, 1980.

_____. "Social Asset or Social Burden: An Analysis of the Treatment of the Aged in Non-Industrial Societies". In <u>Dimensions: Aging, Culture and Health</u>,Edited by Christine L. Fry, New York: Praeger (a J.F. Bergin Book), 1981.

Goulet, L.R. and Baltes, Paul B., Eds. <u>Life-Span Developmental Psychology: Research and Theory</u>. New York: Academic Press, 1970.

Guemple, D.L. "Human Resource Management: The Dilemma of the Aging Eskimo". <u>Sociological Symposium</u> 2 (1969): 59-74.

Gulliver, P. "Age Differentiation". In <u>International Encyclopedia of the Social Sciences</u>. New York: Macmillan, 1968.

Hareven Tamara K. "The Life Course and Aging in Historical Perspective". In <u>Life Course: Integrative Theories and</u>

Exemplary Populations. Edited by Kurt W. Back. AAAS Selected Symposium #41. Boulder: Westview Press, 1980.

_____. Ed. Transitions: The Family and the Life Course in Historical Perspective. New York: Academic Press, 1978.

Hart, C.W. and Pilling, A.R. The Tiwi of Northern Australia, New York: Holt Reinhart and Winston, 1960.

Hendricks, C. Davis and Hendricks, Jon "Concepts of Time and Temporal Construction Among the Aged with Implications for Research". In Time Roles and Self in Old Age, Edited by Jaber F. Gubrium. New York: Human Sciences Press, 1976.

Hill, R. Foote, N. Aldous, J., Carlson, R. and Macdonald, R. Family Development in Three Generations. Cambridge: Schenkman, 1970.

Kalish, Richard A. "The Old and the Young as Generation Gap Allies". The Gerontologist, 9 (1969): 83 - 90.

Keith, Jennie. "Old Age and Age Differentiation: Anthropological Speculations on Age as a Social Border". Elderly of the Future, Edited by Sara Kelser. New York: Academic Press, forthcoming.

_____. "'The Best is Yet to Be' Toward an Anthropology of Age". In Annual Reviews of Anthropology, Vol. 9. Palo Alto: Annual Reviews, 1980.

Kirk, Lorraine, and Burton, Michael. "Meaning and Context: A Study of Contextual Shifts in Meaning of Masai Personality Descriptions". American Ethnologist 4 (1977): 734-61.

Leach, Edmund R. "Chronus and Chronos". In Rethinking Anthropology. By E.R. Leach, New York: Humanities Press, 1961a.

_____. "Time and False Noses". In Rethinking Anthropology. By E.R. Leach, New York: Humanities Press, 1961b.

LaFontaine, J.S. Ed. Sex and Age as Principles of Social Differentiation. New York: Academic Press, 1978.

LeVine, Robert. "Adulthood and Aging in Cross-Cultural Perspective". Items 31/32 (1978a), 1 - 5.

_____."Comparative Notes on the Life Course". In Transitions: The Family and The Life Course in Historical Perspective. Edited by Tamara K. Hareven. New York: Academic Press, 1978b.

Linton, Ralph. "A Neglected Aspect of Social Organization". American Journal of Sociology. 45 (1940): 870 - 886.

_____."Age and Sex Categories". American Sociological Review. 7 (1942): 589 - 603.

Maxwell, Robert, J. "Anthropological Perspectives". In The Future of Time. Edited by H. Yaker, et. al. Garden City, N.J.: Anchor Books, 1972.

Maybury-Lewis, David. Akwe-Shavante Society. Clarendon: Oxford University Press, 1967.

Moore, Alexander. Life Cycles in Atchatlan: The Diverse Careers of Certain Guatemalans. New York: Teachers College, Columbia University, 1973.

Myerhoff, Barbara and Simic, Andrei. Eds. Life's Career -- Aging: Cultural Variations in Growing Old. Beverly Hills: Sage Publications, 1978.

Nadel, S. F. "Witchcraft In Four African Societies". In Cultures and Societies of Africa. Edited by S. Ottenberg and P. Ottenberg. New York: Random House, 1960.

Naroll, Raoul and Cohen, Ronald. Eds. A Handbook of Method in Cultural Anthropology. New York: Columbia University Press, 1973.

Neugarten, Bernice L. Ed. Middle Age and Aging: A Reader in Social Psychology. Chicago: University of Chicago Press, 1968.

Neugarten, Bernice L. "Age Groups in American Society and the Rise of the Young-Old". In Political Consequences of Aging. Edited by F. R. Eisle. Philadelphia: The Annals of the American Academy of Political and Social Science, 1974.

Neugarten, Bernice and Hagestad, Gunhild O. "Age and the Life Course". In Handbook of Aging and the Social Sciences. Edited by R. Binstock and E. Shanas. New York: Van Nostrand Reinhold, 1976.

Neugarten, Bernice L. and Moore, Joan W. "The Changing Age Status System". In Middle Age and Aging. Edited by Bernice Neugarten. Chicago: University of Chicago Press, 1968.

Neugarten , Bernice L., Moore, Joan W. and Lowie, John. "Age Norms, Age Constraints, and Adult Socialization". American Journal of Sociology 70 (1965): 710 -717.

Neugarten, Bernice L. and Peterson, Warren. "A Study of the American Age Grade System". Proceedings of the International Association of Gerontology. 3 (1957): 497 - 502.

Nydegger, Corinne. "Role and Age Transitions: A Potpourri of Issues". In New Methods for Old Age Research: Anthropological Alternatives. Edited by Christine L. Fry and Jennie Keith. Chicago: Center for Urban Policy, Loyola University of Chicago, 1980.

Paulme, Denise. "Blood Pacts, Age Classes and Castes in Black Africa". In French Perspectives in African Studies. Edited by P. Alexandre. Oxford: Oxford University Press, 1973.

Perun, Pamela J. and DelVento Bielby, Denise. "Structure and Dynamics of the Individual Life Course". In Life Course: Integrative Theories and Exemplary Populations. Edited by Kurt W. Back. AAAS Selected Symposium #41. Boulder: West-view Press, 1980.

Plath, David W. and Ikeda, Keiko. "After Coming of Age: Adult Awareness of Age Norms". In Socialization and Communication in Primary Groups. Edited by Thomas R. Williams. The Hague: Mouton (Distributed by Aldine: Chicago, 1975.

Prins, A.H.J. East African Age-Class Systems: An Inquiry into the Social Order of Gallo, Kipsigis, and Kikuyu. Groningen: The Netherlands: Wolters, 1953.

Radcliffe-Brown, A.R. "Age Organization Terminology". Man 29 (1929): 21.

Riley, Matilda White, Johnson, Marilyn and Foner, Anne. Aging and Society: Volume Three: A Sociology of Age Stratification. New York: Russell Sage Foundation, 1972.

Ross, Jennie (Keith). "Social Borders: Definitions of Diversity". Current Anthropology 16 (1975): 53 - 72.

Smith, Robert J. et. al. "Cultural Differences in the Life Cycle and the Concept of Time". In Aging and Leisure. Edited by Robert Kleemeier, New York: Oxford Univerity Press, 1961.

Spencer, Paul. The Samburu: A Study in Gerontocracy in a Nomadic Tribe. London: Routledge and Kegan Paul, 1965.

Uhlenberg, Peter. "Changing Configurations of the Life Course". In Transitions: The Family and the Life Course in Historical Perspective. Edited by Tamara K. Hareven. New York: Academic Press, 1978.

van den Berghe, Pierre L. Age and Sex in Human Societies: A Biosocial Perspective. Belmont, Calif.: Wadsworth, 1973.

van Gennep, A.   The Rites of Passage. Chicago: University of Chicago Press, 1960 (original published in 1909).

Vatuk, Sylvia. "Withdrawal and Disengagement as a Cultural Response to Aging in India".   In Aging in Culture and Society: Comparative Perspectives and Strategies. Edited by Christine L. Fry, New York: Praeger (a J.F. Bergin Book), 1980.

Weatherford, Jack M. "Labor and Domestic Life Cycles in a German Community".   In Dimensions: Aging, Culture and Health. Edited by Christine L. Fry. New York: Prager (a J.F. Bergin Book), 1981.

Whorf, Benjamin Lee.   "The Relation of Habitual Thought and Behavior to Language".   In Language, Culture and Personality, Essays in the Memory of Edward Sapir. Edited by Leslie Spier. Menasha, Wis.: Sapir Memorial Publication Fund, 1941.

Whiting, Beatrice B. and Whiting, John W.M. Children of Six Cultures: A Psycho-Cultural Analysis. Cambridge: Harvard University Press, 1975

Wilson, Monica. Good Company: A Study of Nyakusa Age Villages. London: Oxford University Press, 1951.

Woodcock, G. "The Tyranny of the Clock".   Politics 3 (1944): 265 - 267.

4. Some Consequences of Age Inequality in Nonindustrial Societies

Old age, a common stereotype has it, is relatively glorious in nonindustrial societies: the old occupy seats of power; are lords of the family; and are honored for their wisdom and experience. This stereotype is too simple, however. Relations with the young can complicate the picture. Because age is a basis of structured inequality, strains and conflicts often develop between the advantaged old and disadvantaged young. In addition, in many nonindustrial societies the elderly lose, rather than gain, rewards and privileges.

Focusing on societies where the old are relatively privileged, this paper reports selected findings from my comparative study of age inequalities and age relations in a broad range of nonindustrial societies.[1] I first outline the kinds of rewards and valued roles the elderly can acquire in nonindustrial societies and then discuss the impact of old people's high status on relations with the young. For where the old reap many benefits, the young tend

---

[1]/The larger comparative study on which the analysis in this paper is based draws on material on about 60 nonindustrial societies (Foner, n.d.). This material provides in-depth information on inequalities, tensions, and accommodations between old and young. The comparative study does not investigate the frequency with which the old gain or lose valued roles and rewards in nonindustrial societies. For attempts to develop statistically reliable generalizations about the status or the treatment of the aged in cross-cultural perspective see Glascock and Feinman, 1981; Maxwell and Silverman, 1970; and Simmons, 1945.

to be relatively disadvantaged, often resenting the privileges of their elders and the restraints under which they, themselves, labor. The bulk of the paper concentrates on the privileged old-- and on old people who can still physically and mentally attend to their daily existence and who do not need custodial care. I will, however, briefly comment on the kinds of social losses the old in different cultures experience and how this can create tensions with the young. The concluding remarks are of a more general nature, considering some implications of my analysis of age inequalities and age relations for a general approach to the study of age in nonindustrial societies.

Rewards and Valued Roles

Let me begin with the bright side for the elderly. In many nonindustrial societies, growing old gives individuals the opportunity to occupy valued roles and accumulate rewards. This does not mean that all of the elderly are equally successful. Luck, skill, and personality, to name just three factors, can affect an old person's achievements. In addition, in some societies older people who are, for example, members of particular descent groups may be the only ones who can qualify for certain political roles. But age does limit the competition for rewards and valued roles, and younger people often have to wait their turn to compete.

What kinds of rewards and valued roles can the old acquire in nonindustrial societies?[1] One benefit of aging is that the old often have greater opportunity than the young to control material resources and other property. This is especially marked for old men. Elderly widows in some places, to be sure, control much of the family patrimony in their lifetimes. In some societies, too, aging gives women the opportunity to accumulate movable property. By and large, however, old women's control of key material resources is more limited than old men's. Indeed, in farming and pastoral societies, old men often control-- and have the power to allocate and transfer-- land, livestock, and other property. Such control gives them considerable power over the young, particularly when the resources or property old men administer are in scarce supply.

---

[1] In many nonindustrial societies, middle-aged or mature adults may also obtain the rewards and valued roles discussed below and they may also have strained relations with younger people. My concern in this paper, however, is with the old.

Old men's control of material resources and other property can have far-reaching consequences. Old men may manage property or have the wealth needed for a livelihood; to marry; to provide hospitality and to give generously; to acquire a following; and to gain prestige.

It is often hard to separate old men's control over material resources and other property from their "people power." In nonindustrial societies, the ability to command the labor and support of others often underpins old men's wealth, prestige, and influence. Where land is readily available, where labor cannot be hired, and where one person can, given rudimentary technology, only cultivate or gather a limited amount of food, those who can call on many people have a definite edge. They are the ones with the surplus to entertain or acquire prestige goods; who can build up political support; and who can even retire from the more arduous productive tasks.

Building up large households and followings is thus a key to success in nonindustrial societies. Old men, for one thing, have simply had more time than younger people in which to do this. They also frequently control the material-- as well as reproductive-- resources needed to attract followers and accumulate dependents. Polygyny is important here. In societies with polygyny, it is usually older men who are adding wives while young men must wait (sometimes until their thirties) to marry (see, for example, Douglas, 1963; Hart and Pilling, 1960; Spencer, 1965). (This is often because older men control the wherewithal to marry; or sometimes because other restrictions prevent young men from marrying until relatively late.) Wives provide labor power. So do children and subsequently, daughters-in-law or sons-in-law and grandchildren. Where daughters leave to join their husbands, they usually bring bridewealth into the household. In some societies, sons-in-law provide fathers-in-law with labor for periods of time in the form of bride service. Where sons-in-law join their wives' people at marriage, younger men may give fathers-in-law more lasting help. Marriage also creates affinal bonds which are useful in building up alliances and support.

As heads of domestic groups, older men in many societies have extensive powers over juniors. Older men, for example, may allocate resources and labor as well as settle disputes and punish offenders in the group (see LeVine, 1965). As a woman ages, she also usually has more juniors under her wing. A woman's domestic authority typically increases as her children grow up and marry and, in turn, have their own children. In some societies, women may even head households

in their later years. More commonly, official authority in
the household rests with the male head. Even so, older women
often supervise the activities of younger women in the
household-- daughters, for example, daughters-in-law,
granddaughters and perhaps also junior wives. These older
women command respect and obedience from juniors. And
younger women in many places relieve older mothers or
mothers-in-law of more onerous burdens.

With age, women may also have more influence outside the
domestic group. Old women frequently play a dominant role in
initiation rites, for example. In certain societies they
even have formal power over younger women in the community
(e.g. Ottenberg, 1971). And old women often gain informal
political clout in the community because they can exert
influence over husbands, sons, or brothers.

Old women's political influence in the community tends
to be informal. As men grow old, however, they often have
greater opportunity to hold formal positions of authority
beyond the domestic group. Local leaders are frequently
drawn from the ranks of old men. In many societies,
moreover, old men predominate in councils, informal
assemblies, voluntary associations, and secret societies.
And they often play a crucial role in adjudicating disputes.

Old people's political and domestic authority in
nonindustrial societies is often backed up by beliefs about
their ritual powers. Indeed, we cannot talk about old
people's advantaged position without mentioning the ritual
sphere. Aging in nonindustrial societies tends to bring with
it certain ritual powers so that the old have ritual benefits
and may occupy ritual offices denied-- or less available-- to
younger people. By virtue of their mystical powers, the old
in some societies are believed capable of harming as well as
protecting living juniors-- and thus the old have powerful
mystical sanctions at their command. In many places as well,
ritual specialists (curers, for example) tend to be old, and
the elderly often occupy a central place in religious
ceremonies.

Ritual knowledge is just one part of old people's
expertise. They are also the ones with years of experience
in every-day practical affairs. In preliterate societies,
the elderly are valued as repositories of wisdom--sources of
information about the past and about the way things should be
done.

Quite apart from their property, ritual and secular
authority, and wisdom, age, in itself, frequently commands

deference from the young. In many nonindustrial societies,
the old, on the basis of their age and/or seniority, are
thought to deserve respect. And juniors are supposed to
accord the aged special treatment such as greeting old people
in a deferential way or giving them seats of honor at
ceremonies.

Strains with the Young

This review of the privileges of old age has, by
necessity, been brief. Yet it gives an idea of why we can
say old people in many nonindustrial societies are at the top
of the age hierarchy. It has also hinted at why old people's
relations with the young may be problematic. In short, there
is a negative side to power and privilege. We need to round
out our view of the advantaged old by exploring how they get
along with less fortunate juniors.

While the elderly are accumulating powers, privileges,
and wealth, young people often find themselves subject to and
constrained by old people's authority. As a rule, the young
are supposed to defer to and obey their elders, and they
frequently do. They may also be bound to their elders by
ties of loyalty, identification, and affection; and they may
even accept their disadvantaged position as right and proper.
But-- and this is a crucial but-- the young may also be
bursting over with envy and resentment or at least be
ambivalent towards old folks in control. Nor do tensions
between old and young always lie beneath the surface.
Sometimes they erupt in open conflict.[1]

Which relations are particularly subject to strain?
Much depends on the structural arrangements in the society
under study. In some societies, for example, there is a
general opposition between old and young men in the community
or wide kinship group with young men restricted in their
activities by elders and having little say in matters which
deeply affect them (see, for example, Spencer, 1965).[2]

---

[1] An analysis of the forms such conflict takes as well
as the factors which prevent or minimize open conflicts
between old and young is developed in Foner (n.d.).

[2] Even in these cases, relations between certain old and
young men in the community or wide kinship group may be
especially strained. Among the Samburu, for example, young
men in the moran age grade and older men in the firestick
elder grade had particularly tense relations (Spencer, 1965).

In many nonindustrial societies, however, tensions between old and young are most pronounced between particular close kin or affines. In the case of men, we commonly find serious strains developing where young men succeed and are subject to the authority of certain older men. Most typically these strains develop between fathers and sons in patrilineal societies and between maternal uncles and sister's sons in matrilineal societies.

What are the sources of tension and rivalry between older men and their successors? One source of the younger man's resentment before he marries is his economic dependence on his father or maternal uncle. Although a young man is eager to come out from under, it may be difficult for him to become more independent. We read of many patrilineal societies where a young man's very ability to marry and set up his own household hinges on his father's willingness and readiness to allocate resources to him. Senior men may not be so willing or ready, trying, for example, to delay providing the bridewealth sons need to marry.

Nor does marriage necessarily end younger men's dissatisfactions. Rivalry between fathers and sons and maternal uncles and nephews might actually increase after young men mature and marry. At this time, young men often want more autonomy and become more impatient to replace the older men.

When an older man and his successor live in the same household, the younger man is subject to the old man's constant authority. A resident son, for example, might have to wait for his father's death or extreme old age before he can officially take charge in the household.

Even where young married men are residentially independent of maternal uncles or fathers, their continued dependence on these older men in many societies can rankle. Among the patrilineal Anlo Ewe of southern Ghana, for instance, a man was expected to establish his own compound after he married. His father now gave him part of his, the father's, land (or uncleared bush adjoining it) to use. But this did not liberate a young man from his father's authority. A son built his compound at a place chosen by his father-- usually not far from the father's compound so he could help the older man when needed. And help he did. The father's farming needs came first and he had a claim on his son's labor at sowing, hoeing, and weeding times (Nukunya, 1969: 32-40). Among the Suku of Zaire, to give an example from a matrilineal society, nephews generally lived in separate villages (though not too far) from their maternal uncles. Yet young men chafed under the never-ending demands for contributions from real or classificatory maternal uncles who, as lineage elders, had greater control of lineage wealth (Kopytoff, 1964).

Issues of property inheritance may loom large. Young men are often waiting to come into their full inheritance-- clearly a cause of tension with older men in many societies. Even where seniors allocate land or other property in their lifetime to the younger generation, they may retain considerable property-- the land they themselves farm, for example-- which the young are eager to inherit.

If young men in many societies resent their economic dependence on, and demands for labor and financial assistance from, fathers or maternal uncles, there are also other grounds for discontent. The older man's jural and/or ritual authority can place severe constraints on their actions. Young men, for example, might be unable to make certain decisions without consulting and gaining the approval of the older men. In many patrilineal societies, younger men cannot assume certain ritual powers or roles until their fathers die.

Older men are not oblivious to young men's desires to come into their own. "Look at my oldest son," said one Tallensi man. "He would not care if I should die tomorrow. Then he would inherit all my possessions...." (Fortes, 1949:225; see also Fortes, 1950:272; Harris, 1978:110). A sick man among the Suku preferred to be cared for by his sons rather than his sister's sons: sons had nothing to gain materially from the older man's death whereas sister's sons might be impatient to move up the ladder of authority and take control of lineage property (Kopytoff, 1964:104). In many societies, the older a man got, the more he felt his days on top were numbered and that his heir was simply waiting in the wings to take over.

What about relations between old and young women? Because old men usually have more official authority and control more property than old women does not mean that old women's relations with juniors are trouble-free. Most frequently reported are the strains between mothers-in-law and daughters-in-law who live in the same household (in patrilocal extended families). Although tensions may be severest when the daughter-in-law is a new bride and the mother-in-law may not yet be old (R. LeVine, 1965), in some societies tensions continue well into the mother-in-law's old age (see, for example, S. LeVine, 1978; Vatuk, 1975).

The daughter-in-law -- like younger men mentioned above-- represents a threat from below. If she is slated to take over as mistress of the household when her mother-in-law dies or steps down, then she may be impatiently biding her time. Other daughters-in-law represent a different kind of challenge. The way to autonomy and control for them is to persuade their husbands to set up their own households. The mother-in-law, however, is trying to keep her household together (and her sons with her) and she resents any real or imagined attempts by her daughters-in-law to tear it apart (cf. Collier, 1974).

Younger women often have good reason to want to leave. They are supposed to help their mother-in-law and accede to her demands, but the older woman's domination can be quite repressive, especially when there are severe limitations on the daughters-in-law autonomy. The older woman's demanding and even sometimes abusive behavior may stem from her jealousy of the daughter-in-law's tie with the son/husband and the fear that the daughter-in-law is trying to lure the young man away (see, for example, Wolf, 1972). The older woman may also relish her new-found opportunity to order other adults to do her bidding. Whatever the reason, a daughter-in-law's lot is frequently a difficult one. In an urbanized village of metropolitan Delhi, for example, a daughter-in law did the heaviest duties in the house (Vatuk, 1975). The mother-in-law controlled the purse strings so that a daughter-in-law had to ask for money for any routine purchases. And an old woman expected her daughter-in-law to serve her-- to perform such tasks as massaging her legs at night. "Young women," Vatuk (1975:153) tells us, "often relate how their sas (mother-in-law) makes them press her legs... for hours at a stretch each night, until they drop off to sleep from exhaustion, at which point the old woman is perversely brought back to wakefulness, demanding that the massaging continue."

Whether we are talking about mothers-in-law, fathers or maternal uncles on top, it is clear that old people pay a price for privilege. Relations with young subordinates are frequently in a state of uneasy peace, and sometimes open conflict. Moreover, the old usually have to be careful not to be too greedy or to press their demands too far, particularly where it is fairly easy for dissatisfied young dependents to withdraw their labor and political support by moving to other communities (see Douglas, 1965; Terray, 1972: 170-172).

Social Losses

If all is not a bed of roses for the advantaged old, things tend to be worse for the elderly who give up valued roles and rewards they have worked so hard to obtain.

First consider the still alert and fairly active old. In some age-set societies, for example, these old men must relinquish formal political roles when their set moves on to the next grade (see Kertzer and Madison, 1981). In societies without age sets, the still active old may find themselves losing authority. This loss of authority can be quite a formal process. In some peasant societies, for example, the capable old formally cede control of property and headship of the household to the younger generation.

Just when and how this transfer occurs differs from place to place. It may be effected by a legal contract and the whole estate may pass to a designated heir when he marries (e.g. Arensberg and Kimball, 1968). Sometimes, the family property is slowly whittled away as each child marries. Among the Sherpa, each son was given a share of the family's land and ideally a house when he married; each daughter was given a dowry. The youngest son stayed on in the parents' house-- which he would inherit-- and he was supposed to feed and care for his parents out of this last share of their estate. In practice, Sherpa parents were, Ortner (1978:20,44-47) says, often reduced to the status of dependents-- sometimes almost servants-- in the youngest son's household. When they had turned over all their remaining property to the youngest son, they worked in his fields and received food from him. In some cases, the old people clung to independence for as long as possible by buying or building a small hut for themselves and by retaining a small piece of land to cultivate.

Where the old transfer property and household control to the young during their lifetime, tensions can arise with the young over the timing of the transition. The young wait with bated breath while the old often try to delay giving up control. In the Sherpa case, for example, parents connived to postpone their children's marriages. In general, once the property and household control have passed to the younger generation, there are different sources of trouble.

The old may be resigned to their lot. Like the Sherpa old described by Ortner (1978:47), they may expect little of their children. But reports on other societies indicate that the old often have greater expectations. They may have a hard time adjusting to their new role and continue to try

to dominate even though formal control is gone. This can
lead to strains with the young heir and his wife who want to
fully take over and who may resent having to restrain
themselves, for the sake of harmony, until the old couple die
(see Douglass, 1969).

In many nonindustrial societies, however, people only
begin to experience significant social losses when advanced
physical debility or senility set in. The elderly usually
find their physical incapacity distressing. Physical
declines also mean they tend to become increasingly marginal
in daily affairs. And they are more and more dependent on
the young for support and custodial care.

The quality of the care the elderly receive varies
widely, depending in part on the relationship with their
caretakers. We read, for example, of adult children in many
societies looking after incapacitated parents with devotion
up until the end. But there are also many examples where the
incapacitated aged are defined as second-class citizens whose
needs come last. And there are cases where the aged are
abused and neglected, sometimes even killed or abandoned (see
Glascock and Feinman, 1981). Even young people with the best
intentions may find they are too busy with productive and
other tasks to attend to frail old people's every need. And
factors beyond young folks' control-- such as drought, a poor
food supply, or the group's need to move-- can lead to poor
treatment of the elderly.[1]/

Although the evidence is scanty, it appears that
tensions between the incapacitated old and their younger
caretakers can develop around the issue of care and support.
The elderly may have difficulty coming to terms with their
physical condition and resent the still healthy young-- who
are also taking over. The old may also feel they are not
being supported properly. As for younger folks, caring for

---

[1]/Of course, the question arises as to whether the old
perceive this as ill-treatment. There are indications that
in some societies they may resent their situation (e.g.
Colson and Scudder, 1981) and see themselves as sufferers
(e.g. Simmons, 1945:234). But there is also evidence from
other societies that the aged may accept their second-class
status as legitimate and feel that because they are
incapacitated they deserve what they get. And there are
reports that the decrepit old may even request to be killed
or abandoned when their strength gives out and they become
too great a burden (e.g. Simmons, 1945; Watson and Maxwell,
1976:38).

the aged may be a burden and they may resent what they
believe are exorbitant or unfair demands from the old.

Conclusion

In sum, the preceding discussion has shown that a simple
view of the old in nonindustrial societies-- luxuriating in
their power and privilege-- clearly will not do. In the
first place, the influential and privileged elderly often
have strained relations with the disadvantaged young.
Moreover, the old frequently suffer considerable social
losses and this, too, can create tensions with the young.

If this analysis warns against idealizing the situation
of the elderly in nonindustrial societies, it also has
implications for the general anthropological study of old
age. A perspective which emphasizes age as a basis of
structured social inequality-- or social stratification--
opens up new lines of inquiry and highlights social processes
that have received relatively little attention in
cross-cultural studies of aging.[1]

When age systems are seen as systems of social
inequality, the old are viewed as part of the whole age
system rather than in isolation. After all, the very
existence of an age hierarchy assumes that individuals in one
age stratum are better or worse off in certain ways than

----

[1]Although many ethnographies discuss tensions between
young and old, anthropologists writing about aging in
cross-cultural perspective have tended to neglect this
subject. In the main, gerontological anthropologists have
focused on such topics as: factors leading to high (or low)
status among, and good (or bad) treatment of, the aged (e.g.
Goody, 1976; Maxwell and Silverman, 1970; Simmons, 1945);
societal and self conceptions of aging (e.g. Kleemeier, 1961;
Myerhoff and Simic, 1978); old age communities (e.g. Keith,
1977, 1979); and the importance of cross-cultural evidence in
evaluating sociological and psychological theories of aging
(e.g. Clark, 1973; Myerhoff and Simic, 1978).

LeVine's (1965) paper on intergenerational tensions in
African patrilocal extended families and French Marxist
anthropologists' (e.g. Terray, 1972, 1975) analyses of
elder-youth relations are the main anthropological
contributions to the cross-cultural study of relations
between old and young. A. Foner and Kertzer (1978), in
addition, have utilized the age stratification model to
analyze anthropological material on age-set societies.

individuals in other age strata. Age strata (socially recognized divisions based on age), as age stratification theorists write, not only differ in age or life stage but they also have unequal access to highly valued roles and social rewards (see Riley, Johnson, and Foner, 1972; A. Foner, 1975, 1979). It is important to know how social rewards and roles are allocated among all the age strata in a society and not only among the old.

Furthermore, once the perspective of age inequality or stratification is introduced, the possibility of conflict and tension between age strata arises. Of course, we know from our own society that social inequalities-- class, race, or sex, for instance-- do not inevitably produce open conflict between the advantaged and disadvantaged. But the potential for discord and strain is ever present (see A. Foner, 1979). In terms of age inequalities in nonindustrial societies, those at the top of the age hierarchy may be resented by those below. And downwardly mobile individuals-- who have suffered social losses with age-- may resent the more successful young and be bitter about their own declines.

In this paper I have begun to specify some of the consequences of age inequality in nonindustrial societies by analyzing certain trouble spots between young and old. It thus not only dispels the notion of an idyllic old age in these societies but emphasizes the importance of age inequalities as a source of strain and conflict.

References

Arensberg, Conrad and Solon Kimball
  1968 Family and Community in Ireland. Second edition.
     Cambridge: Harvard University Press.

Clark, Margaret
  1973 "Contributions of Cultural Anthropology to the Study
     of the Aged," Cultural Illness and Health, ed. by Laura
     Nader and Thomas Maretzki. Washington, D.C.: American
     Anthropological Association.

Collier, Jane F.
  1974 "Women in Politics," Woman, Culture and Society, ed.
     by Michelle Z. Rosaldo and Louise Lamphere. Stanford:
     Stanford University Press.

Colson, Elizabeth and Thayer Scudder
  1981 "Old Age in Gwembe District, Zambia," Other Ways of
     Growing Old, ed. by Paula Amoss and Stevan Harrell.
     Stanford: Stanford University Press.

Douglas, Mary
  1963 The Lele of the Kasai. London: Oxford University
  Press.

Douglass, William A.
  1969 Death in Murelaga: Funerary Ritual in a Spanish
  Basque Village. Seattle: University of Washington
  Press.

Foner, Anne
  1975 "Age in Society: Structure and Change," American
  Behavioral Scientist 19: 144-166.
  1979 "Ascribed and Achieved Bases of Stratification."
  Annual Review of Sociology 5: 219-242.

Foner, Anne and David Kertzer
  1978 "Transitions over the Life Course: Lessons from
  Age-Set Societies," American Journal of Sociology 83:
  1081-1104.

Foner, Nancy
  n.d. Old Age: A Comparative View of Inequality and
  Conflict.

Fortes, Meyer
  1949 The Web of Kinship among the Tallensi. London:
  Oxford University Press.
  1950 "Kinship and Marriage among the Ashanti," African
  Systems of Kinship and Marriage, ed. by A.R.
  Radcliffe-Brown and Daryll Forde. London: Oxford
  University Press.

Glascock, Anthony and Susan Feinman
  1981 "Social Asset or Social Burden: An Analysis of the
  Treatment of the Aged in Non-Industrial Societies,"
  Dimensions: Aging, Culture and Health, ed. by Christine
  Fry. New York: J.F. Bergin.

Goody, Jack
  1976 "Aging in Nonindustrial Societies," Handbook of Aging
  and the Social Sciences, ed. by Robert Binstock and Ethel
  Shanas. New York: Van Nostrand Reinhold.

Harris, Grace Gredys
  1978 Casting Out Anger: Religion among the Taita of
  Kenya. Cambridge: Cambridge University Press.

Hart, C.M.W. and Arnold Pilling
  1960 The Tiwi of North Australia. New York: Holt,
  Rinehart and Winston.

Keith, Jennie
   1977 Old People, New Lives. Chicago: University of
   Chicago Press.
   1979 (ed.) The Ethnography of Old Age. Special Issue of
   Anthropological Quarterly.

Kertzer, David I. and Oker B.B. Madison
   1981 "Women's Age-Set Systems in Africa: The Latuka of
   Sudan," Dimensions: Aging, Culture and Health, ed. by
   Christine Fry. New York: J.F. Bergin.

Kleemeier, Robert W. (ed.)
   1961 Aging and Leisure. New York: Oxford University
   Press.

Kopytoff, Igor
   1964 "Family and Lineage among the Suku of the Congo," The
   Family Estate in Africa, ed. by Robert F. Gray and Philip
   H. Gulliver. London: Routledge and Kegan Paul.

LeVine, Robert A.
   1965 "Intergenerational Tensions and Extended Family
   Structures in Africa," Social Structure and the Family:
   Generational Relations, ed. by Ethel Shanas and Gordon
   Streib. Englewood Cliffs, N.J.: Prentice-Hall.

LeVine, Sarah
   1978 Mothers and Wives: Gusii Women of East Africa.
   Chicago: University of Chigago Press.

Maxwell, Robert and Philip Silverman
   1970 "Information and Esteem: Cultural Considerations in
   the Treatment of the Aged," Aging and Human Development
   1: 361-393.

Myerhoff, Barbara and Andrei Simic (eds.)
   1978 Life's Career-- Aging: Cultural Variations in
   Growing Old. Beverly Hills, Ca.: Sage.

Nukunya, G.K.
   1969 Kinship and Marriage among the Anlo Ewe. London:
   The Athlone Press.

Ortner, Sherry
   1978 Sherpas Through Their Rituals. New York: Cambridge
   University Press.

Ottenberg, Simon
   1971 Leadership and Authority in an African Society.
   Seattle: University of Washington Press.

Riley, Matilda W., Marilyn Johnson, and Anne Foner
    1972 Aging and Society, Volume III: A Sociology of Age
          Stratification. New York: Russell Sage.

Simmons, Leo
    1945 The Role of the Aged in Primitive Society. New
          Haven: Yale University Press.

Spencer, Paul
    1965 The Samburu: A Study of Gerontocracy in a Nomadic
          Tribe. London: Routledge and Kegan Paul.

Terray, Emmanuel
    1972 Marxism and Primitive Societies. New York: Monthly
          Review Press.
    1975 "Classes and Class Consciousness in the Abron Kingdom
          of Gyaman," Marxist Analyses and Social Anthropology,"
          ed. by M. Bloch. London: Malaby Press.

Vatuk, Sylvia
    1975 "The Aging Woman in India: Self-Perceptions and
          Changing Roles," Women in Contemporary India, ed. by A.
          deSouza. Delhi: Manohar.

Watson, Wilbur and Robert Maxwell
    1976 Human Aging and Dying. New York: St. Martin's
          Press.

Wolf, Margery
    1972 Women and the Family in Rural Taiwan. Stanford:
          Stanford University Press.

5. Subgroup Variations in Early Life Transitions

The passage of twentieth century American males from youth to adult status involves the completion of key age-graded transitions. These transitions include the completion of formal education, the achievement of relative economic independence through the beginning of the first, full-time civilian job, and the formation of a family of procreation through first marriage (Winsborough, 1978; Modell et al., 1976). The achievement of these three transitions transform American males from nonproductive, dependent members of the society into largely self-supporting, reproductive members of the society.

The timing of these transitions is not determined exactly by society. Rather, the school completion, beginning of first job, and first marriage transitions are achieved transitions that tend to be self-initiated (Neugarten and Hagestad, 1976). Although the society does not set exact ages for these early life transitions, there do appear to be normative expectations about the appropriate age-ranges for these transitions, outside of which a person is "early" or "late" (Neugarten et al., 1965). Persons achieving a transition within the prescribed age range are viewed as "on-time" in that transition, whereas persons who complete the transition early or late are viewed as "off-time". These normative expectations not only specify the appropriate age range for each transition, but also prescribe an appropriate

Support for this study provided by a Spencer Foundation Research Grant to the Division of Social Sciences, University of Chicago, is gratefully acknowledged. Table 1 and its discussion are adapted from Transitions and Social Change: The Early Lives of American Men by Dennis P. Hogan (New York: Academic Press, 1981).

sequence of transitions (Elder, 1974, 1978). For example,
most persons agree that it is desirable to delay marriage
until after schooling is completed and the couple is self-
supporting (Modell, 1980). Furthermore, American males
tend to conform to this ordering norm in their actual transition behavior (Hogan, 1978). Thus, the range of options
available to individuals initiating these early life transitions are constrained by normative timetables.

The timing of early life transitions varies substantially among cohorts and social groups. In part, these
differentials in transition behavior are associated with
intercohort and intergroup variability in educational attainment. In order to complete a high level of education men are
forced to prolong their school enrollment, delaying the completion of schooling. A later first job entry and first
marriage are associated with delays in school completion
(Hogan, 1978). Rates of marriage before the completion of
schooling are higher among men with advanced levels of education (Hogan, 1978). Thus, men from higher status social
classes tend to have a later age at school completion, first
job, and marriage and are more likely to marry prior to the
completion of schooling. Men born in more recent cohorts
also display a later age at school completion and first job
and higher rates of marriage prior to finishing school,
although they do not have later ages at marriage (Hogan,
1981).

The timing and sequencing of transition events may vary
among population subgroups because of differential access to
resources which facilitate transitions. Social class, size
of community of residence, and ethnic ancestry are three
characteristics of family background frequently mentioned as
affecting transition behavior (Neugarten and Hagestad, 1976;
Elder, 1978; Katz and Davey, 1978). Each of these characteristics affect aspirations for educational attainment, as
well as the ability to complete the level of education to
which persons aspire (Sewell and Shah, 1968; Sewell, 1964,
1971; Blau and Duncan, 1967). Thus, men from subgroups with
control of relatively few social and economic resources are
less likely to aspire to a college education, and relatively
few of those who do wish to complete college will achieve
that ambition. As a consequence, the men from these lower
status social groups tend to finish school, begin work, and
first marry at an earlier age, as noted above.

But the problems of coordinating and managing transition behavior are likely to be greatest among those men who
complete college. The effects of subgroup membership on

transition behavior would be most pronounced among college graduates, since a college education must be financed and the economic resources of population subgroups vary. Subgroup differences in transition behavior thus are hypothesized to persist when controls are introduced for educational attainment, and the largest differentials are anticipated among men with four or more years of college.

Social class, community size, and ethnic ancestry are correlated variables. Men who are black or Hispanic are more likely to be of farm or blue-collar backgrounds. Men from rural communities tend to have lower social class positions than men from metropolitan areas. To an extent, therefore, the effects of each characteristic on transition behavior is a result of its association with the other background characteristics. For example, ethnic differences in transition behavior in part result from the differing social class compositions of the ethnic groups.

However, these background variables are theoretically distinct, and each is hypothesized to have unique effects on transition behavior. Social class of family or origin indicates the availability of social and economic resources of the family in which a man grew up. Men from higher status social class backgrounds (i.e., white collar origins) will, on average, have the greatest access to resources facilitating a normative transition to adulthood. Men from lower status social class backgrounds (i.e., blue collar or farm) will have the least access to family resources facilitating their early life transitions, and are expected to display the highest rates of nonnormative transition behavior. The size of community of residence is associated with a greater availability of resources facilitating the transition to adulthood. For example, a larger community is more likely to have a college which a man could attend while living at home, and the high schools in the community are more likely to include college-preparatory curricula. The occupational opportunity structures of large communities are more diversified, and thus may facilitate labor force entry. Ethnic groups vary in their degree of integration with the American value system. Although empirical evidence is not available, it seems probable that ethnic groups vary in the degree to which they adhere to societal norms about transition behavior (Elder, 1978; Neugarten and Hagestad, 1976). Also, fertility differentials produce ethnic variability in the number of children drawing upon family resources. Family consumption strategies may vary among ethnic groups in ways which facilitate or hinder early life transitions (see Modell, 1978).

Hypotheses

This paper reports empirical tests of three hypotheses about subgroup variations in the timing and sequencing of early life transitions among twentieth-century American males:

1. Conformity to societal norms about the timing and sequencing of early life transitions varies uniquely among social class, community size, and ethnic subgroups.

2. These subgroup variations in transition behavior vary by level of education, and are most pronounced among men with four or more years of college.

3. The subgroups with the fewest social and economic resources and the least integration into the American value system most frequently violate transition norms.

Data

The data for this study are drawn from the Occupational Changes in a Generation II (OCG-II) survey, which was carried out in conjunction with the March demographic supplement to the Current Population Survey (CPS) in 1973. The eight-page OCG-II questionnaire was mailed out six months after the March CPS and followed by mail, telephone, and personal callbacks. The respondents, comprising 88 percent of the target sample, included more than 33,500 men aged 20 to 65 in the civilian noninstitutional population. Blacks and Hispanics were sampled at about twice the rate of other men, and almost half of the black men were interviewed personally. (See Featherman and Hauser [1978] for a complete description of the survey.)

Methods

No existing data describes the actual population normative prescriptions about transition behavior. Therefore, I operationally defined transition behavior as normative or nonnormative according to its statistical normativity in the transitions of American men. That is, the modal transition behavior of American men was taken to be that which is normative, and transition behavior that was statistically rare was defined as nonnormative.

Five measures of nonnormative early life transition
behavior are examined: an interruption in schooling, off-
time school completion, first job, and first marriage, and
marriage before the completion of schooling. Men who report
at least one interruption in schooling lasting six months or
longer are defined as having a nonnormative educational
history. For each level of education, survival table estimates of the age at school completion, first job, and first
marriage were calculated. The ages at which one-quarter and
three-quarters of the men at each level of education completed each transition was calculated. Men who completed a
transition earlier than the first quartile or later than the
third quartile age at that transition for men at the same
level of education were classified as "off-time" on that
transition. Finally, men who marry prior to the completion
of school are viewed as having a nonnormative sequence of
transitions.[1]

Five levels of educational attainment are distinguished:
fewer than twelve years of high school; high school graduate;
some college; college graduate; and one or more years of
graduate or professional education. Social class is defined
according to the occupation of the father (or other household head) when the respondent was about age 16. Three
social classes are defined: white collar; blue collar; and
farm. Size of community of residence at age 16 is defined
as: metropolitan (large city or suburb); small city or town;
and rural. Ethnic ancestry is based on the respondent's
race and his first response to the question, "What is the
original nationality of your family on your FATHER's side?
That is, what was it before coming to the United States?
(Example: Polish, German, Spanish, Russian)." Four paternal
ethnic ancestry groups are distinguished: Northern and

---

[1] In the log-linear models estimated, the relative timing of
school completion, first job, and first marriage actually
distinguished among men completing a transition in the first,
second, third or fourth quartile of men at their level of
education. The odds ratios calculated for these models were
combined to provide the estimates of the probability of an
off-time versus an on-time transition reported in this paper.
Also, three categories of the temporal ordering of events
were distinguished in the models estimated. In this paper,
men who first completed school, then began work and lastly
married were combined with men who have one inversion from
this normative order. Therefore, this paper contrasts the
probability of marrying before school completion versus
marrying after school completion.

Table 1. Models of the net effects of social background variables on the timing of transition events: U.S. males born 1907-1952.

Dependent Variable	Model[a]					X^2_{LR}[b]	df[c]	p[d]	e
School interruption. . . .	(LSPE)	{TLS	{TLP	{TLE	(TSP)	102.1	136	>.5	1.6
Age at school completion. .	(LSPE)	{TLS	{TLP	{TLE		307.0	420	>.5	3.7
Age at first job. . . .	(LSPE)	{TLS	{TLP	{TLE		311.3	420	>.5	3.7
Age at first marriage. . .	(LSPE)	{TLP	{TLE	{TSP		309.0	414	>.5	3.5
Temporal ordering of events .	(LSPE)	{TLS	{TLP	{TSP	{TLE (TPE)	187.1	280	>.5	2.7

a Each model shown was selected using reverse stepwise procedures to include all statistically significant (p<.05) parameters in the model and to exclude all parameters not statistically significant (p>.05) from the model.

T = Timing variable. School interruption (No/Yes); age at school completion; age at first job; age at first marriage (first quartile/second quartile/third quartile/fourth quartile); temporal ordering of events (normative/intermediate nonnormative/extreme nonnormative).

L = Level of education (0-11/12/13-15/16/17 or more).

S = Social class (white collar/blue collar/farm).

P = Size of place of residence (large city or suburb/small city/rural).

E = Paternal ethnic ancestry (Northern, Western, and Central European/Eastern European and Russian/Southern European/Hispanic and Black).

X^2_{LR} is the likelihood ratio chi-square statistic.

c df are the degrees of freedom.

d p is the probability level that the chi-square statistic is due to chance.

e is the index of dissimilarity between the observed sample frequencies and the expected sample frequencies obtained with that model.

Western European; Eastern European, including Russian;
Southern European; Hispanic or black.[2]

There are five different dependent variables in the
analysis. The relation of each of these dependent variables
to education, social class, community size, and paternal ethnic ancestry is examined separately. Both the dependent and
independent variables are categorical, and the effects of
social class, community size and ethnicity are hypothesized
to vary by level of education. In this situation, log-linear
modified multiple regression modeling procedures are appropriate (Goodman 1971, 1972). The log-linear analysis of each
transition proceeds as follows. The multi-way cross-classification of the dependent variable by education by social
class by community size by ethnicity is produced. The
association among education, social class, community size,
and ethnicity are included in a baseline model, as is a
variable indicating the proportion of persons in each category of the dependent variable. The appropriate hierarchical
model that explains all of the statistically significant
associations of the independent variables with the dependent
variable is selected following the reverse of stepwise modeling procedures discussed by Goodman (1971). The model
selected incorporates the direct effects of an independent
variable on the dependent variable, as well as any joint
effects between two or more independent variables on the
dependent variable.

Results

The model which best fits the association between the
independent variables and the dependent variable, for each
of the five dependent variables of interest, is shown in
Table 1. The baseline model for the effects of education
and subgroup membership on school interruption includes a
parameter for the association among the four independent
variables (LSPE). The model selected additionally incorporates parameters for the direct effect of each independent
variable on school interruption. For example, the (TS)
parameter that is hierarchically included in the (TLS) parameter indicates that social class has a direct effect on

----

[2] In order to simplify the tables, only the results for
high school graduates, college graduates, and five or more
years of college are shown. These are the groups of greatest theoretical interest, and they also are the categories
of the education variable within which years of schooling
completed are homogeneous.

school interruption. The inclusion of the (TLS) parameter
instead of a simple (TS) parameter indicates that the effect
of social class on school interruption varies among levels
of education. In addition, both size of community and ethnic ancestry affect the probability of a school interruption,
and these effects vary among men at different levels of
education. Finally, the inclusion of the (TSP) parameter
in the school interruption model indicates that the effects
of social class on school interruption vary among men from
different community sizes. The model selected with reverse
stepwise procedures fits quite well (X^2_{LR} = 102.1 with 136
degrees of freedom, p > .5), misallocating only 1.6 percent
of the total number of cases.

The first hypothesis states that conformity to societal
norms about the timing and sequencing of early life transitions varies uniquely among social class, community size,
and ethnic subgroups. For each of the five dependent variables, the model selected includes (TS), (TP) and (TE)
parameters (see Table 1). This confirms that social class,
community size, and ethnic ancestry each have statistically
significant, independent effects on the conformity of men
to societal norms about the timing and ordering of transition events.

The second hypothesis states that the subgroup
differences in transition behavior vary by level of education, and are most pronounced among men with four or more
years of college. The effect of community size and ethnic
ancestry vary among levels of education for each of the five
transition variables. The effect of social class on transition behavior varies among levels of education for every
transition variable except age at marriage. This provides
strong support for the hypothesis that subgroup differences
in transition behavior vary by level of education.

In order to determine whether the subgroup differentials in transition behavior indeed are greatest among men
with four or more years of college, it is necessary to
examine the effect parameters estimated for each model.
These odd probabilities (gammas) are greater than 1.0 when
the probability of being in a nonnormative category of a
transition variable are greater than average among men in
that subgroup and less than 1.0 when the probability of
being in a nonnormative category of a transition variable
are less than average among men in that subgroup. A gamma
coefficient equal to 1.0 means that membership in that subgroup does not affect the likelihood of a nonnormative transition. For example, the net odds probability that a
college educated man will interrupt his schooling is 2.267

to 1.0 if he is from a farm background, but 1.442 to 1.0 if he is from a white collar background (Table 2). The odds probability of an interruption in schooling thus are 57 percent higher (2.267/1.442 = 1.57) among college-educated men of farm backgrounds compared with college-educated men from white collar origins.

For each level of education, I calculated the largest percentage difference in each type of nonnormative transition behavior for each subgroup (calculations not shown). The largest social class, community size, and ethnic subgroup differential among high school graduates was then compared with the largest subgroup differentials among college graduates and men with five or more years of college. The subgroup differentials are larger among men with four or more years of college in only eleven of the twenty-eight possible comparisons. The hypothesis that subgroup differentials in nonnormative transitions will be greatest among men with four or more years of college therefore must be rejected. Thus, there are subgroup differentials in nonnormative transition behaviors, and these differences vary by level of education, but the strength of subgroup differentials among levels of education cannot be described summarily.

The third hypothesis states that the subgroups with the fewest social and economic resources and the least integration into the American value system most frequently violate transition norms. Looking at the net effects of social class origins on transition behavior, blue collar and farm origin men have higher rates of school interruption among men with four or more years of college (Table 2) and, among men with four years of college, are more likely to be off-time in their completion of schooling (Table 3). The blue collar and farm origin men, at all levels of education, more frequently are off-time in the beginning of their first job (Table 4). Despite their off-time school and first job transitions, men from lower social class origins are no more likely to be off-time in their first marriage (Table 5). Partly as a result, among men with four or more years of college, the rates of marriage before school completion are much higher among blue collar and farm origin men (Table 6). The net effects of social class, therefore, tend to be in the hypothesized direction.

Among high school graduates, men from metropolitan communities more frequently interrupt their educations and are more often off-time in their school completion. This pattern of community differentials in the school transition is not found among men with four years of college, and the

Table 2. The net odds probability of an interruption in schooling by social class, community, and ethnic background, U.S. males born 1907-1952, with selected levels of education.

Social Background	Level of Education		
	High School (4 years)	College (4 years)	College (5 or more yrs.)
Social Class			
White Collar	0.457	1.442	2.878
Blue Collar.	0.399	2.053	3.816
Farm	0.429	2.267	3.039
Community			
Metropolitan	0.486	1.849	2.568
Small City	0.457	1.732	3.007
Rural.	0.353	2.098	4.323
Ethnicity			
Northwestern European	0.456	2.445	3.704
Eastern European . .	0.392	1.886	2.474
Southern European. .	0.372	2.014	3.638
Hispanic or Black. .	0.504	1.363	3.224

Class Community Interaction

	Metropolitan	Small City	Rural
White Collar	0.896	1.112	0.002
Blue Collar.	1.079	1.077	0.979
Farm	0.975	0.846	1.079

Note: The odds probability of an interruption in schooling versus no interruption in schooling are shown. These odds reflect the direct effects of education and social background on an interruption in schooling, as well as their joint effects. The odds shown for each social background variable are net of the effects of the other social background variables.

Table 3. The net odds probability of an off-time completion
of schooling by social class, community, and ethnic background,
U.S. males born 1907-1952, with selected levels of education.

Social Background	Level of Education		
	High School (4 years)	College (4 years)	College (5 or more yrs.)
Social Class			
White Collar	0.709	1.229	1.031
Blue Collar.	0.717	1.609	1.011
Farm	1.558	2.121	0.796
Community			
Metropolitan	1.159	1.719	0.819
Small City	1.105	1.861	0.848
Rural.	0.619	1.311	1.195
Ethnicity			
Northwestern European	0.522	1.094	0.847
Eastern European . .	0.783	1.538	0.628
Southern European. .	1.050	2.050	0.853
Hispanic or Black. .	1.708	1.962	1.721

Note: The odds probability of an off-time versus on-time
completion of schooling are shown. The odds reflect
the direct effects of education and social background
on the timing of school completion, as well as their
joint effects. The odds shown for each social
background variable are net of the effects of the
other social background variables.

Table 4. The net odds probability of an off-time beginning of first job by social class, community, and ethnic background, U.S. males born 1907–1952, with selected levels of education.

Social Background	Level of Education		
	High School (4 years)	College (4 years)	College (5 or more yrs.)
Social Class			
White Collar	0.492	1.055	1.071
Blue Collar.	0.538	1.594	1.883
Farm	0.947	1.678	1.377
Community			
Metropolitan	0.6771	1.349	1.302
Small City	0.733	1.575	1.567
Rural.	0.505	1.328	1.485
Ethnicity			
Northwestern European	0.449	1.052	0.727
Eastern European . .	0.610	1.135	1.075
Southern European. .	0.767	1.606	1.687
Hispanic or Black. .	0.754	2.079	2.107

Note: The odds probability of an off-time versus on-time age at first job are shown. The odds reflect the direct effects of education and social background on the timing of first job, as well as their joint effects. The odds shown for each social background variable are net of the effects of the other social background variables.

Table 5. The net odds probability of an off-time first
marriage by social class, community, and ethnic background,
U.S. males born 1907-1952, with selected levels of education.

Social Background	Level of Education		
	High School (4 years)	College (4 years)	College (5 or more yrs.)
Community			
Metropolitan	1.465	1.079	0.799
Small City	1.021	1.084	0.657
Rural.	0.918	0.841	0.819
Ethnicity			
Northwestern European	1.138	0.935	1.277
Eastern European . .	1.058	1.218	0.545
Southern European. .	0.813	0.740	0.584
Hispanic or Black. .	1.298	1.162	0.800

Class-Community Interaction

	Metropolitan	Small City	Rural
White Collar	1.098	0.930	0.842
Blue Collar.	1.147	0.890	0.951
Farm	1.395	0.954	9.847

Ethnic-Community Interaction

Northwestern European	1.164	1.159	1.236
Eastern European . .	1.243	0.780	1.040
Southern European. .	1.230	0.662	0.357
Hispanic or Black. .	1.192	1.322	1.300

Note: The odds probability of an off-time versus on-time age
       at first marriage are shown. The odds reflect the
       direct effects of education and social background on
       the timing of first marriage, as well as their joint
       effects. The odds shown for each social background
       variable are net of the effects of the other social
       background variables.

Table 6. The net odds probability of marriage prior to the completion of schooling by social class, community, and ethnic background, U.S. males born 1907–1952, with selected levels of education.

Social Background	Level of Education		
	High School (4 years)	College (4 years)	College (5 or more yrs.)
Social Class			
White Collar	0.210	2.649	6.943
Blue Collar.	0.174	4.602	13.063
Farm	0.279	3.313	17.884
Community			
Metropolitan	0.249	2.272	9.496
Small City	0.239	3.761	12.750
Rural.	0.172	4.727	13.400
Ethnicity			
Northwestern European	0.251	4.526	20.206
Eastern European . .	0.173	2.564	8.004
Southern European. .	0.135	3.468	9.820
Hispanic or Black. .	0.378	3.446	12.003

Note: The odds probability of marriage prior to the completion of schooling versus marriage after the completion of schooling are shown. These odds reflect the direct effects of education and social background on marriage prior to school completion, as well as their joint effects. The odds shown for each social background variable are net of the effects of the other social background variables.

reverse pattern is observed among men with five or more years
of college. At every level of education, men from small
cities and towns more frequently have an off-time first job.
Metropolitan origin men especially are likely to have an
off-time first marriage. Rates of marriage prior to school
completion are lowest among high school graduates from
rural origins, but highest among college graduates from
rural origins. Controlling for social class and ethnicity,
therefore, the effects of community size on conformity to
transition norms depends upon the transition behavior
examined, and the level of education completed.

There are no systematic ethnic differentials in rates
of school interruption, but there is a tendency for blacks
and Hispanics and, to a lesser extent, southern Europeans,
to be off-time in their school completion and first job
transitions. Ethnic differentials in off-time first
marriages fluctuate among levels of education. Contrary to
expectations, college-educated men of northwestern European
ancestry are more likely than other ethnic groups to marry
prior to the completion of schooling. Controlling for social
class and community size, therefore, the effects of ethnic
ancestry on conformity to transition norms depends upon the
transition behavior examined, and the level of education
completed.

This analysis identified three interactions among the
independent variables in their effects on conformity to
transition norms. First, the effect of social class on the
probability of an interruption in schooling varies by size
of community of residence. Especially high rates of school
interruption characterize blue collar origin men in metropolitan areas, men of white collar origins in small towns,
and men from farm families in rural areas. Second, blue
collar and farm origin men in metropolitan areas experience
especially high rates of off-time marriages. Third, in
nonmetropolitan communities, the probability of an off-time
first marriage is especially high among blacks and Hispanics
and especially low among southern European ancestry men.
These interactions among social class, community size, and
ethnic ancestry conform to no readily discernible pattern.

Conclusions

Utilizing the idea of normative timetables with on-
time and off-time transitions, this analysis has demonstrated that social class, community size, and ethnic ancestry
each independently influence the probability of an interruption in schooling, an off-time school completion, beginning
of first job, and first marriage, and marriage prior to the

completion of schooling. The net effects of each of these subgroups on transition behavior vary among levels of education. It was hypothesized that the effect of subgroup membership on the probability of nonnormative transition behavior would be greatest among men with college educations, but the empirical evidence did not support this. Men from lower social class origins are more likely to complete the transition to adulthood in a nonnormative fashion insofar as men from blue collar and farm origins more frequently interrupt their schooling, are off-time in their school completion and first job transitions, and marry prior to the completion of schooling. The hypothesis that men from rural communities and small towns more frequently experience non-normative transitions due to a lack of community resources was rejected. Also rejected was the hypothesis that lower status ethnic groups are more likely to experience nonnormative timing and sequencing of early life transitions. Thus, community size and ethnic ancestry affect the probability of nonnormative transitions, but the nature of the effects varies among men at different levels of education and according to the transition behavior examined.

References

Blau, Peter M. and Otis Dudley Duncan, 1967. The American Occupational Structure. New York: Wiley.

Elder, Glen H., Jr., 1974. "Age Differentiation and the Life Course." Pp. 165-90 in Annual Review of Sociology, 1975, Vol. 1. Edited by Alex Inkeles et al. Palo Alto, California: Annual Reviews.

Elder, Glen H., Jr., 1978. "Approaches to Social Change and the Family." American Journal of Sociology 84 (Supplement): S1-S38.

Featherman, David L. and Robert M. Hauser, 1978. Opportunity and Change. New York: Academic.

Goodman, Leo A., 1971. "The Analysis of Multidimensional Contingency Tables: Stepwise Procedures and Direct Estimation Methods for Building Models for Multiple Classifications." Technometrics 13:36-61.

Goodman, Leo A., 1972. "A Modified Multiple Regression Approach to the Analysis of Dichotomous Variables." American Sociological Review 37:28-46.

Hogan, Dennis P., 1978. "The Variable Order of Events in the Life Course." American Sociological Review 43:573-86.

Hogan, Dennis P., 1981. Transitions and Social Change: The Early Lives of American Men. New York: Academic.

Katz, Michael B. and Ian E. Davey, 1978. "Youth and Early Industrialization in a Canadian City." American Journal of Sociology 84 (Supplement): S81-S119.

Modell, John, 1978. "Patterns of Consumption, Acculturation, and Family Income Strategies in Late Nineteenth-Century America." Pp. 206-240 in Family and Population in Nineteenth-Century America. Edited by Tamara K. Haravan and Maris A. Vinovskis. Princeton University Press.

Modell, John, 1980. "Normative Aspects of American Marriage Timing Since World War II." Journal of Family History 5:210-34.

Modell, John, Frank E. Furstenberg, Jr., and Theodore Herschberg, 1976. "Social Change and Transitions to Adulthood in Historical Perspective." Journal of Family History 1:7-32.

Neugarten, Bernice L. and Gunhild O. Hagestad, 1976. "Age and the Life Course." Pp. 35-55 in Handbook of Aging and the Social Sciences. Edited by Robert H. Binstock and Ethel Shanas. New York: Van Nostrand Reinbold.

Neugarten, Bernice L., Joan W. Moore, and John C. Lowe, 1965. "Age Norms, Age Contraints, and Adult Socialization." American Journal of Sociology 70:710-17.

Sewell, William H., 1964. "Community of Residence and College Plans." American Sociological Review 29:24-38.

Sewell, William H., 1971. "Inequality of Opportunity for Higher Education." American Sociological Review 36: 793-809.

Sewell, William H. and Vimal P. Shah, 1968. "Social Class Parental Encouragement, and Educational Aspirations." American Journal of Sociology 73:559-72.

Winsborough, Halliman H., 1978. "Statistical Histories of the Life Cycle of Birth Cohorts: The Transition from Schoolboy to Adult Male." Pp. 231-59 in Social Demography. Edited by Karl E. Taeuber et al. New York: Academic.

6. "Aged Servants of the Lord": Changes in the Status and Treatment of Elderly Ministers in Colonial America

Until very recently, the analysis of the status and treatment of the elderly in our past was almost totally neglected. Despite the outpouring of studies in social and family history during the 1960s and 1970s, the elderly were mentioned only in passing. But with the growth of concern about aging today, historians are now beginning to consider how our colonial ancestors dealt with the aged in the seventeenth and eighteenth centuries. Unfortunately, the recent scholarship on the elderly in colonial America has been rather limited to date. Historians are treating the seventeenth and eighteenth centuries as one unit without really considering if there were major changes in societal reactions to aging during that period. David Fischer (1978), for example, writes of the continued exaltation of the elderly throughout the colonial period and only sees a significant change in the attitudes and behavior toward the elderly in the last two decades of the eighteenth century. Similarly, John Demos (1978, p. S248) analyzes old age in early New England with "little attention...to issues of chronological development and change." This static view of the status and care of the elderly in early America is reinforced by the tendency of scholars from other disciplines to analyze age-relations in pre-industrial societies as relatively constant and unchanging over time.

In an effort to construct a more detailed picture of

This research was supported by NIA Grant No. AG02692-01. I am grateful to David Hollinger, Kenneth Lockridge, Gerald Moran, Martin Pernick, and John Shy for helpful comments on an earlier version of this paper and to Donna Gotts for typing the manuscript.

the elderly in early America, this paper will focus on one
particular group--the Puritan ministers of New England.
They are an appropriate focus of attention not only
because they frequently revealed their ideas about the
elderly in published sermons, letters, and diaries, but
also because their own lives exemplified the ambiguous
treatment that was accorded to the elderly in colonial
America. Though historians have devoted much time and
effort to recreate the intellectual and social experiences
of Puritan ministers, they have paid almost no attention
to the process of aging--especially among the different
generations of ministers (Elliott, 1975; Hall, 1972;
Lucas, 1976; Schmotter, 1973, 1975; Youngs, 1976). Yet
their analyses present a more dynamic portrayal of the
experiences of Puritan ministers than the one given by the
recent historians of aging in colonial America.
Therefore, in this essay I will draw upon the recent
literature on Puritan ministers as well as on aging in
colonial America in order to suggest some of the possible
changes in the status and treatment of elderly ministers.

First-Generation Ministers

To understand the status and treatment of elderly
Puritan ministers in New England, it is necessary to
reconstruct the lives of the first-generation ministers
who came to the New World in the initial waves of the
"Great Migration" during the 1630s and early 1640s. These
first-generation Puritan ministers and settlers
established the New England churches as well as formulated
the relationship between the minister and his congregation
which provided the basis for religious practices and
controversies for future generations. Though many of the
experiences of these first-generation New England
ministers were atypical of that of their successors, they
set the standards by which subsequent ministers judged
their own lives and achievements. As a result, the aging
experiences of the first-generation of Puritan ministers
in America had a particularly important influence on the
way colonial society dealt with their elderly ministers in
the seventeenth and eighteenth centuries. 1/

---

1. There is a vast literature of Puritans in early
American (see McGiffert, 1970; Moran and Vinovskis,
forthcoming). While this essay cannot hope to interact
with most of these studies, it will focus on the most
recent work specifically dealing with the role of
ministers in New England.

There is no simple definition of elderly in colonial
America, but the term was usually first applied to
individuals in their sixties (Demos, 1978).

The first-generation of Puritan ministers came to New England in their twenties and thirties (Stout, 1974). While they fled from the increasing persecution of King Charles and Archbishop William Laud in England, they brought with them the social and cultural heritage of that struggle. Yet in America these ministers and their congregations were forced to create their own system of churches based not only upon their religious beliefs, but also taking into consideration the particular social and economic conditions in early New England (Hall, 1972). Though the first-generation Puritans were united in their opposition to the existing Anglican Church, they strongly disagreed amongst themselves on how to create and run their own churches. Given the congregational form of church organization which they adopted, emphasizing the autonomy of each individual church, their early efforts led to a variety of different practices (Lucas, 1976). Yet certain basic features of the Puritan church in New England emerged which had an important bearing on the lives of their ministers in their old age.

One of the fundamental factors in shaping the experiences of elderly ministers is the way in which a religion selects and maintains its clergy. Some religions minimize the role of a separate clergy altogether and simply rely upon members of the congregation to conduct services. Others designate a separate clergy but treat them as part-time ministers who are expected to provide for themselves. Support of ministers in their old age is not a particular problem for these groups since they do not have a separate or full-time ministry which needs to be maintained by the congregation. In situations where a separate clergy exists the relationship of the ministers to their congregation becomes very important in determining who provides support for the aging ministers and under what conditions.

The relationship between a Puritan minister and his congregation was never resolved in colonial America. On the one hand, the Puritans believed that the minister was set apart from his congregation and derived his sacredotal authority from above. On the other hand, Puritans allowed congregations to select their own ministers and encouraged them to participate in many of the decisions of the church such as the admission of new members or the disciplining of sinners. Throughout the seventeenth and eighteenth centuries the tension between the clergy and their congregations continued over the exact responsibilities and powers of the minister which sometimes encouraged parishioners to withhold support from their aging minister (Hall, 1972; Lucas, 1976; Youngs, 1976).

Once a minister was settled in a particular parish, it was assumed that he would remain there for life unless, in extraordinary circumstances, both the minister and the congregation mutually agreed upon a termination of his tenure. It was not clear according to Puritan theology, however, who should pay for the maintenance of the clergy. Initially, the Massachusetts Bay Company paid for the ministers out of its "Common Stock" but it soon shifted that responsibility to the local towns where it remained throughout the colonial period. The decision to have the local areas pay for their own ministers was important because it passed control of the salaries of ministers from the colony as a whole to the individual towns. In the first decades of settlement, ministers preferred to collect their salaries through voluntary weekly contributions, but most communities quickly abandoned this practice since it became increasingly difficult to raise sufficient funds unless everyone in the town, whether a church member or not, was taxed for the support of the minister. Since the salary of the minister often comprised at least one-half of the town budget, any decisions involving the support of the minister soon became an issue for all of the citizens rather than just members of the congregation (Lucas, 1976).

Despite the hardships of settling in a new land, the first-generation Puritan ministers did exceedingly well in America. Whereas most Puritan ministers in England had not enjoyed high socio-economic status, those who migrated to New England in the 1630s and 1640s became prominent social as well as religious leaders of their local communities (Hall, 1972). In the initial and subsequent divisions of land, ministers usually received among the largest allotments. Reverend John Allin of Dedham, for example, received the largest share of land of anyone in every division before 1656. His overall wealth of over 1000 pounds was unequalled by most men in Dedham before 1700 (Lockridge, 1967). The prominence of the first-generation ministers was the result not only of their spiritual leadership, but also of their unusually high socio-economic standing within the community--an achievement all the more satisfying to them because of their rapid upward social mobility from their low status in England.

The first-generation ministers enjoyed many other advantages besides access to wealth. Many of them like Thomas Hooker migrated to the New World with their old congregations--thus benefiting from continued close association with their old friends and parishioners with

whom they had endured so many hardships in England
(Shuffelton, 1977). Furthermore, since one of the major
motivations for Puritans to migrate to the New World was
to be able to practice their religion, the ministers could
assume a much larger role than if they had remained in
England where most people were either indifferent or
hostile to them. The importance of their spiritual
leadership was reinforced by the heightened sense of
excitement and anticipation during the 1630s and early
1640s among the New England Puritans due to the expected
imminent return of Christ and the inauguration of the
Millennium. Finally, and perhaps most important of all,
the first-generation of Puritan ministers as a whole were
unusually charismatic and provided the type of personal
leadership for their congregations which was rarely
matched by their successors. Ministers such as John
Cotton, Thomas Hooker, and Thomas Shephard dominated their
congregations by the sheer force of their personalities
and intellect while their successors pleaded
unsuccessfully with their parishioners to obtain the same
authority that the first-generation ministers had
commanded. Thus, though the first-generation of Puritan
ministers probably experienced just as many religious
controversies, such as the Antinomian Crisis, as other
generations, they were in a much stronger religious and
socio-economic position to deal with these problems both
individually and collectively.

Since the local towns were responsible for
maintaining ministers throughout their entire lives, any
illnesses associated with aging presented a major crisis
for the community if the minister could no longer perform
his duties. With such a large proportion of the town
budget already expended for maintaining the present
minister, it was financially difficult, if not impossible,
simply to bring in another minister while at the same time
continuing to pay the incapacitated one his normal salary.
If the illness was of short duration the town often either
invited neighboring clergymen to fill in temporarily for
their stricken colleague on a voluntary and
nonremunerative basis or survived without a few Sunday
services. But if the illness was more permanent, the town
faced a very difficult and unpleasant quandry since they
did not want to (nor legally could) stop supporting their
old minister while at the same time they could not afford
to bring in a paid assistant--especially since the harmony
of the town was often disrupted over the choice of any
potential successor to the ailing minister.

The anguish and cost of dealing with incapacitated

ministers was to plague future generations, but it does
not seem to have been particularly troublesome for the
first-generation. This can be explained partially by the
fact that many New England ministers remigrated back to
England with the outbreak of the English Civil War in 1640
and the availability of positions for Puritans in
Cromwellian England (Stout, 1974). Many New England
communities were thus spared the cost of caring for their
aging minister. But even those who remained did not seem
to create much of a problem--perhaps because they had
accumulated sufficient personal wealth so that they could
afford to retire gracefully from office if they became
incapacitated and because the community was more willing
to shoulder the extra financial burden since they were
such outstanding social as well as religious leaders. The
combination of the closeness of the remaining
first-generation ministers to their parishioners as well
as their own financial ability to care for themselves in
old age appears to have minimized much of the difficulty
experienced by subsequent generations of aging ministers.

To fully understand the impact of the
first generation of Puritan New England ministers on their
successors we must look beyond their actual experiences to
the ways in which they were remembered. What is most
striking about the first-generation ministers is that
their achievements and spiritual purity were greatly
exaggerated not only by their successors, but even by
themselves. They created a myth about themselves and
their accomplishments which minimized any of the conflicts
amongst themselves and over-emphasized the religious zeal
of the early settlers (Bercovitch, 1975). This myth was
widely accepted and fostered an image of the
first-generation ministers that made all subsequent ones
pale into insignificance by comparison. As a result, the
very real achievements of the first-generation of Puritan
ministers was even magnified for their successors through
the lenses of their own narratives of the past.

Historians are currrently debating amongst themselves
whether the elderly were really venerated in colonial
America (Achenbaum, 1978; Demos, 1978; Fischer, 1978;
Haber, 1979; Smith, 1978). Perhaps some of the
differences of opinion may stem from the highly favorable
image of the role of the elderly in colonial America as
exemplified and created by the rather unique experiences
of the first-generation ministers. Since much of the
material on the portrayal of the elderly in early America
is based on the writings and experiences of the New
England clergy, it is important to note that for the

first generation of Puritan ministers, old age, wealth,
and social status were highly correlated in their own
lives--certainly much more than they might have expected
if they had remained in England. This relatively
favorable personal image of aging was reinforced by the
exaggerated exaltation of their achievements and
importance by their contemporaries and successors. As a
result, it is not surprising that this particular
generation emphasized the role of the elderly in society
by the example of their own lives as well as in their
writings. Perhaps subsequent generations of New England
ministers accepted their image of the proper role of the
elderly in society even though, as we shall soon see,
their own experiences of aging did not live up to the high
expectations created by the first generation.

Second-Generation Ministers

If we define the first generation of New England
ministers as those who migrated to the New World in the
1630s and 1640s, the second generation can loosely be
designated as their successors who assumed office mainly
in the 1660s and 1670s. While the concept of generations
quickly loses its analytical rigor as we move much beyond
the early years of settlement, it is a useful distinction
initially since the first generation of ministers saw
themselves passing on their spiritual leadership to the
next generation of clergymen. 2/ Yet the socio-economic
and religious conditions under which their successors
labored were much more disadvantageous for fulfilling that
trust than the situation which had confronted the
first-generation ministers in the 1630s and 1640s.

----

2. There are many problems as well as advantages in
the use of generations as an analytical construct in early
America (Vinovskis, 1977). While some of the
second-generation ministers, who were quite old when they
assumed office in the New World, experienced old age in
the 1660s and 1670s, others, who began their careers in
New England at a much younger age, became old only in the
late seventeenth or early eighteenth century. In
addition, though a minister might be considered
second generation in relation to the colony as a whole, he
might be of the first generation of settlers in his
particular community. Nevertheless, the distinction of
generations is worth preserving for the first and
second generations of settlers to New England because they
viewed themselves in those terms and because the overall
age spread within those first two generations was not so
broad as to be meaningless.

The first generation of Puritan ministers had risen
to prominence during a period of high population growth
and economic prosperity due to the rapid influx of
settlers. But the "Great Migration" to New England peaked
in 1638 and with the start of the English Civil War,
immigration to New England dropped off dramatically
(McManis, 1975; Pomfret, 1970; Smith, 1972). While new
towns had multiplied rapidly during the 1630s and early
1640s, by the 1650s and 1660s very few new settlements
were established. As a result, the need for new churches
and additional ministers to staff them dropped from a high
of eighteen new churches founded between 1638 and 1640 to
only one new church established between 1647 and 1649
(Stout, 1974). Though the economy gradually recovered as
New England merchants developed trade with the West
Indies, the overall economic conditons facing the
second generation were not as favorable as those
encountered by the first generation (Bailyn, 1955;   Walton
and Shepherd, 1979).

The economic opportunities available to second
generation ministers were disappointing--especially when
compared to the economic success of the first-generation
ministers. While the first-generation ministers benefited by
receiving some of the largest shares of land in the initial
divisions, their successors in the more settled areas were
fortunate to receive any land at all since by the 1660s and
1670s much of the town lands had already been allocated.
Secondly, though the tax-base of the older towns was
increasing due to population growth and economic development,
the amount available for any particular minister in many
areas may have actually diminished since towns were
subdivided to form new communities or additional parishes
were created in the same town to accommodate the increasingly
dispersed population. Finally, by the 1660s and 1670s, most
of the older communities had developed an established social
elite which had prospered from the early land divisions as
well as the economic improvements made on their property
during the past twenty or thirty years. Any young ministers
who were now hired by the congregation simply could not match
the wealth and social status of many of these earlier
settlers or descendents--even if the community tried to be as
generous as possible in its provisions for the new
minister.3/   Thus, the second-generation ministers who

---

3.   One factor which may have helped some of the
second-generation ministers was an inheritance of substantial
funds from their fathers--especially for those sons whose
parents had become prominent and wealthy in the New World.
Some historians (Greven, 1970) emphasize the importance of

settled in the older communities of New England found it more difficult, if not impossible, to achieve the same social and economic status as their predecessors had attained earlier.

If the second-generation ministers assuming office in the settled communities did not fare as well as their first-generation counterparts, perhaps those who went to the frontier communities, where land was still plentiful and which had no entrenched social elite, did much better. Though this may have been true in a few instances, overall the second-generation ministers settling in the frontier areas faced at least equally formidable problems. While more land was available, it was less valuable because frontier areas were more distant from the markets (Walton and Shepherd, 1979). Many of the frontier areas were also considered unsafe as New England tried to cope with the continued threats from the Indians which culminated in the bloody King Philip's War in 1675 (Leach, 1958; Vaughan, 1965). Finally, whereas the new settlements along the eastern shore of New England in the 1630s and 1640s were in the mainstream of colonial development from the very beginning those established in the interior were more socially as well as physically isolated from the rest of society--not only in terms of distance but also psychologically (Clark, 1970). Second-generation ministers who were offered positions in frontier communities often preferred to risk unemployment or under-employment in order to wait for a post in one of the older settlements (Lucas, 1976). Thus, whether one looks at the settled or frontier areas, most second-generation ministers did not have as attractive opportunities available to them as their predecessors.

If second-generation ministers did not fare as well economically as their predecessors, they also faced an audience which seemed less enthusiastic spiritually than the first settlers. Most of the excitement and anticipation of the impending return of Christ had dissipated by the 1660s and 1670s. Many of the sons and daughters of the first settlers did not possess the same religious zeal and self-assurance that had characterized their parents. Whereas New England was the center stage of the Puritan world in the 1630s and early 1640s, by the post-Restoration period it had lost its special glamor and promise. Though part of this seeming lack of religious interest by the second-generation can be seen as the

---

inheritance as a means for the first generation to control the behavior of their children, but others (Vinovskis, 1971) have questioned this interpretation.

result of the exaggeration of the piety and achievements of the first settlers, it does reflect some real changes that were occurring in that society. 4/ Furthermore, while the early congregations had been willing to submit to the strong leadership of the first-generation ministers, parishioners as well as non-church members later openly and vociferously challenged the second-generation ministers for the leadership of the parish (Lucas, 1976). As a result, the young ministers who climbed into their pulpits in the 1660s and 1670s faced congregations which were less eager and willing to be guided by the new spiritual leaders of their communities.

If the residents of the New World seemed less pious than their forefathers, their new leaders as a whole were also less capable of inspiring them. While the first-generation ministers were dynamic individuals who led their congregations by the force of their personalities and intellect, their successors were less charismatic and less effective as leaders. Whether this was due to the adverse circumstances under which they labored or the type of training they had received at Harvard is not clear (Hall, 1972). In any case, contemporaries as well as most historians have accepted the notion that these second-generation ministers were less capable--a failing which was magnified by the exaggerated stature and achievements of their predecessors (Elliott, 1975; Hall, 1972; Lucas, 1976; Rutman, 1970). 5/

As the second-generation ministers grew older, they did not possess the same socio-economic or religious

---

4. While there were real changes occurring in New England society, the effort of earlier historians to portray the experiences of Puritans in terms of declension have not been satisfactory. For a critique of the use of declension see McGiffert, 1970; Moran, 1972; Moran and Vinovskis, forthcoming; Pope, 1969-70.

5. While most second-generation ministers were regarded as inferior in talent and stature compared to the first-generation, a few such as Solomon Stoddard, pastor of the church at Northampton, were regarded as outstanding leaders in their own communities. But even someone like Stoddard found himself more constrained in what he could achieve within his congregation than the earlier ministers (Lucas, 1976; Tracy, 1979).

status in their community not did they inspire the same
awe as their first-generation counterparts. The
communities they served also were no more capable or
willing to assist them in their old age than they had
helped their precedessors. Yet the problems associated
with the aging of the second-generation ministers may have
been greatly reduced if most of them died before reaching
old age. While most first-generation ministers lived well
into their sixties (Stout, 1974), perhaps their
successors, who entered the ministry at a younger age than
when their predecessors assumed office in the New World,
had much lower life expectancies.

The burden of providing assistance for elderly
ministers is greatly reduced in many pre-industrial
societies which have high adult as well as high infant
mortality rates. In fact, some scholars argue that the
issue of retirement does not exist in pre-industrial
societies since very few individuals survive into their
sixties or seventies. This was certainly the case in the
colonial South. In seventeenth-century Middlesex County,
Virginia, for example, twenty-year-old males could only
expect to live another twenty-nine years and their female
counterparts only twenty years (Rutman and Rutman, 1976).
If northern ministers also experienced such high adult
mortality rates, their parishioners would encounter the
problems of an aging minister only infrequently.

Though earlier historians accepted the idea of very
high mortality rates in colonial New England, recent work
by demographic historians emphasizes the high life
expectancy of adults--especially in rural areas (Demos,
1970; Greven, 1970; Vinovskis, 1972, 1976). Yet these
findings are being challenged by some scholars who
question the validity of such high life expectancy for
adults in colonial America (Fischer, 1978). Therefore, in
order to set the proper demographic context for this
analysis, it was necessary to establish more precisely the
life expectancy of colonial New England ministers. 6/

The life expectancy at age twenty of Harvard
graduates who went into the ministry, temporarily or
permanently, from the classes of 1642 through 1749 was

---

6. While some of the early demographic studies of
rural New England towns (Demos, 1970; Greven, 1970) may
have exaggerated the expectations of life of adults,
Fischer (1978) probably has under-estimated it. For a
review of the studies of mortality in early America, see
Vinovskis, 1972, 1978.

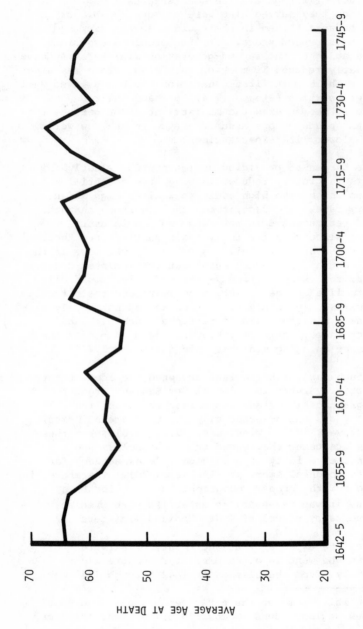

Figure 1. Average age at death of Harvard graduates who preached, by class, 1642-1749. Calculated from Shipton and Silbey, 1873-1972.

41.1 years. 7/ Thus, the average Harvard graduate who preached at least during part of his career could expect to live at least to age sixty. 8/ While there are variations in the average age of death of Harvard graduates who went into the ministry over time, there are no strong trends (see Figure 1).

According to these figures, 58.7 percent of these Harvard graduates from the classes of 1642 through 1749 survived to age sixty. Since most Harvard students were ordained only several years after graduation, the percentage of permanently settled ministers who lived to at least age sixty was even higher. 9/ In other words, though in many pre-industrial soceities the problem of caring for the elderly is lessened by high adult mortality rates, the demographic pattern of New England meant that most ordained ministers were likely to serve their congregations in their sixties and many even in their seventies (36.7 percent of these graduates lived to age seventy).

While it is impossible to estimate what proportion of second-generation ministers became incapacitated, temporarily or permanently, in their old age, it is clear from the fragmentary surviving records that this may have been a more common occurrence among ministers in their sixties, seventies, and eighties than we have suspected. It is certainly evident even among those elderly ministers who continued to work until they died,

---

7. To keep the mortality data comparable, it was necessary to calculate the expectation of life at the age of graduation from college. In order to make certain that changes in the mean age of death of ministers were not affected by a rise or fall in the age of college graduation, those data were also gathered and analyzed.

8. Fischer found a mean age of death of 64.9 years for thirty-five New England ministers in the seventeenth century which is similar to that presented in this analysis (Fischer, 1978, p. 45). Yet Fischer in his discussion of the life expectancy of colonial Americans repeatedly relies on other data which gave him a considerably lower estimate.

9. In 1700 the average minister could expect to wait 7.9 years; in 1710, 7.2 years; in 1720, 6.8 years; in 1730, 5.7 years; and in 1740, 5.5 years (Schmotter, 1973, p. 184).

old age often brought with it a limitation of their
activities. 10/ This diminution of the effectiveness of
their elderly ministers was generally tolerated by the
congregations both out of respect for their ministers as
well as from an unwillingness to pay the extra cost of
bringing in an assistant.

There is no evidence that the second-generation elderly
ministers were mistreated because of their age. But some of
them did suffer in their old age because of the growing
contentiousness between the ministers and their congregations
over issues of church policy and authority. The newly
founded community of Middletown dismissed, with the reluctant
acquiesence of the Connecticut General Court, its aged
minister, Nathaniel Stow, because he proposed innovations in
church discipline. Since Stow was too old to acquire another
post and too poor to fend for himself, he appealed to his
opponents in the town for a pension; they refused (Lucas,
1976, p. 78). Though the dismissal of ministers because of
disagreements was not commonplace, it was sufficiently
frequent to demonstrate how far antagonisms between the
ministers and their congregations had developed. In the case
of Reverened Stow it is interesting to observe that neither
his age nor his helpless condition elicited any sign of

---

10. While Fischer (1978, p. 44) stresses that only
three of the thirty-five colonial New England ministers in
his sample retired, nearly fourteen percent of them who
survived to age sixty-five retired. Furthermore, since
many incapacitated ministers continued in their office as
long as possible in order to collect their salaries, that
fourteen percent figure probably is a very low estimate of
the likelihood of an elderly minister being incapacitated,
partially or totally, in colonial America.

It will be very difficult to ascertain the nature and
extent of physical and mental limitations of aging
ministers in colonial America. One might be tempted, for
example, to extrapolate from current studies of aging and
visual perception or motor performance in order to
estimate the disabilities of elderly ministers in the
past. But any such simple-minded use of contemporary studies
of elderly might be very misleading since the functioning of
the elderly is affected by their social environment. In the
past, when the elderly were expected to be productive and
active members of society, they may not have experienced the
same rate of diminution of abilities which is characteristic
of societies which encourage or even force its elderly into
inactivity and early retirement.

support or compassion from his enemies in the town. While
old age was not despised or penalized by these early
settlers, neither was it sufficiently venerated or exalted
always to help someone who was poor and needed the town's
assistance. 11/

   Despite the difficulties encountered by
second-generation ministers, often in their older years,
most of them continued to publicly praise the virtues of
aging and the elderly. In fact, they often seemed, if
anything, to exaggerate the importance of the elderly in
society. In part this was undoubtedly simply a
continuation of the praise of the elderly which had
characterized the sermons and writings of the
first generation. Perhaps it also reflected the efforts
of ministers in the second half of the seventeenth century
to bolster order and stability in general as well as to
promote their own positions in society as they aged.

   Yet underneath this widespread public praise of aging
and the elderly there were also indications that the
Puritans recognized and abhored the negative aspects of
aging (Demos, 1978; Haber, 1979; Smith, 1978). In fact,
some ministers like Increase Mather, upon his retirement
in the early eighteenth century at the age of eighty-two,
complained about his loss of identity and uselessness and
advised others that "it is a very undesirable thing for a
man to outlive his work" (quoted in Haber, 1979, p. 31).

   Compared to the experiences of their predecessors,
the process of aging for second-generation ministers was
often a real disappointment. Their hopes for themselves
and their society had been raised to a very high level by
the achievements and rhetoric of the first-generation
Puritan ministers--so that their failure to live up to
those expectations grated all the more. Though most
second-generation ministers probably managed to achieve a
reasonably comfortable living in their community, very few
of them managed to obtain the same social status and
admiration that their forefathers seemed to have attained.
But while most second-generation ministers fell short of

---

   11. Though early Americans may have venerated the
elderly, they did so only if they were not dependent upon
taxpayers for support or assistance (Demos, 1978; Haber,
1979). While Fischer (1978) acknowledges that the elderly
poor did not fare well, the tone of his discussion of the
elderly in colonial America tends to exaggerate the positive
image and benevolent treatment of elderly in that culture.

their own expectations, their local communities were remarkably supportive of them in their old age unless they became embroiled in a bitter factional fight. Though there were disputes over the payment of the salaries of ministers, especially in the economically backward areas of Plymouth Colony, congregations were usually willing to support their aged minister even when he became partially or totally incapacitated. 12/

Eighteenth-Century Ministers

While the concept of generations had considerable utility in comparing the experiences of first- and second-generation Puritan ministers, it is not of much analytical assistance when we move into the eighteenth century since the wide range of ages represented by the third and fourth generations make any distinction between them very arbitrary and misleading. Instead, we will focus on the cohorts of ministers in the first half of the eighteenth century based on their year of graduation from Harvard or Yale. 13/

Historians generally are in agreement that the second-generation ministers were disappointed by their religious and socio-economic achievements compared to those of the first-generation. There is little consensus, however, on the well-being of New England ministers in the first half of the eighteenth century. Some scholars (Calhoun, 1965;   Scott, 1978) emphasize the stability and prosperity of the New England ministers during this period while others (Schmotter, 1975;   Shipton, 1933;   Youngs, 1976) note the disruptions caused by inflation and the Great Awakening. Part of the difference is one of perspective. Those who minimize the difficulties of the ministers in the first half of the eighteenth century

---

12. Unfortunately there are no systematic studies of aging of first- and second-generation ministers in regard to their relationship to congregations. There is little indication in the secondary literature of major disputes over matters of continued support simply because a minister had reached age sixty or seventy and was no longer as capable of performing his duties as a younger person.

13. Most of the colonial New England clergy were trained at either Harvard or Yale and fortunately Schmotter (1973, 1975) has completed a very useful analysis of their careers.

write from the vantage point of the nineteenth century while those who see it more negatively usually do so from the point of view of the seventeenth century. But it also reflects differences in evidence with those who see a more prosperous and less tumultuous early eighteenth century providing much less evidence and analysis than those who differ with them. 14/

In the early eighteenth century, the ministry was becoming a less attractive profession. Whereas most American college graduates in the seventeenth century became clergymen, a much smaller proportion of them did so in the eighteenth century. While 53 percent of Harvard graduates of 1691-1700 became ministers, only 35 percent of Harvard and Yale graduates of 1731-1740 climbed into the pulpit (Schmotter, 1975). Part of this shift in career choices of college graduates reflects the growing popularity and opportunities in law and medicine rather than in the ministry (Gawalt, 1979; Kett, 1968).

Not only were college graduates less likely to enter the ministry, those that did were no longer the most prominent or promising individuals. Whether measured by the social background of their parents, their birth order, or their class placement, the quality of individuals who went into the ministry declined relative to that of those who entered the other professions (Schmotter, 1975). As the eighteenth century progressed, the brightest and most socially advantaged young men no longer pursued a career in the church (Shipton, 1933).

New England ministers in the first half of the eighteenth century did not prosper economically. Though the second-generation ministers did not do as well as those of the first generation, most of them managed to make a reasonable living and accumulate a modest estate. Their successors in the eighteenth century fared even worse economically since by that time most towns had already distributed almost all of their land. But even more damaging to the ministers was the effect of inflation on their fixed salaries.

---

14. Most of the work on eighteenth-century clergy are highly impressionistic or based only on a few ministers. Only a few studies have tried to reconstruct in detail the careers of eighteenth-century New England ministers (Harris, 1969; Schmotter, 1973, 1975; Stout, 1974a).

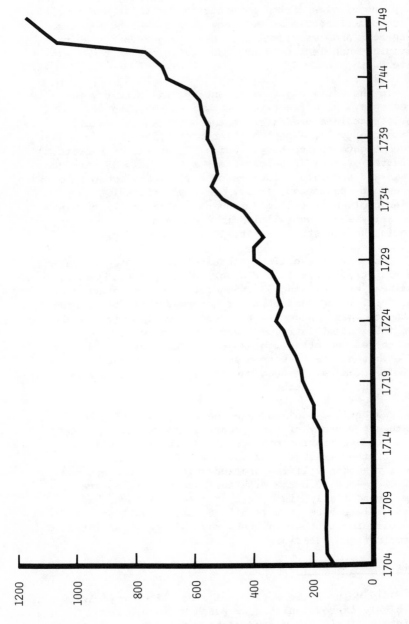

Figure 2. Rate of exchange of Massachusetts paper currency on sterling, 1704-1749.
From Nash, 1979, pp. 405-406.

Most ministers in the eighteenth century, as earlier, served in only one parish once they had been ordained. Among the Congregational minister cohort of 1691-1700, only eight percent served in more than one charge after ordination and among those of the 1731-1740 cohort only nine percent (Schmotter, 1973). At the time of ordination, the minister usually received some type of settlement, such as land or a house, and was placed on a fixed annual salary which often included payment in kind as well as cash. By the end of the seventeenth century most ministers and their congregations relied upon a written contract which could only be renegotiated by mutual agreement of both parties. As a result of these arrangements, the ordained minister was highly dependent upon the stability of the economy or the goodwill of his congregation to agree to any adjustments necessitated by economic fluctuations in the cost of living.

Unfortunately for the well-being of the ministers as well as their parishioners, the New England economy was badly damaged by the cost of King William's War (1689-1697) and Queen Anne's War (1702-1713). In order to finance these wars, Massachusetts began to issue paper money for the first time in 1690 and continued to do so. Since taxes were not raised sufficiently to retire the money and because of a growing trade deficit which necessitated additional specie, the value of the Massachusetts paper currency steadily deteriorated (see Figure 2).

The loss in the purchasing power of Massachusetts paper currency severely affected the clergy since they were on fixed incomes. While many workers were able to negotiate higher wages to offset some of the decline in the value of the Massachusetts paper currrency, the ministers were in a particularly weak position since their contracts were not renegotiated on a regular basis and their bargaining power with their congregations was limited since they could not leave their parish for another one as long as the congregation lived up to the terms of the written contract (Youngs, 1976). 15/ Many congregations did try to increase the salaries of their

---

15. In some situations, the minister's salary was granted on an annual basis, but not subject to renegotiation. Jonathan Edwards, for example, was so distressed that the townspeople continued to question his expenditures and style of living that he petitioned them to put him on a fixed annual salary (Tracy, 1979).

ministers, but they were limited themselves by the general
economic hardships that affected all of them individually
as well as collectively. The citizens of many communities
could not afford to raise their taxes at a time when their
own wealth had depreciated and their colony taxes had
increased to retire the war debts. Though the economic
situation of the colony varied from year to year in the
first half of the eighteenth century, the position of the
ministers, which usually was so heavily dependent upon
fixed salaries, continued to suffer
disproportionately. 16/

The declining fortunes of ministers in the eighteenth
century meant that many of them were not able to provide
adequately for their children as they came of age. Most
ministers hoped that at least one of their sons would
follow in their footsteps. Therefore, it was important
for them to be able to send at least one of their sons to
either Harvard or Yale. But, as Reverend John Cleaveland
of Chebacco Parish in Ipswich, Massachusetts was to
discover, it was often impossible anymore to raise
sufficient funds to send one of their children to college
(Jedrey, 1979). 17/ In fact, while sixty-three percent of
all Congregational ministers from the classes of 1691-1700
sent at least one son to college, those who graduated from
the classes of 1721-1730 or 1731-1740 were able to send at
least one son to college in only forty-nine percent of the
cases (Schmotter, 1973). As a result, the percentage of
ministers' sons following their father's occupation
dropped steadily--undoubtedly contributing to the
frustration of their parents with their increasingly
precarious economic position in society.

---

16. For a discussion of New England economic
conditions in the eighteenth century, see Jones, 1980;
Nash, 1979; Walton and Shepherd, 1979.

17. Even as prominent a minister as Cotton Mather in
1720 admitted to Thomas Hollis, the English
philanthropist, that because of his small ministerial
salary and the rapid increase in inflation he would have
been unable to send his son to college without outside
assistance (Youngs, 1976, p. 105). A surprisingly
significant proportion of college students, particularly
those training for the ministry, received outside support
from charitable groups because their own parents could not
afford to send them to school (Allmendinger, 1975).

In the seventeenth century there were conflicts
between individual ministers and congregations over issues
ranging from church policy to payment of salaries. Yet
the number of such controversies as well as their severity
seems to have increased in the eighteenth century
(Schmotter, 1975). The number of serious disputes between
ministers and their local congregations increased
dramatically from 22 per 100 ministers of the cohort of
1691-1700 to 50 for the cohort of 1721-1730 (see Figure
3). Throughout the first half of the eighteenth century,
the major cause of these disputes was over the salary of
the minister--reflecting the tensions created by the
runaway inflation. 18/

Another event which was to prove very disruptive of
the lives of these eighteenth-century New England
ministers was the Great Awakening which split churches and
undermined the authority of many clergymen in the 1740s
and 1750s (Goen, 1962; Stout, 1974a; Tracy, 1979).
Ministers who did not agree with the revival risked
dismissal or having their congregations split while those
who embraced the New Lights incurred the wrath of their
Old Light parishioners. Though initially many of the
ministers had welcomed the revival because it reawakened
interest in religion, the bitter controversies generated
by the Great Awakening weakened the respect and authority
that ministers had hoped would come automatically with
their office. Ministers who had been in their pulpits for
many years were suddenly called upon by many of their
parishioners to defend their own Godliness (Youngs, 1976).
Disputes over church doctrine rose steadily among the
cohorts of eighteenth-century New England ministers and
even exceeded those created by controversies over salaries
for the cohort of 1731-1740 (see Schmotter, 1975).

The net result of the increases in the number of
controversies between ministers and their parishioners in
the eighteenth century was the growing number of clergymen

---

18. While Schmotter (1973, 1975) acknowledges the
negative impact of inflation on the salaries of ministers,
he seems to under-estimate the seriousness of it.
Instead, he tends to explain the increasing concern about
the salaries of ministers in the 1720s as a reflection of
their growing professional orientation. The stress on the
growing professionalism of the clergy in the early
eighteenth century is also a theme emphasized by Youngs
(1976).

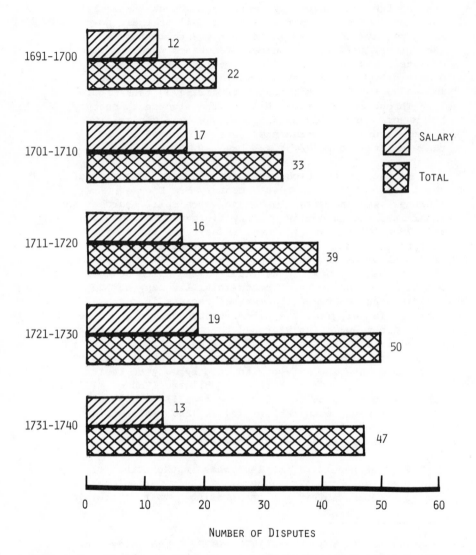

Figure 3. Number of disputes per 100 ministers by decade of
college graduation, 1691-1740. Schmotter, 1973, p. 160.

who were dismissed--sometimes by mutual agreement but
often unilaterally (Schmotter, 1973). The likelihood of
dismissal increased over time with over one-fourth of
those ministers graduating from the classes of 1721-1740
severing their connections with their churches (see Figure
4). Furthermore, only about a third of those clergymen
dismissed continued a career in the ministry by finding
another congregation. Thus, while some scholars (Calhoun,
1965; Scott, 1973; Youngs, 1976) emphasize the
permanence of the eighteenth-century clergy, especially
when compared to their nineteenth-century counterparts,
there was a trend toward church dismissals that affected a
significant proportion of the clergy and alarmed the rest.
The eighteenth century was anything but a tranquil and
stable period for New England ministers.

The adverse economic and religious conditions of the
first half of the eighteenth century undoubtedly hurt many
if not most of the elderly ministers. Since they had
often signed their contracts well before anyone could have
anticipated the runaway inflation, they were particularly
hard hit by the depreciation of the paper money. Though
many of them did receive some increases in their salaries
or special supplements, often they did not keep pace with
the depreciation of the currency. While some of the
entering ministers did manage to include clauses in their
contracts to protect them from inflation, most of the new
contracts did not have such provisions and even many of
them that did were not sufficient to alleviate entirely
the problems caused by the depreciated currency
(Schmotter, 1975). Furthermore, since fewer and fewer
clergy received any land or housing when they were
settled, the clergy were less likely to have extensive
real estate which would have acted as a hedge against
inflation (Schmotter, 1973). Since the salary of
ministers consisted of a combination of payment in kind as
well as cash, it is impossible to know exactly how badly
the elderly clergy were hurt by the inflation of the first
half of the eighteenth century. Yet if we can believe
their own statements as well as those of their
contemporaries, most clergymen faced severe cutbacks in
their real incomes during these years--a factor which
helps to account for the increasing tendency of college
graduates to pursue careers in other fields (Winslow,
1952; Youngs, 1976).

The Great Awakening has sometimes been described as a
conflict between different age-groups with the young
generally favoring it while older individuals opposing

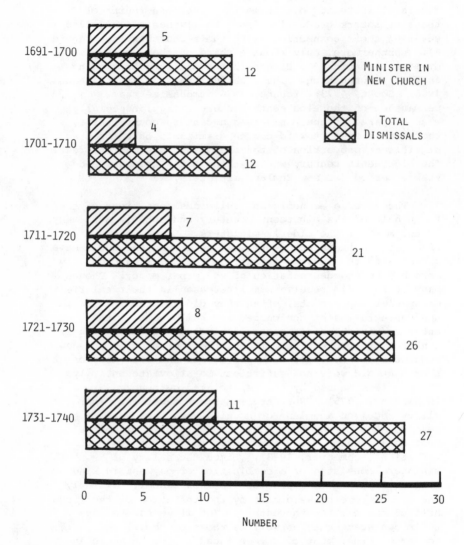

Figure 4. Number of dismissals and subsequent vocation per
100 ministers by decade of college graduation, 1691–1740.
Schmotter, 1973, p. 164.

it. 19/ As a result, one might expect that elderly
ministers might have been more willing to oppose the
revival and therefore perhaps more likely to suffer from
it. This is not the case, however, since the age of the
minister, somewhat unexpectedly, does not appear to have
any influence on the likelihood of favoring or opposing
the Great Awakening (Stout, 1974a). Though the economic
disruptions of the first half of the eighteenth century
may have hurt the elderly clergy more than their
counterparts, the religious turmoil caused by the Great
Awakening seems to have affected everyone more equally in
terms of age.

Elderly ministers in the first half of the eighteenth
century suffered economically and religiously not because
of their age, but due to the adverse conditions many of
them experienced--though in some areas such as their
economic well-being elderly ministers may have been
particularly vulnerable to these outside forces. Most of
them continued, however, to praise the virtues of aging
just as their predecessors had done in the seventeenth
century and as their successors would continue to do in
the early nineteenth century. 20/ But the gap between the
ideals of aging they espoused and the reality of their own
lives probably widened.

Most communities continued to support aging ministers
even when they became incapacitated--though some of them
tried to reduce their salaries or even pressured them to
retire in order to make way for a successor. One of the
major reasons that elderly clergymen refused to retire
from office was because few towns were willing to provide
adequate pensions for their former ministers and most of
these individuals did not have sufficient wealth to
support themselves and their families. Even more
distressing and commonplace was the neglect of the widows
of elderly ministers. While a very small minority of
parishes provided regular pensions for widows, most only
granted them an additional six to twelve months of their
former husband's salary to help them make that transition.
Since many eighteenth-century ministers had been unable to

---

19. There is an extensive literature on the issue of
age and the Great Awakening. For a good introduction to
the field, see Greven, 1972; Moran, 1972.

20. On the images of aging in the nineteenth
century, see Achenbaum, 1978; Fischer 1978; Range and
Vinovskis, forthcoming; Rosenkrantz and Vinovskis, 1978.

accumulate a very large estate for their surviving
spouses, widows were often forced into a rapid
remarriage--frequently, if they were relatively young,
with the successor to their husband (Youngs, 1976). As a
result, in the late eighteenth century some New England
ministers tried to develop an annuity scheme for the
support of their widows (Vinovskis, 1971a).

There is one interesting change in the eighteenth
century in how towns provided for their ministers.
Increasingly in the eighteenth century, as opposed to the
seventeenth, the town was expected to show its final
respect for its minister by providing him with an
elaborate funeral. Whereas the first and even
second generation of Puritan ministers opposed the idea of
elaborate funerals for anyone, including themselves, their
eighteenth-century counterparts expected them. 21/ In
fact, while public opinion was not outraged by the idea
that a widow of an elderly minister did not receive a
pension, it was often aroused against any congregaton that
did not provide for an adequate funeral for its minister.
When Reverend John Newmarch of Portsmouth died at age
eighty-one in 1749, his children published an accusatory
obituary in the Boston newspapers chastising his
congregation for failing to provide him with a proper
funeral. 22/ Though parishioners in eighteenth-century
New England may not have accorded their spiritual leaders
the same respect and reverence that their forefathers had
received, they now remembered them more lavishly at their
funerals. 23/

---

21. On the ways in which colonial Americans dealt
with death and dying, see Moran and Vinovskis,
forthcoming; Stannard, 1977; Vinovskis, 1976.

22. The town replied defensively that they had meant
to cover the costs of the funeral at the next town
meeting, but then counterattacked by arguing that the
minister had done quite well in his years in office and
that his estate was quite capable of bearing the costs of
the funeral if necessary (Shipton and Sibley, IV, 1933,
pp. 73-75).

23. It is not clear how much of the willingness of
the congregation to spend large sums on the funerals of
its members in the eighteenth century was in part an
effort to soothe their own conscience for any slights they
may have accorded him while he was alive. It sometimes
does appear that in congregations which are badly split,

Conclusion

Historians as well as other scholars have tended to
see the elderly in colonial America in rather static
terms--usually stressing the high status and favorable
treatment that the aged received. Our examination of the
lives of elderly Puritan ministers, however, casts doubt
on this traditional interpretation. The status and care
accorded elderly colonial ministers varied over time and
cannot be accurately characterized simply by the use of
the terms veneration and exaltation.

The first generation of Puritan ministers come
closest to fitting our stereotype of elderly in
pre-industrial societies being praised and rewarded for
their achievements and leadership. The unique set of
circumstances by which the first-generaton ministers
assumed office as well as their personal characteristics
insured most of them respect, admiration, and power as
they aged in the New World. Their substantial
accomplishments were quickly glorified into legendary
proportions so that the expectations for the role of
elderly ministers in society that they created for the
next generations were almost impossible for anyone to
attain.

The second generation of Puritan New England
ministers experienced a lot of frustration in their lives.
Though they achieved relatively comfortable and
respectable positions in society, they never were able to
attain the religious or socio-economic position of their
immediate predecessors--a failing for which they blamed
themselves as well as their parishioners. The increasing
conflicts between the ministers and their congregations
further eroded the authority of the second-generation
clergymen and left some of them vulnerable in old age to
bitter attacks from within their churches. Nevertheless,
though many of the elderly ministers of the
second generation saw their own lives as less than
adequate, on the whole they fared well and did not
experience any unusual hardships in their old age.

Compared to their seventeenth-century counterparts,
New England elderly ministers in the eighteenth century
did not do as well. The ministry no longer attracted as

------

the funeral may have become an important ritual to
reintegrate the parish as well as to say goodbye to their
minister.

talented or socially prominent individuals because it
could not compete as effectively with the newly emerging
professions of law and medicine. Those that did enter the
ministry found themselves battling against runaway
inflation and the disruptions caused by the Great
Awakening. All of these difficulties left the elderly
Congregational minister in a weaker religious and
socio-economic position in his community. Though the
elderly ministers still did well in eighteenth-century New
England compared to the experiences of many, if not most,
of their elderly parishioners, they had suffered a
significant loss of status from that of the
first-generation ministers--a fact which they frequently
and bitterly lamented.

While this essay of necessity has been exploratory
rather than definitive in its analysis of the lives of
elderly in colonial America, it does point to the need for
further work in this area from a more dynamic perspective.
The tendency of scholars to view the status and treatment
of elderly in all pre-industrial societies as fixed and
given needs to be modified using a life-course approach
which places the aging process within its proper
historical context. Though this will necessitate a much
more detailed and laborious effort than simply treating
pre-industrial societies as static entities, it will yield
a richer and a much more accurate picture of the
experiences of the elderly.

References

Achenbaum, W. Andrew. 1978. Old Age in the New Land:
    The American Experience Since 1790. Baltimore:
    Johns Hopkins Press.

Allmendinger, David. 1975. Paupers and Scholars: The
    Transformation of Student Life in Nineteenth
    Century New England. New York: New York
    University Press.

Bailyn, Bernard. 1975. The New England Merchants in
    the Seventeenth Century. Cambridge, Mass.:
    Harvard University Press.

Bercovich, Sacvan. 1975. The Puritan Origins of the
    American Self. New Haven: Yale University Press.

Calhoun, Daniel H. 1965. Professional Lives in
    America: Structure and Aspiration, 1750-1850.
    Cambridge, Mass.: Harvard University Press.

Clark, Charles E. 1970. The Eastern Frontier: The
Settlement of Northern New England, 1610-1763.
New York: Alfred A Knopf.

Demos, John. 1970. A Little Commonwealth: Family
Life in Plymouth Colony. New York: Oxford
University Press.

Demos, John. 1978. "Old Age in Early New England."
In Turning Points: Historical and Sociological
Essays on the Family, eds. J. Demos and S. S.
Boocock. Chicago: University of Chicago Press.

Elliott, Emory. 1975. Power and the Pulpit in Puritan
New England. Princeton: Princeton University
Press.

Fischer, David H. 1978. Growing Old in America.
Expanded edition. New York: Oxford University
Press.

Gawalt, Gerald W. 1979. The Promise of Power: The
Emergence of the Legal Profession in Massachusetts
1760-1840. Westport, Conn.: Greenwood Press.

Goen, C. C. 1962. Revivalism and Separation in New
England, 1740-1800. New Haven: Yale University
Press.

Greven, Philip J. Jr. 1970. Four Generatitons:
Population, Land, and Family in Colonial Andover,
Massachusetts. Ithaca, N.Y.: Cornell University
Press.

Greven, Philip J. Jr. 1972. "Youth, Maturity, and
Religious Conversion: A Note on the Ages of
Converts in Andover, Massachusetts, 1711-1749."
Essex Institute Historical Collections. 108
(April): 119-134.

Haber, Carole R. 1979. "The Old Folks: Conceptions
of Senescence in Nineteenth-Century America."
Unpublished Ph.D. Thesis. University of
Pennsylvania.

Hall, David D. 1972. The Faithful Shepherd: A
History of the New England Ministry in the
Seventeenth Century. Chapel Hill: University of
North Carolina Press.

Harris, P.M.G. 1969. "The Social Origins of American
     Leaders: The Demographic Foundations."
     Perspectives in American History. III: 159-344.

Jedrey, Christopher M. 1979. The World of John
     Cleaveland: Family and Community in
     Eighteenth-Century New England. New York: W. W.
     Norton.

Jones, Alice S. 1980. Wealth of a Nation to Be: The
     American Colonies on the Eve of the Revolution.
     New York: Columbia University Press.

Kett, Joseph F. 1968. The Formation of the American
     Medical Profession. New Haven: Yale University
     Press.

Leach, Douglas E. 1958. Flintlock and Tomahawk: New
     England in King Philip's War. New York: W. W.
     Norton.

Lockridge, Kenneth. 1967. "The History of a Puritan
     Church." New England Quarterly. 40 (Winter):
     399-424.

Lucas, Paul R. 1976. Valley of Discord: Church and
     Society Along the Connecticut River, 1636-1725.
     Hanover, N.H.: University Press of New England.

McGiffert, Michael. 1970. "American Puritan Studies
     in the 1960s." William and Mary Quarterly. 17
     (January): 36-67.

McManis, Douglas R. 1975. Colonial New England: A
     Historical Geography. New York: Oxford
     University Press.

Moran, Gerald F. 1972. "Conditions of Religious
     Conversion in the First Society of Norwich,
     Connecticut, 1718-1744." Journal of Social
     History. V (Spring): 331-343.

Moran, Gerald F. and Maris A. Vinovskis.
     Forthcoming. "The Puritan Family and Religion: A
     Critical Reappraisal." William and Mary Quarterly.

Nash, Gary B. 1979. The Urban Crucible: Social
     Change, Political Consciousness, and the Origins
     of the American Revolution. Cambridge, Mass.:
     Harvard University Press.

Pomfret, John E. 1970. Founding the American
    Colonies, 1583-1660. New York: Harper and Row.

Pope, Robert G. 1969-70. "New England versus the New
    England Mind: The Myth of Declension." Journal
    of Social History. 3 (Winter): 95-99.

Range, Jane and Maris A. Vinovskis. Forthcoming.
    "Images of the Elderly in Popular Literature: A
    Content Analysis of Littell's Living Age,
    1845-1880." Journal of Social Science History.

Rosenkrantz, Barbara G. and Maris A. Vinovskis.
    1978. "The Invisible Lunatics: Old Age and
    Insanity in Mid-Nineteenth-Century Massachusetts."
    In Aging and the Elderly: Humanistic Perspectives
    in Gerontology, eds. S. F. Spicker, et al.
    Atlantic Highlands, N.J.: Humanities Press.

Rutman, Darret B. 1970. American Puritanism. New
    York: W. W. Norton.

Rutman, Darret B. and Anita H. Rutman. 1976. "Of
    Agues and Fevers: Malaria in the Early
    Chesapeake." Reprinted in Studies in American
    Historical Demography, ed. M. A. Vinovskis.
    New York: Academic Press.

Schmotter, James W. 1973. "Provincial
    Professionalism: The New England Ministry,
    1692-1745." Unpublished Ph.D. Thesis.
    Northwestern University.

Schmotter, James W. 1975. "Ministerial Careers in
    Eighteenth Century New England: The Social
    Context, 1700-1760." Journal of Social History.
    9 (Winter): 249-267.

Scott, Donald M. 1978. From Office to Profession:
    The New England Ministry, 1750-1850.
    Philadelphia: University of Pennsylvania Press.

Shipton, C.K. 1933. "The New England Clergy of the
    'Glacial Age.'" Publications of the Colonial
    Society of Massachusetts. 32 (December): 24-54.

Shipton, C.K. and J.L. Sibley. 1873-1972. Sibley's
    Harvard Graduates. Vols. 1-16. Cambridge,
    Mass.: Harvard University Press.

Shuffelton, Frank. 1977. <u>Thomas Hooker, 1586-1647</u>.
Princeton: Princeton University Press.

Smith, Daniel S. 1972. "The Demographic History of
Colonial New England." Reprinted in <u>Studies in
American Historical Demography</u>, ed. M. A.
Vinovskis. New York: Academic Press.

Smith, Daniel S. 1978. "Old Age and the 'Great
Transformation': A New England Case Study." In
<u>Aging and the Elderly: Humanistic Perspectives in
Gerontology</u>, eds. S. F. Spicker, et al.
Atlantic Highlands, N.J.: Humanities Press.

Stannard, David E. 1977. <u>The Puritan Way of Death: A
Study in Religion, Culture, and Social Change</u>.
New York: Oxford University Press.

Stout, Harry S. 1974. "University Men in New England,
1620-1660: A Demographic Analysis." <u>Journal of
Interdisciplinary History</u>. 4 (Winter): 375-400.

Stout, Harry S. 1974a. "The Great Awakening in New
England Reconsidered: The New England Clergy As a
Case Study." <u>Journal of Social History</u>. 8
(Fall): 21-47.

Tracy, Patricia J. 1979. <u>Jonathan Edwards, Pastor:
Religion and Society in Eighteenth-Century
Northampton</u>. New York: Hill and Wang.

Vaughan, Alden T. 1965. <u>New England Frontier:
Puritans and Indians 1620-1675</u>. Boston: Little,
Brown and Company.

Vinovskis, Maris A. 1971. "American Historical
Demography: A Review Essay." <u>Historical Methods
Newsletter</u>. 4 (September): 141-148.

Vinovskis, Maris A. 1971a. "The 1789 Life Table of
Edward Wigglesworth." <u>Journal of Economic
History</u>. 31 (December): 570-590.

Vinovskis, Maris A. 1972. "Mortality Rates and Trends
in Massachusetts Before 1860." Reprinted in
<u>Studies in American Historical Demography</u>, ed. M.
A. Vinovskis. New York: Academic Press.

Vinovskis, Maris A. 1976. "Angels' Heads and Weaping
Willows: Death in Early America." Reprinted in

Studies in American Historical Demography, ed. M. A. Vinovskis. New York: Academic Press.

Vinovskis, Maris A. 1977. "From Household Size to the Life Course: Some Observations on Recent Trends in Family History." American Behavioral Scientist. 21 (November/December): 263-287.

Vinvoskis, Maris A. 1978. "Recent Trends in American Historical Demography: Some Methodological and Conceptual Considerations." Reprinted in Studies in American Historical Demography, ed. M. A. Vinovskis. New York: Academic Press.

Walton, Gary M. and James F. Shepherd. 1979. The Economic Rise of Early America. Cambridge, England: University of Cambridge Press.

Winslow, Ola L. 1952. Meetinghouse Hill, 1630-1783. New York: MacMillan.

Youngs, J. William T. Jr. 1976. God's Messengers: Religious Leadership in Colonial New England, 1700-1750. Baltimore: Johns Hopkins Press.

7. Families and Early Industrialization: Cycle, Structure, and Economy

Three attributes characterize all families: a cycle, a structure, and an economy. Families all pass through a sequence of stages from formation through dissolution; all are formed by a set of relationships between people with different roles and statuses; and all must acquire and allocate the means for their subsistence. These three attributes have assumed different forms and related in various ways to one another. In fact, five major changes took place in the organization of family life during the development of industrial capitalism. These were: the nuclearization of the household (a word used deliberately to distinguish household from family); the separation of home and work; the prolonged period during which children lived in the home of their parents; the decline in marital fertility, and the prolonged period during which husbands and wives lived together after their youngest child left home. The first four of these had begun to happen by the early years of industrialization.

Here I will discuss three of these changes. The two that I will not discuss in detail are the prolonged co-residence of children in the home of their parents--which I have written about a length elsewhere--and the new phase in the life-course of couples, which began after this period. I will compare the situation in Hamilton, Ontario, with that in Buffalo, New York, and rural Erie County, attempting to show in what social classes change occurred and to convey a sense of the family always as an institution in process, moving through a sequence of relatively well-demarcated stages, reflecting the pressures and the inequalities of the social order of which it was a part.

The data for this paper come from a larger study of Hamilton, Ontario, between 1851 and 1871, and of Buffalo and rural Erie County, New York, in 1855. In 1851 Hamilton was a

commercial city of about 14,000 people. Within twenty years
it underwent significant industrialization, most notably
during the 1860's. The leading industrial sector was the
metal industry, and very little textile was manufactured in
the city. Industrialization was spurred by a number of
factors, including a conscious policy adopted by city leaders
who believed that the weakness of an economy based solely
upon trade had contributed to the devastating impact of the
depression of the late 1850's upon the city. By 1871 the
city's population had grown to about 26,000, drawn mainly from
England, Scotland, and Ireland with a small American born
group and a small but increasing German community.

As the terminus of the Erie Canal, Buffalo was an
exceptionally prosperous city. Its rapidly increasing
population had reached about 60,000 by 1855. In that year
ten railroads passed through the city, which was a launching
point for travel to the West and an important center for the
transhipment of goods between regions. Indeed, the city
itself was at the center of a rich agricultural area which it
serviced. Although more of Buffalo's population than of
Hamilton's was native born, the American city also had a
substantial proportion of immigrants. There, the largest
share, about forty percent of the city's household heads, had
been born in Germany rather than in Ireland.

The data for the study of Hamilton consist of the entire
manuscript censuses of 1851, 1861, and 1871 put into
machine-readable form. As well, the assessment rolls for the
same year plus 1881 also have been put into machine-readable
form and joined to the census. Master artisans and
manufacturers have been identified by tracing people with
artisanal titles from the census and tax rolls to the
manufacturing censuses and city directories. The data-base
also includes nominal level records from schools, jails,
newspapers, churches, and credit investigations. People who
remained within the city have been traced from one census to
another and linked records created. The Buffalo data
consist of the entire 1855 manuscript census of the city put
into machine-readable form, with, again, artisans traced to
city directories to identify master craftsmen and
manufacturers. The final records are a twenty per cent
sample of the 1855 manuscript census of the area of Erie
County outside of Buffalo. This sample consists of a ten per
cent sample of entire villages.

The Family Cycle

The family cycle begins with the formation of the family
through marriage. Throughout the years between 1851 and 1871

the average age at marriage for men in Hamilton was 27 and
for women 23. These figures were identical in Buffalo and
Erie County. By contrast, in the English cases reported by
Peter Laslett women married between the ages of 25 and 27
and men a few years later. In this respect, the North
American pattern diverged quite sharply. Very likely
scarcity of land, inheritance practices, and the consequent
problem of acquiring the means to a livelihood delayed
marriage in England. All of these factors operated with
relatively less intensity in the more abundant setting of the
New World (Laslett, 1977; Demos, 1970; Smith, 1972).
Although class differences in marriage age were emerging,
they had not yet begun to affect the estimates for age at
birth of first child very much.

Once couples are married, the delineation of the next
phase of their family cycle becomes less straightforward.
For the choice of categories with which to describe the
experience of families is partially arbitrary and the scheme
selected obviously affects the results. Here the
classification is based on the age of women, since the family
cycle is connected so closely with the age of children.
Three stages immediately come to mind: young families who do
not yet have children; families whose children all have left
home; and women who have passed beyond their child-bearing
years. Here the conventionally employed age of 45 marks the
start of this period.

Given the analytical purposes the categories should
serve, it was important to distinguish between phases of the
cycle in which families would be under the greatest and the
least financial strain. The greatest strain should have been
when no children dwelled at home or when at least one child
was old enough to contribute to the family income. Within
these categories, another significant division separated
families all of whose children of working age were females.
The application of these principles yielded twelve family
cycle categories (one of which was residual) which were used
in the analysis of cycle, structure, and economy.

The proportion of families in each category was
relatively stable throughout the period, with the exception
of shifts due to the general aging of the population (Table
1). Likewise, the distinctions between Hamilton, Buffalo,
and rural areas all can be explained by the different age
structures of the populations. Most notable was the
difference in the proportion of late-cycle families, a
reflection of the older population in the more stable rural
areas.

Table 1.   Characteristics of households by family cycle,
Hamilton, Ontario, 1851, 1861, and 1871.

	Year	Number	Percent
Young: Wife less man 25			
(1) No children	1851	98	5.0%
	1861	111	3.6
	1871	187	4.3
(2) All children 1-6	1851	160	8.2
	1861	188	5.9
	1871	252	5.7
Early Mid-Cycle: Wife 25-34			
(3) No children	1851	115	5.9
	1861	185	6.0
	1871	246	5.6
(4) All children 15	1851	636	32.5
	1861	927	30.2
	1871	1079	24.5
Mid-Cycle: Wife 35-44			
(5) No children	1851	64	3.3
	1861	102	3.3
	1871	168	3.8
(6) All children 15	1851	250	12.8
	1861	396	12.9
	1871	596	13.6

Table 1, continued

	Year	Number	Percent
(7) At least one male child, 15+	1851	133	6.8%
	1861	230	7.5
	1871	371	8.4
(8) All children 15+ female	1851	87	4.4
	1861	109	3.6
	1871	191	4.3
Late Cycle: Wife 45+			
(9) At least one male child, 15+	1851	202	10.3
	1861	409	13.3
	1871	639	14.5
(10) All children 15+	1851	96	4.9
	1861	176	5.7
	1871	254	5.8
(11) No children	1851	67	3.4
	1861	153	5.0
	1871	316	7.2
(12) Other	1851	48	2.5
	1861	86	2.8
	1871	97	2.2

The family cycle ended with dissolution, most often the result of death. By and large it was husbands who died first, and widowhood formed an important part of the life experience of many women. In Hamilton, of all the people who became widowed between 1861 and 1871, 72% were women and only 28% men. The experience of widowers and widows differed. Men often were able to re-marry; widows far more often remained single. Given the relative lack of life insurance or social security and the lack of any substantial property among the great majority of the population, widows without working age children usually were poor, and those with young children often were in desperate poverty. Thus, the combination of demographic patterns and economic circumstances explains the preoccuaption of much nineteenth-century philanthropy with widows. Indeed, in Hamilton the major charitable organization was the Ladies' Benevolent Society.

Two other points about the family cycle require emphasis: first, most married couples had children living with them throughout almost their entire--or the vast portion--of their married life. In 1871, only 4.6% of all Hamilton families, and this is an absolute maximum, consisted of a man and a woman whose children all had left home.

Second, because women commonly bore children until the close of their fecund years and because death came earlier than it does today, an extraordinarily high proportion of children could expect to be orphaned before they reached adulthood, and very few people knew all their grandparents. As a result, a combination of demographic constraints and geographic mobility severely limited the number of married couples who had a living parent whom they might take into their households. That is why one should expect to find few three generation families, why few couples could expect to dwell together alone after their children had left home, why very many children would be orphans, and why only a small proportion of people could expect to know their grandparents.

Orphanage is a subject about which little is known. How many orphans went to live with kin or relatives, how many became the wards of public or private orphan asylums are questions whose answers remain obscure. Certainly, the establishment of orphanages in nineteenth-century cities hints that an increased number, if not a greater proportion, of young children had nowhere to turn after the deaths of their parents. In Hamilton, the Ladies Committee of the Hamilton Orphan Asylum attempted to apprentice orphans to families for the duration of their minority. The families

were supposed to care for the children and to deposit a sum
each year into a bank account on their behalf. The records
of the asylum make difficult the estimation of just how well
the children were treated. Some ran away, a very few
complained of harsh treatment, but in most cases the books
show the payment of the annual deposit year after year. And
in a number of cases the arrangement obviously worked well.
Indeed, some families actually adopted the child they had
apprenticed (Ladies Committee of Orphan Asylum, Hamilton
Orphan Asylum, 1872-1898. Manuscripts, Hamilton Public
Library).

Consider the following case, which speaks eloquently of
both the affection that existed within working-class families
at this time, the anxieties of parents, and the particular
problems of women. When only a little over two years old in
1881, Minnie Nichol was apprenticed to John L. Tomlinson, a
moulder who lived at 107 McNab Street and later moved to
Toronto, residing at three different addresses there by 1889.
The Tomlinsons almost immediately adopted Minnie whom they
baptised Edna May Tomlinson. On August 23, 1889, Mrs. Mary
Tomlinson wrote to the head of the Ladies Committee of the
orphanage (Mary Tomlinson to Hamilton Orphan Asylum,
Hamilton Orphan Asylum Manuscripts).

Dear Madam:

I am sending you $4.00 on my little Daughter's
account and would like to have sent more but could not on
account of my Husband being sick for nearly 2 weeks which
leaves us rather short of funds, however, I hope to get it
settled as soon as possible then on the new year pay in
advance you will hear from me again on the 23 of Septbr.

We are paying for a ... piano for Edna and giving her
a good Musical education so that if anything should happen
to her Papa or I she will be able to earn a living for
herself and be independent of the world of course she
knows no different but that we are her own parent we love
her dearly and could not part with her unless called away
to another world...

Mary Tomlinson

Family Structure and the Family Cycle

The major reinterpretation of family structure in recent
years did not account for the family cycle. Peter Laslett's
assertion that most Western families at all times were
nuclear rested on aggregate figures that did not break down
family structure by age. (Laslett, 1977) As his critics

have pointed out, most families commonly could have
incorporated extensions at certain points in their cycles.
This was the case with the Austrian peasant families studied
by Lutz Berkner and with the working-class families in
nineteenth-century Lancashire, reconstructed by Michaeal
Anderson. It was not, by and large, the situation in
Hamilton (Berkner, 1972; Anderson, 1972).

In his recent book, Family Life and Illicit Love in Earlier
Generations, Laslett noted the force of the objection that he
had ignored the life cycle in his discussions of family
structure. Nonetheless, he was unable to estimate the
probability that given households would be extended or
multiple at some point in their domestic cycle (Laslett,
1977).

The issue, nonetheless, remains important. For there
are reasons why the composition of the domestic group might
have altered during its cycle. One is that in some places,
such as mid-nineteenth century Lancashire, it was customary
for young people to live with their parents for a short time
after marriage. This pattern probably characterized areas
with a shortage of housing. Certainly, in other places it was
common for elderly or infirm parents to live with their
married children. Because parents had more than one child
and because death came relatively early, only a small
minority of married couples would have a parent living with
them at any one point in time (Anderson, 1972).

From a different perspective, changes in domestic
organization could reflect the economic requirements of the
family. At certain points of strain--when children were
young--a female relative, often a mother, might live with a
family in order to permit the wife to work outside the home.
Or on peasant farms the labor requirements of families with
young children could require the incorporation into the
household of individuals who could participate in the
operation of the farm. Extending this line of argument, and
assuming, as most studies have shown to be the case, that one
working class income was not sufficient to support a family,
working-class families, all of whose children were young,
might have supplemented the family income through the
incorporation of boarders or kin who could contribute in some
way. In the same way, we should expect to find fewest kin or
the smallest proportion of boarders among those families with
the least economic need, namely, either those with no
children or with children of working age. Finally, given the
paucity of job opportunities for women and the under-
development of life insurance, we should expect to find

women who headed households especially likely to have people other than children dwelling with them.

As it happens, only the last of these expectations was met fully by the situation in Hamilton. Female-headed households did have a high proportion of boarders. Some other relations did exist between life cycle and domestic organization (defined by the number and identity of people dwelling together), but they were by and large minor and sometimes in the opposite direction from those which the forgoing arguments would lead us to expect.

To summarize a great deal of evidence briefly, the relationship between the presence of boarders and relatives and the family cycle was tenuous. There was little pattern to their distribution. Boarders and relatives did not compensate for the strain undergone by young working-class families; grandmothers did not live in enough homes to assist with child care; very few children lived with their parents after marriage; most families did not contain an elderly relative. To some extent families without children were more likely to have boarders than others. Undoubtedly, they had more room and might have felt more responsibility. But the differences by and large were not great.

At various points in their histories many families were likely to house a boarder or relative, probably for a relatively brief period. The same is true of servants. During the course of early industrialization, however, families were much more likely to lose than acquire extensions. Indeed, the proportion containing either a boarder, relative, or servant diminished sharply. This is what I refer to as the nuclearization of the household (Table 2).

This does not mean that boarding or living as kin was random. In particular, two patterns should be stressed. Life-cycle boarding, to use Peter Laslett's apt phrase, was common. Boarders and relatives were most often young unmarried people between the ages of 15 and 29, and the boarders, more often than relatives, were men. Boarding was a common phase in the life course, a routine experience of young men between leaving home and marrying. It began to decline partly because young people started to remain longer than ever before in the homes of their parents, a practice facilitated by the introduction of large industrialized work settings which enabled young men and women to find work within walking distance of their parents' homes (Laslett, 1977. Katz, Doucet, and Stern, In press).

Table 2. Changes in household composition among families traced from 1851–1861 and 1861–1871: Hamilton, Ontario.

A. Change in Household Membership

	Lost All		At Least One 61 or 71		Acquired One or More	
	51–61	61–71	51–61	61–71	51–61	61–71
Children	6.7	14.4	91.8	89.1	57.6	40.7
Boarders	71.8	65.3	42.7	34.8	11.8	19.6
Relatives	71.2	90.1	26.1	19.7	16.1	4.7
Boarders or Relatives	34.4	62.4	56.4	46.0	24.9	21.7
Servants	29.6	54.5	46.1	27.9	16.3	6.7

B. Percent with At Least One Member in Different Statuses

	1851–61 Group		1861–71 Group	
	51	61	61	71
Children	80.8	85.1	83.3	78.1
Boarders	31.7	20.0	19.9	22.5
Relatives	16.2	14.6	16.7	5.6
Boarders or Relatives	42.0	31.2	31.1	26.7
Servants	35.6	28.8	22.7	15.5

Second, elderly widows dwelled more frequently with their children than did elderly widowers. Indeed, just the opposite patterns characterized poor-houses, which contained more elderly men than women (Katz, 1980). It is unmistakable that children were more willing to house their mothers than their fathers, a pattern whose significance for family history deserves much more exploration (Table 3).

Patterns in Hamilton and Buffalo were quite similar. The major difference was that fewer families had boarders in the American city, probably a reflection of the fact that housing supply was much tighter. However, large differences separated the two cities from the rural areas, where families were much more likely to contain relatives, even though as in the cities, very little relation existed between the cycles of farm families and the likelihood that they would contain kin. They simply had more relatives at every stage. This pattern may have reflected greater population stability. Since people had remained in the same place longer—a pattern my colleagues and I have shown elsewhere—it is more likely that children lived near their siblings or parents had a married child nearby (Katz, Stern, and Doucet, In press). For these reasons it is not surprising that the farm families had more co-resident married children and contained larger proportions of elderly relatives. The other major difference between city and country is that in rural areas there were almost no households headed by women. There are probably two reasons for this. First, when a husband died, one of the children very likely took over the family farm. Second, younger widows with farms undoubtedly found it easier to re-marry than did their propertyless peers in the cities.

The Family Cycle and the Family Economy

The relation between family composition and property brings me to the question of the family economy. The economy of the family is a product of its class, its cycle, and its cultural context. Its class determines the rewards that the family receives, the life-chances of its members, the necessity for more than one income. The family cycle determines whether or not there are in fact members of the family other than the household head who can earn wages to supplement the family income. The cultural context affects a variety of issues: the acceptability of wage-work by women outside the home, attitudes toward education, the age at which children legitimately may work, the role of family members in the allocation of family income, the proportion of children's wages turned over to the family, and the requirements of an adequate standard of living.

Table 3. Proportion of women among inmates age 50 or more in Erie County, New York, Poorhouse, 1829–1886.

Years	Percent
1829	28.0%
1830–34	25.0
1835–39	10.0
1840–44	21.9
1853–54	22.4
1855–59	22.2
1860–64	21.6
1865–69	10.5
1870–74	14.7
1875–79	11.0
1880–86	24.0

Source: Registers of Inmates, Erie County, New York, Poorhouse.

The theme of most accounts of the relation between the family and the economy, of course, is the increasing separation between the two. In this interpretation, the functions of the family split apart as work came to be carried on outside the home which no longer was the setting of both production and residence.

There are serious problems with this interpretation. One is that its emphasis on the family as a retreat, as a "haven in a heartless world," sometimes neglects to emphasize that families always have an economy, whether or not all members are engaged in either the production of food, commodities, or wages. The nature of that economy and its internal relationships vary greatly, but all families must meet their needs for subsistence and all must establish patterns for the allocation of resources. Moreover, the separation of home and work usually is considered a middle-class or bourgeois practice. Indeed, it sometimes is assumed that the bourgeoisies were the first people to manifest all modern family traits. That assumption, however, has no foundation whatsoever.

In Hamilton, and elsewhere as well, the class which virtually to a person worked away from home was the working class. With the exception of the transitional and diminishing outworkers, the working-class consisted of wage-workers hired to work in a shop, on the streets, on the docks, on the railway, but not in the home. Clearly, the working-class was the first urban people for whom home became separate.

By contrast, during its early industrialization a substantial proportion of Hamilton's business class continued to combine their place of work with their place of residence. In 1871, about half of the professionals, 29% of the agents and merchants, 75% of the grocers, 86% of proprietors of services and semi-professionals, and 51% of masters and manufacturers still lived at their place of work.

Between 1851 and 1871, as already observed, young people began to live at home more often during their early working years. In 1851 one-half of the young men in Hamilton had left home by the age of 17; in 1861 one-half did not leave until the age of 21; in 1871, until 22. In 1851, 24% of the 20-year-old men lived at home; that proportion rose to 54% in 1861 and 61% 10 years later. By the latter year, 1871, 27% of the 25-year-old young men lived at home compared with 14% and 19% in the two earlier decades. Similar trends marked the experience of young women. Although their places of work and residence remained separate, the existence of

Table 4. Occupational designations by work/consumption and wage/consumption indexes, mean household size, and mean number of children: Hamilton, Ontario, 1851 and 1871, summary statistics.

Selected Occupational Categories	Number of Families		Mean Work/Consumption Indexes				Mean Wage/Consumption Indexes			
			Family		Household		Family		Household	
	51	71	51	71	51	71	51	71	51	71
Professional & Rentier	90	110	.63	.62	.68	.67	.38	.34	.45	.41
Agent & Merchant	133	297	.58	.60	.66	.62	.36	.39	.46	.41
Services & Semi-Professional	69	127	.58	.61	.72	.71	.36	.56	.52	.58
Business Employee	69	213	.58	.59	.62	.62	.34	.37	.39	.40
Master/Manufacturer	120	339	.57	.58	.65	.60	.33	.35	.45	.38
Skilled Worker	670	1447	.59	.59	.61	.59	.35	.38	.39	.38
Transport Worker	78	187	.60	.57	.63	.57	.35	.36	.40	.37
Laborer	357	694	.58	.59	.60	.59	.33	.38	.35	.37

larger workplaces enabled young people to find employment relatively close to their parents' homes and to continue to live with their families. This co-residence meant that working-class families had a greater number of incomes at particular points in their cycle. This is how the family cycle and the family economy intersected.

The economic strain on families varied with their stage of development. Young families with children faced the greatest economic burdens; families in which children worked had a potentially greater household income. The variation affected wage-earning families most since the income of adult male workers was both irregular and low. Men with higher incomes more easily could absorb the strain that existed when they were the sole income earners in their families. In Hamilton and Bufflo, moreover, very few married women worked outside their homes.

In order to test the relationship between these periods of strain and the composition of households more precisely—to test again the notion that families compensated for strain by incorporating additional members—I derived a series of indices, called work/consumption and wage/consumption indices, and applied them to both families and households separately.

Again, it is clear that families experiencing the greatest strain did not compensate through the addition of extensions to their households. Within occupational groups two patterns were evident. Among those families experiencing the period of greatest strain, indices showing the balance of workers to consumers were highest for those in the most prosperous occupations. That is, these families were the most likely to have additional incomes provided by boarders or kin. However, among those families with working-age children, the wage-indices were highest in the working class. In other words, the working class families were least able to compensate for the burden of young children through the incorporation of another wage-earner into the household. They were, however, the most likely to have more than one wage-earner in the family when children reached the age at which they could work for wages outside their home (Table 4).

The indices in Buffalo and Erie County closely resembled their counterparts in Hamilton. Especially striking was the similarity of indices on farms and in the cities. It might have been thought that farm families with young children more often would supplement their labor supply with resident relatives or employees, but this definitely was not the case.

Apparently, farms even at this period operated with wage-
labor, hiring laborers on a seasonal basis rather than
retaining a resident workforce. This was true even of
farmers with relatively large properties, over 100 cultivated
acres. For they were no more likely than smaller farmers to
supplement their household with resident laborers during the
years when all their children were young.

Although no relation existed between ethnicity and
household composition in either Hamilton or Buffalo, one
important ethnic distinction in the Canadian city's family
patterns must be stressed: the proportion of families at
different points in their cycles with at least one employed
child in 1871. For a greater proportion of late mid-cycle
Irish Catholic homes generally contained a working child age
15 or over, a function, without doubt, of their poverty.

One other pattern, though, was not related to ethnicity.
It is that daughters worked far more frequently in families
that did not contain sons of working age. This pattern
occurred in most ethnic groups within the working class. In
1871 the comparative proportions with a working daughter were
4% and 27% among laborers' families with and without sons
aged 15 or over. Clearly, most families expected a
contribution from their children. When sons were present,
they most often worked, when no sons were at home, daughters
had to enter the labor market.

Fertility

To some extent the economic utility of children was
reflected in fertility patterns. The years of early
industrialization, of course, were a period during which
marital fertility declined, though at exactly what pace and
among which groups remains largely unknown. At least one
part of the story, though, is clear. Fertility history is
not simply the tale of a growing discovery of better modes of
contraception. Contraceptive techniques have been available
and fairly widely understood for centuries, and demographic
history has made it clear that peasant populations
customarily regulated fertility through late marriages.

The acceptability of family limitation is not,
certainly, a story of calm, rational decisions reached
mutually by husbands and wives, reinforced by medical advice
and changed cultural standards. Its history is one of
conflict between accepted values and new problems, between
the shrill prophets of race suicide and the dilemnas of men
and women struggling to raise and educate children. It is

especially noteworthy that the decline in marital fertility
occurred in the face of determined disapproval from most
medical, cultural, religious, and political authorities (Katz
& Stern, In press; Stern, 1979).

The limitation in family size was, in a very real sense,
a movement that began despite, not because of, ideology or
policy. It originated in the adaptions of ordinary people to
the changed circumstances of their lives.

The development of a satisfactory theory relating
fertility to economic and social change remains an unsolved
task, one which I will not try to attempt here. Rather, I
want to summarize briefly the principal conclusions of a
detailed analysis of fertility in Hamilton.

These are, first: the relation between fertility and
class altered during early industrialization between 1851 and
1871. At the start, marital fertility within the business
class was higher than within the working class. By the
close, working class fertility was higher (Table 5). This
was accounted for by both an absolute decline within the
business class and an absolute rise within the working class,
a rise which cannot be accounted for either by infant
mortality or marriage age. Within the business class, the
group that led the decline were the business employees,
especially those with specialized occupational titles such as
bookkeeper, accountant or salesman, as opposed to the older
general title of clerk. These were the people in the most
modernized sector of the economy. The group whose fertility
rose most sharply was the Irish Catholics. Among them not
only fertility but illegitimacy increased during these years.
At the same time the fertility of other immigrant groups
declined. Finally, there were distinct differences between
immigrants and their children. Children of immigrant
backgrounds had lower fertility than their parents. An
extensive analysis of Buffalo between 1855 and 1915 supports
these trends, pointing out that children of immigrant parents
had a fertility ratio usually between that of immigrants and
the native-born children of native parents (Stern, 1979).

The increasing differences between the fertility of
ethnic groups arose from the group occupational or ethnic
standing. The great rise in Irish Catholic fertility was at
least partially a function of its working-class character,
and the decline among the other immigrant groups related to
the prominence of business class occupations among them.
Ethnicity, in short, served as a mediation between class and
fertility.

Table 5. Percentage change in standardized child-woman ratios, Hamilton, Ontario, 1851-1871.

	1851-1861	1861-1871	1851-1871
Occupation			
Prof. & Rentier	18.0%	-9.7%	6.7%
Agents & Merchants	0.9	-9.4	-8.6
Service & Semi-Prof.	-2.2	0.5	- .17
Business Employee	-7.5	-4.5	-11.7
Government Employee	45.0	-25.5	8.1
Masters & Manufactures	-6.5	3.4	3.3
Skilled Workers	4.5	1.0	3.5
Transport Workers	35.6	-3.3	31.0
Other Working Class	2.5	-11.7	-9.5
Laborer	9.7	-1.6	7.9
Business Class	-0.4	-4.0	-4.3
Working Class	7.2	-1.1	6.0
Ethnicity			
Irish Catholics	18.3	6.9	26.5
Irish Protestants	11.6	-4.5	6.6
Scottish Presbyterians	-10.9	-4.8	-15.2
Other Scottish	3.9	-3.1	0.8
English Anglicans	4.5	-0.2	4.3
English Methodists	-5.8	2.4	3.6
Other English	3.7	-13.4	-10.3
Canadian Protestants	-10.2	-4.3	-14.1
Canadian Catholics	-48.2	-27.9	6.8
U.S. Non-Whites	-47.3	7.7	-43.2
U.S. Whites	9.9	-4.7	4.7
Other	-6.9	9.3	1.7

Like all social behavior, fertility is learned through socialization, not the result of mechanical forces. The milieu in which socialization occurs, thus, is of critical importance. Attitudes toward fertility, moreover, probably are acquired relatively early in adulthood or in adolescence and may not change very dramatically later in life. Thus, it would be the dominant attitudes within the milieu in which young men and women grew up, not so much their adult occupations, which contributed most to their attitudes toward fertility.

The most homogeneous settings for socialization in nineteenth-century Hamilton were the sub-communities in which ethnicity and class overlapped. Thus, the son of an Irish Catholic laborer who managed to become a clerk or grocer may well have retained the approach to fertility more common among Irish Catholic laborers than among the members of the class which he had entered. Similarly, a downwardly mobile Scottish Presbyterian might have spent his youth and young adulthood in a higher class than the one in which he eventually found himself. This hypothesis about the importance of the setting in which socialization takes place makes understandable the lower fertility of the native-born children of immigrants. More likely than their foreign-born contemporaries to attend school, they would come of age in a more ethnically and socially diverse setting. Never having lived in Ireland, England, or Scotland, ethnicity would have a less direct impact upon their lives. The agencies that mediated between class and fertility in their case would extend beyond their ethnic group and embrace the school, peers, and the culture of urban North America, which interacted in ways which we remain unable to trace.

Speculative though the reasoning about the mediating effect of ethnicity upon the relation between class and fertility may be, it is clear that class trends in fertility were consistent with the forces influencing the family economy already described. Those families most actively limiting their fertility were the commercial employees in the upper middle sectors of the economic rank order. Their adolescent children were dwelling longer at home and remaining longer in school, not contributing by and large to the family's income. The aspirations that many of these families held and the economic pressures upon them are evident in the inverse relation between property ownership and servant employment among them. It was precisely the business class families of middling means, unable to both purchase a home and employ a servant, that more often chose a resident domestic, the conventional sign of affluence and gentility. Caught thus within a squeeze between their aspiration for their children--a realistic assessment of the relation of prolonged schooling to jobs in commerce and the professions--and their aspirations for themselves, these are the families that began to limit their fertility. 1/

Working-class families of similar economic standing more often chose to purchase a home. For them the prolonged residence of their children at home was not a drain but, on the contrary, a source of prosperity because teenage sons and sometimes daughters worked and contributed to the family income. During the early years of industrialization jobs near home for young men became more widely available and industrial work opened to young women as well. With no pressure to keep their children at school beyond the age at which they could enter industrial work, working-class families could view an additional child as another potential source of support. Thus, it is important to remember that in Hamilton the prolongation of adolescent residence at home, the increase in the proportion of working-class adolescents employed, and the rise in working-class fertility all happened at about the same time.

Conclusion

Families in Hamilton followed a cycle that altered only a little over the course of the two decades of early industrialization. Some people began to marry a bit earlier and others to have fewer children. However, the proportion of families in different phases of their cycle remained relatively constant, altered only by a slight aging of the population. Households, however, did alter notably. Relatives, boarders, and servants dwelled with far fewer families in 1871 than in 1851. Thus, the balance of potential workers to consumers within families remained constant while within households the proportion of potential workers declined. To some extent the prolonged residence at home and increased employment of adolescent children compensated for the decline in other household members.

By and large, only minimal relations existed between the structure of households and their cycle, and this was true in Buffalo and in Erie County towns and villages as well. The major exceptions occurred among families with no children and families headed by women, both of whom were more likely to contain relatives or boarders. Families experiencing their

---

1/ This thesis concerning the squeeze on middle-class income leading to fertility restriction was first proposed by Banks, 1954.

phases of greatest strain--when all children were too young to work--usually were unable to compensate for their difficulty through the incorporation of other people into the household. Throughout the various phases of the family cycle, affluent households more often contained members other than parents and children. The distinction was greater in 1851 than in 1871 when the general decline in the proportion of households with non-conjugal family members had lessened the degree of difference between groups. This distinction also was almost entirely one of class. In virtually no instance did ethnicity appear a significant factor differentiating the family cycle, structure, or economy.

Households, it must be stressed, were fluid. The composition of most of them changed during a decade, probably much more often. Throughout the period a sizeable, though diminishing, portion occasionally housed a relative or boarder.

Class also affected the likelihood that children would work. Before jobs for adolescents had become widely available, little class distinction existed in rates of adolescent employment. Working-class families probably experienced enormous strain during these years, and the unavailability of local jobs undoubtedly influenced the frequent early departure of young men and women from home. When employment opportunities became more widely available, working-class children entered the labor force earlier. By contrast, more affluent young people remained more often in school. Families, especially those in the working-class, clearly expected a contribution from their adolescent sons. Indeed, families apparently preferred to have their sons rather than their daughters employed, and only in instances when no son of employable age lived at home did a sizeable fraction, though still a minority, of families send their daughters to work.

At the conclusion of the family cycle few couples could expect to live very long together after their children had left home. In fact, a very high proportion of women over the age of 45 were widows, and at all ages women were widows more often than men. Men who had been widowed found it much easier than women to re-marry. Thus, women realistically could expect a phase in their lives when they would have to support children who remained at home or find a way of earning their own livelihood. Few of them left home to work, for in Hamilton there were few job opportunities to which they could turn. Rather, they more often took in boarders to supplement their income or were supported by a working child. Those in dire need were given charity by the Ladies

Benevolent Society, and some elderly women moved in with
relatives or other families, a practice much more common on
farms than in the city and probably a result of the presence
of more kin in rural than in urban areas. However, very few
elderly widowed men dwelled with their kin. When unable to
maintain their own households, they more often lived as
boarders with another family or in a poorhouse.

Few simple statements can summarize the relations
between families and industrialization. One reason is that
industrialization itself is an imprecise concept, too often
confused with capitalism. Clearly though, at least one major
contrast must be made: namely, between industrialization in
the textile industries and industrialization in metals and
machinery. In textile producing areas whole families
sometimes worked in mills and the rate of employment among
women and young children was quite high. In towns like
Hamilton which industrialized without a significant textile
industry almost no married women worked for wages and little
employment existed for young children. Whether differences
in total family wages also existed remains unknown. However,
the two employment patterns had very different impacts upon
the organizaton of family life (Anderson, 1972; Hareven,
1977).

Another reason that simple summary statements about the
relation of families to social change are difficult to make
is that they obscure the intimate relation between families
and class. For centuries, the timing, direction, and causes
of changes in family organization have differed by class.

Only a model which examines the family by class can
explain the contrast between their contemporary and their
pre- and early capitalist predecessors. That model,
moreover, cannot be one which is based upon a diffusion of
innovation from higher to lower classes. For different types
of changes begin at various points in the class structure.
The five great changes in family organization that have
occured are: (1) the separation of home and workplace; (2)
the increased nuclearity of household structure; (3) the
decline in marital fertility; (4) the prolonged residence of
children in the home of their parents; and (5) the lengthened
period in which husbands and wives live together after their
children have left home. The first two began among the
working-class and among the wage-earning segment of the
business class (clerks and kindred workers). The third
started among the business class, particularly among its
least affluent, most modernized and mobile sectors. The
fourth began at about the same time in both the working and
business class, though the children of the former usually

went to work and the latter to school. The date at which the
fifth began and its relation to class remains unknown;
certainly, it began well beyond the early industrial era.
Clearly, it is not possible to argue that the bourgeoisie
pioneered a modern family form later imitated by the
working-class.

To some extent the adoption of new patterns of domestic
organization has reflected shifts in values, but by itself
value change contributes very little to any understanding
of why the great alterations in family organization took
place. The key lies, rather, in the family economy, in the
strains, opportunities, and anxieties induced by the
differential social impact of capitalist development upon
domestic life. Individual people, surely, never have been
automatons, and deterministic models do not explain human
experience adequately. Yet, people are not completely free,
either, and it is the reasons why they chose as they did
among limited alternatives that historians must discover. In
that choice the values which justified traditional cultural
patterns, or those which challenged them, mediated between
the great forces of social change and family behavior.

The process of family change is not evolutionary but
dialectical. For family forms partly generate the
contradictions which lead to their supercession. Within the
family formations characteristic of industrial capitalist
society in North America, for instance, the emergence of
newly dependent and exploited strata among women and young
people has unleashed the profound social change which public
policy lamely tries to tame, moderate, or modify. However,
though containing an inherent dynamic, families never drift
free of their anchor in a class structure and economic
system, now increasingly secured by the intrusive authority
of the state, either directly through the schools, courts,
and welfare system or indirectly as in the sanctioned impetus
to consumption and debt carefully cultivated by the media
from childhood through old age. For a brief historical
moment as they firmed up the boundaries between themselves
and their community bourgeois families were very private. By
contrast, consistently scrutinized and regulated by newly
emergent state and charitable authority, working-class
families never secured similar autonomy, even fleetingly. It
is the myth of the private family that has been diffused, not
its reality. In truth, we have returned to a point at which
the boundaries between families in all classes and their
surrounding social, economic, and political context have
become tenuous and indistinct. Whether this should be
counted a gain or a loss is not an objective question (Lasch,
1977).

References

Anderson, Michael, 1972. Family Structure in Nineteenth-Century Lancashire, London: Cambridge University Press.

Banks, J. A., 1954. Prosperty and Parenthood: A Study of Family Planning Among the Victorian Middle Classes. London: Rutledge & Keagan Paul.

Berkner, Lutz K., 1972. "The Stem Family and the Development Cycle of the Peasant Household: An Eighteenth-Century Austrian Example," American Historical Review, 77: 398-418.

Demos, John, 1970. A Little Commonwealth: Family Life in Plymouth Colony, New York: Oxford University Press.

Hareven, Tamara K., 1977. "Family Time and Industrial Time: Family and Work in a Planned Corporation Town, 1900-1924." In T. K. Hareven (ed.), Family and Kin in Urban Communities, 1700-1930, New York: New Viewpoints, 187-206.

Katz, Michael B., 1980. "A Demographic History of the Erie County, New York, Poorhouse, 1829-1886," Institutions and the Casualties of Industrial Society Project, Working Paper No. 1.

Katz, Michael B., Michael Doucet, and Mark J. Stern, in press. The Social Organization of Early Industrial Capitalism, Cambridge, Mass: Harvard University Press.

Katz, Michael B., and Mark J. Stern, in press. "Fertility, Class and Early Industrial Capitalism," American Quarterly.

Ladies Committee of Orphan Asylum, Hamilton Orphan Asylum, (1872-1898) Manuscripts, Hamilton Public Library.

Lasch, Christopher, 1977. Haven in a Heartless World, New York: Basic Books.

Laslett, Peter, 1977. Family Life and Illicit Love in Earlier Generations, London: Cambridge University Press.

Lindert, Peter H., 1978. Fertility and Scarcity in America, Princeton, N.J.: Princeton University Press.

Smith, Daniel Scott, 1972. "The Demographic History of Colonial New England," Journal of Economic History, 32: 165-183.

Stern, Mark J., 1979. "The Demography of Capitalism: Industry, Class, Fertility in Erie County, New York, 1855-1915." Unpublished Ph.D. dissertation, York University: Toronto, Ontario.

Albert Simkus

8. Socioeconomic Careers in the Context of Radical Social Change: Evidence from Hungary

The passage of time is accompanied by changes in the social statuses of individuals through the processes of aging and historical change. Aging and historical change not only have their own independent effects, they also interact. Historical events have different impacts on different age groups, and the cohort differences thus created often persist through subsequent historical eras. In this paper, I describe the relationships between several aspects of socioeconomic careers and fairly radical historical changes in socio-economic structure. More specifically, I discuss a few cohort-specific career consequences of historical changes in Hungary during the period between 1932 and 1973.

In modern societies, there exist various socio-occupational strata associated with different levels of authority, expertise, and life chances. The reproduction of systems of social stratification involves processes for maintaining or replacing the incumbents of these strata. The continuity of social orders requires continuity in the processes of intra- and intergenerational transmission of social status, while radical change requires that these processes be disrupted. The costs and magnitudes of such disruptions are subject to a number of constraints common to most modern societies. Among these constraints are problems related to the relative difficulties of changing social structure through intragenerational social mobility versus through the alternative process of cohort replacement. Examining the experiences of radically changing societies can help show us how much change is possible and how universal are these constraints on the mode of change.

The Hungarian case offers an unusual opportunity to examine changes in the distribution and transmission of social statuses resulting from changes in social policy and organization.   The degree of historical social change has been awesome.   The transition from a largely agricultural to an industrial society was unusually rapid; the rate at which labor was moved out of the agricultural sector during the early 1950s has been matched by only a few other countries, such as the USSR and Japan during their periods of most rapid structural change.   At the same time, the Hungarian case has also involved unusually strong state policies specifically directed at changing the process of the transmission of social status and the relationship between ascribed characteristics and socio-economic careers.   In short, Hungarian history has been poignantly rich in what writers on aging call "non-normative" (Baltes and Willis, 1979) influences on individual careers.   The present limitations on the length of this paper preclude describing these historical events in the detail they merit.   I can only list the most important of these influences in Hungary between 1932 and 1973.

A largely agricultural country with extremely conserva-tive political and social institutions, Hungary experienced a financial crisis and depression in 1930.   This depression had partially abated by 1939, the beginning of Hungary's involve-ment in World War II.   After the end of the war, Hungary be-gan a series of profound structural changes.   Beginning with a major land reform in 1945, a variety of left-wing populist policies were implemented between 1945 and 1948, including the nationalization of large industrial enterprises and a major reform of the educational system.

Following the consolidation of control by the communist party, Hungary underwent a period of Stalinist political consolidation and economic development.   In many ways, Stalinist policies were pursued to greater extremes in Hungary between 1949 and 1953 than in the other East European states.   Various policies were directed at declassement of much of the previous administrative leadership, enlargement of the labor force by increasing the involvement of women, partial collectivization of agriculture, "extensive" indus-trial development, and the use of class and political cri-teria in the control of socio-economic careers.

A period of moderation and shifting policies between 1954 and 1956 ended with a national uprising, followed by economic and political reconsolidation.   Agricultural collec-tivization was renewed in 1960 and completed by 1963.   The subsequent period is referred to within Hungary as the period of "consolidated socialist society" and the "alliance policy." This period has involved various educational and economic reforms, a shift from "extensive" to "intensive" economic development, and a considerable lessening of the influence of

political and class criteria in the determination of socio-
economic careers.

Data

In the face of such events and changes, it is fortunate
that there exist for Hungary an unusually rich collection of
data describing changes in the national labor force and
changes in the transmission of social status.   In this paper
I wish to show certain kinds of changes in three different
aspects of socio-economic careers: 1) the kinds of positions
persons were likely to hold, 2) gender-based differences in
the types of positions held, and 3) the intergenerational
association in social status.   This is done somewhat indirectly, by describing cohort-specific historical changes in
the distribution of social strata, the sex composition of
certain strata, and the association between fathers' social
strata and those of their offspring.   Note that while the
implications of these changes for the individuals involved
are fairly clear, these data refer to cohort, rather than
individual, careers.

Each of these three topics deserves and is receiving
more extensive treatment than can be presented here (see
Andorka and Harcsa, 1981; Simkus, 1981b).   A few pictures
have been selected from the larger story in order to highlight some points about careers and great social change.   The
data considered here are all derived from a large scale
national survey of retrospective occupational life-histories
conducted in Hungary in 1973 (N=40,000) (see Andorka et al.,
1975; Andorka and Harcsa, 1981).   These data share many of
the problems of retrospective data in general--the absence of
those who have died or emigrated and inadequacies in the
recollections of those who have not.   Yet, these shortcomings
are more than compensated for by such advantages as cohort-
specific information for single years covering an extended
period of time and based on similarly defined social
categories.   The measures presented are intentionally quite
simple.   All the same, such a description of change is
extremely rare, particularly for countries having experienced
such extraordinary rates of social change.

In each of the graphs to follow, the historical period
involved begins with 1932 and ends with 1973.   The employed
civilian labor force in each year of this interval has been
divided into five birth cohorts, based on the following
intervals of year of birth: 1) 1901-1910, 2) 1911-1920,
3) 1921-1930, 4) 1931-1940, and 5) 1941-1950.   Each cohort
only appears in the figures beginning in that year in which
the cohort's youngest members have become at least 23 years

of age. Note that most of the first cohort reached age 18,
a crucial point in the completion of education and entrance
into the labor force, between 1919 and 1928--during the
interwar period and before the depression. The second cohort
became age 18 between 1929 and 1938--during the depression,
but just before the war. The third cohort became eighteen
between 1939 and 1948, during the war and just prior to the
Stalinist period. The fourth reached this age between 1949
and 1958, during the Stalinist period and its immediate
aftermath. The fifth and last became eighteen between 1959
and 1968, the period including the completion of collectivization and the beginning of the alliance policy and developed
socialism.

Changes in the Distribution of Social Strata

First, let us consider the pattern of cohort-specific
changes in Hungary's social structure. In Hungary as elsewhere, the process of industrial development involved a large
scale transformation of the labor force (see Andorka and
Zagorski, 1979; M.S.Z.M.P., 1979; Singelman, 1978; Simkus,
1981b). This included massive decreases in the proportion of
the labor force employed in agriculture, followed by increases in the industrial labor force and increases in the
sizes of the nonmanual strata. In the first stage of this
transition, much of the growth in the industrial strata was
concentrated in the less skilled types of jobs. Subsequently,
the skilled industrial-manual and nonmanual strata continued
to grow at the expense of both the unskilled manual and
agricultural strata. These changes involved a great deal of
intergenerational and intragenerational mobility.

It can be argued whether or not various forms of this
mobility, such as moves from certain agricultural positions
to unskilled industrial jobs, constituted "upward" mobility;
thus, such mobility is sometimes called "mobility in the main
direction" (Andorka, 1970). Whether upward or not, such
mobility involved awesome changes in life experiences; and
the expansion of the skilled manual and upper nonmanual strata
clearly did involve upward moves.

How were these structural changes in the labor force
accomplished? By intragenerational mobility involving shifts
within individuals' own careers, or by cohort replacement
with new labor force cohorts with more "modern" occupational
distributions replacing older cohorts with older occupational
distributions? To the extent that within-cohort shifts
occurred, how great were they and within which age ranges
were they concentrated? Since the rate of structural change
in Hungary during the early 1950s was near the upper limits

of such changes as have been observed in cross-national data,
the Hungarian case presents somewhat of an "acid-test" of how
much such intragenerational mobility is likely to occur.

The answers to the preceding questions are complex, but
largely in line with what we might expect. <u>Cross-cohort</u>
differences were important in nearly all aspects of changes
in the socio-occupational structure. However, the magnitude
of <u>within-cohort</u> shifts in structure varied, depending upon
the particular social strata concerned and the age of the
cohorts potentially subject to such mobility. Substantial
within-cohort shifts at late ages were only apparent in regard to increases in the <u>unskilled</u> industrial-manual stratum.
This was particularly true for women and the two oldest cohorts of men. Figure 1 displays the proportion of employed
women in each cohort within the unskilled manual category in
each year. Obviously, both cross-cohort differences and
within-career shifts have been important in the expansion of
this stratum. For both men and women, the scope of within-
cohort stratum shifts at late ages were a negative function
of the education and skill   required for each socio-
occupational category. Compare Figure 1 with Figure 2, which
shows the corresponding changes for women in regard to the
proportion employed in the lower nonmanual stratum.

The possibility of within-career shifts into the higher
social strata was reasonably great for those who were young
at the time of particularly rapid increases in these
categories. For example, notice the substantial increase in
the proportion of women in lower nonmanual positions occurring between 1946 and 1952 among those women in the second
cohort (aged approximately 27-42 during that period). Also
note the small increases in the proportion of men in the
skilled manual stratum between 1952 and 1960 among those in
the second and third cohorts (Figure 3). Increases in the
proportion of men in the upper nonmanual stratum during the
youngest five years of age displayed are observable in all
five cohorts (Figure 4). However, the magnitude of both
these early increases, and somewhat later increases (continuing for at least the first 19 years of age shown), were
greatest for the third and fourth cohorts--those who were
young during the great expansion in the upper nonmanual
stratum. For women, such intragenerational increases in the
upper nonmanual category during the early ages were much less
apparent.

In brief, there were significant within-career shifts
involving all social strata during periods of unusually great
change, particularly during the period between 1945 and 1963.
For those strata associated with relatively high levels of

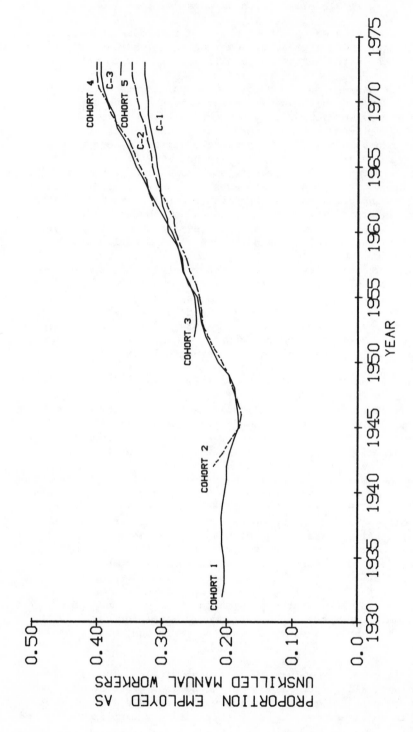

Figure 1. The proportion of employed women who were unskilled manual workers, by year and birth cohort.

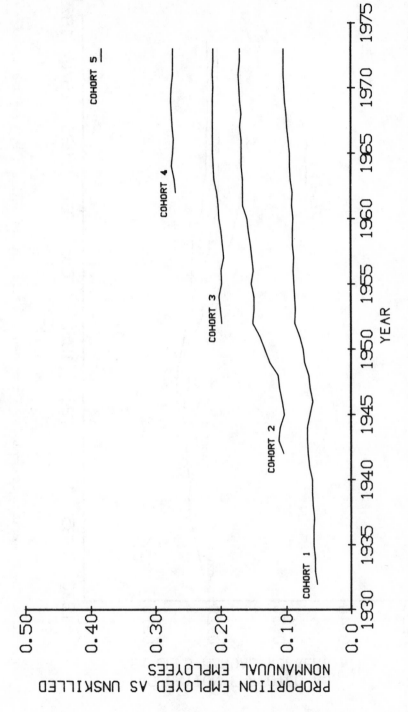

Figure 2. The proportion of employed women who were lower nonmanual employees, by year and birth cohort.

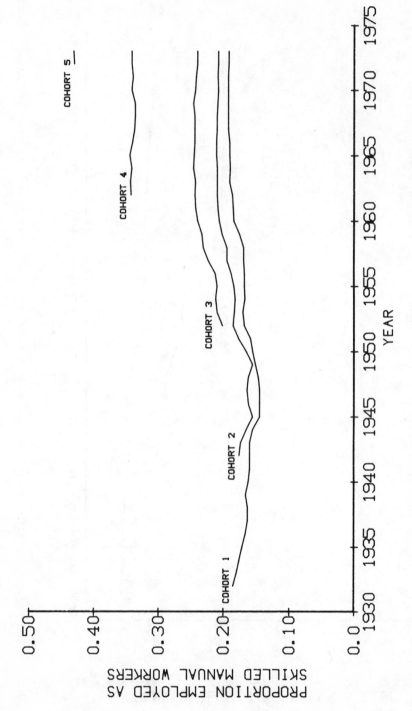

Figure 3. The proportion of employed men who were skilled manual workers, by year and cohort.

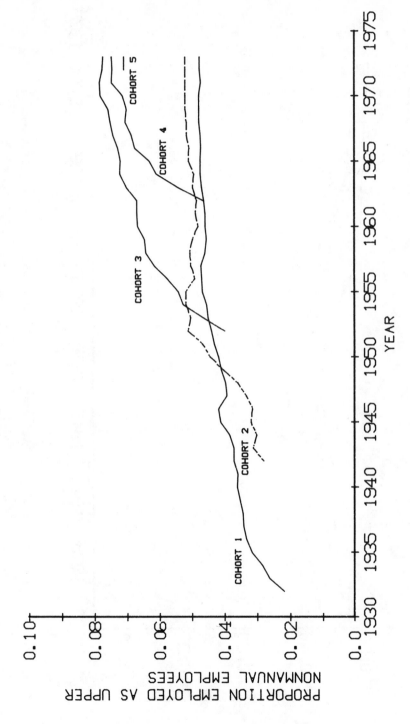

Figure 4. The proportion of employed men who were upper nonmanual employees, by cohort and year.

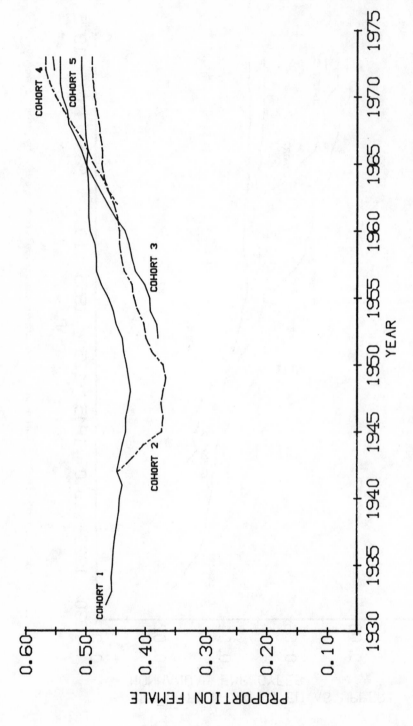

Figure 5. The proportion of unskilled manual workers who were female, by birth cohort and year.

education and skill, such shifts are observable during young ages and even during middle ages. Although there is not space to describe these policies, let me point out that Hungary developed numerous policies facilitating continuing education and skills training at relatively late ages during this period. These policies and the high rate of change brought about shifts at relatively old ages. However, during the older ages, cohorts were unable to benefit from the expansion of the upper social strata. During more normal periods, structural shifts in all but the least skilled strata took place primarily through cross-cohort shifts.

Changes in the Sex-Composition of Social Strata

Now let us consider a related aspect of structural change and individual careers--changes in the sex composition of each socio-economic category. Such changes occurred as a result of both changes in women's labor force participation and changes in the gender-specificity of the occupational distribution. Were such changes accomplished through abrupt changes within the careers of cohorts of women? Or, did they occur through the addition to the labor force of new cohorts of men and women with quite different starting characteristics than those which had passed before? As we might expect from the previous discussion, the answer is that within-cohort shifts in sex composition were important only within the unskilled manual stratum (see Figure 5). Several cohorts which began with a preponderance of men in the unskilled stratum had a preponderance of women in this category by the 1970s. But, with regard to the upper nonmanual stratum, although within-cohort increases in the proportion of women occurred, women benefitted most from cross-cohort improvements (Figure 6).

Changes in the Intergenerational
Association in Social Status

Finally, let us briefly take up a somewhat different issue--the degree to which individuals' social attainments were associated with those of their fathers. How did the relative attainments of persons from different social backgrounds change over time? Did the great changes in Hungary attentuate disparities through within-career changes in social status? Or, did such disparities only change as new cohorts, having entered first jobs through a new mobility regime, replaced older cohorts who began their careers under vastly different circumstances? Imposing a great oversimplification on a complex story, both forms of change were significant, but changes involving intragenerational shifts were important only during the periods of most extreme change and

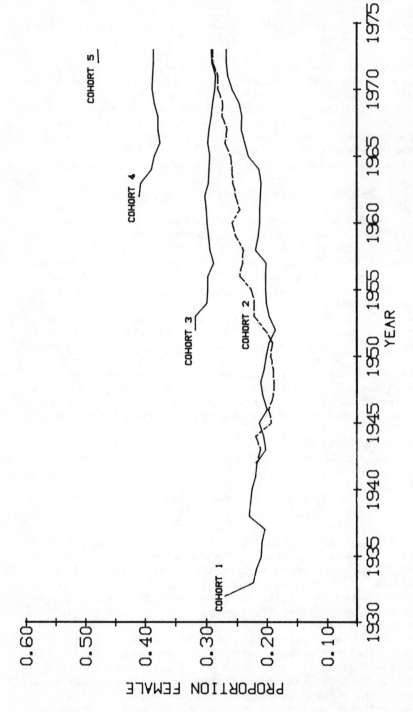

Figure 6. The proportion of upper nonmanual employees who were female, by cohort and year.

extreme policies (Simkus, 1981a; 1981b). Once more "normal"
conditions returned, cross-cohort differences were more
apparent than within-cohort shifts.

In reaching this conclusion, I have analyzed intergenerational social mobility tables classifying sampled respondents by their father's social stratum (when the respondent
was 16 years old) and by their own social stratum in each
year, for each category of birth cohort by gender. Given
these tables, changes in the relative odds of persons from
either of two categories of social origins ending up in
either of two categories of social destinations can be
assessed by calculating odds-ratios for appropriate subtables
drawn from the complete tables (see Goodman, 1969;
Goldthorpe, 1980; Simkus, 1980).

Such odds-ratios have an intuitive interpretation. If
the odds-ratio for two categories of origins and destinations,
such as the upper nonmanual and lower manual categories,
equals 5, we can say that the odds of a person from upper
nonmanual origins being in the upper nonmanual (versus the
lower manual) category are exactly five times as great as
the corresponding odds for a person from lower manual origins.
This measure, whose endearing properties are most familiar to
social mobility researchers, has the advantage of not being a
function of structural changes in origins and destinations
mutually benefiting those from all social backgrounds.

Figure 7 displays changes in the natural logarithms of
such odds-ratios, calculated from subtables relevant to
mobility between the upper nonmanual and lower manual strata.
Only the changes for the five cohorts of males are shown.
There is evidence of both cross-cohort differences and within-
cohort shifts. This aspect of inequality in attainments
decreased through intragenerational mobility among those in
the two oldest cohorts between 1944 and 1950--the time of the
post-war changes and the beginning of the Stalinist period.
Though the estimates between 1952 and 1962 appear unstable,
the indices for all four of the oldest cohorts increased after
1963--the onset of the alliance policy and lessened "class
struggle." By 1973, the cross-cohort differences largely
reflected those differences observable at the start of each
cohort's career.

Other aspects of intergenerational mobility showed
significantly different patterns of change, yet it is reasonably accurate to say that with regard to those aspects of
mobility which involved substantial degrees of "upward" or
"downward" movement, cross-cohort differences were more
apparent and long lasting than within-cohort shifts.

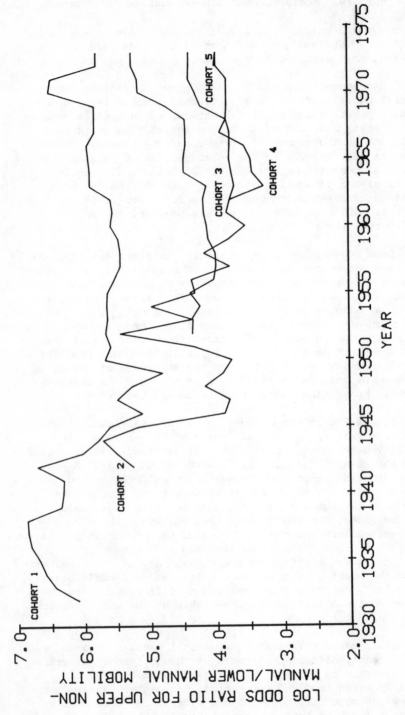

Figure 7. Log odds-ratios indicating openness between the upper nonmanual and lower manual strata (in terms of intergenerational social mobility), for men by cohort and year.

Conclusions and Implications

Three different aspects of the careers of these Hungarian birth cohorts have been considered and the conclusions in each case have been similar. Radical social change can indeed bring substantial changes through within-career shifts; but, in regard to the higher social positions requiring above average education and training, cross-cohort differences are likely to be the greatest source of change; and those within-career shifts which do occur tend to take place during relatively young ages. If such patterns are apparent even in the case of a country which has experienced such rapid transformations of its labor force as has Hungary, they should be even more clear in societies going through more gradual changes.

Why should these patterns be nearly universal? Apart from age-graded norms concerning career changes, there are economic constraints governing the costs of various types of career shifts. First, since investments in education and training are expected to have longer-run payoffs for the young than for the old, it is to be expected that both individuals and societies will find such investments most attractive during early stages of the life-cycle. Second, while modern states, and particularly socialist states, are assuming more and more of the costs of economic dependency during periods of training and education, such costs to the individual and to the state are still smallest during those life-cycle stages during which parental families typically bear the brunt of these expenses.

Third, since human capital, once acquired by individuals, cannot be easily expropriated and redistributed, changes in the distributions of social statuses are most easily brought about by policies directed at the initial distribution of such capital. If highly trained individuals are cast downward into unskilled positions, their capabilities are largely simply thrown away. Apart from critical revolutionary periods, it is unlikely that the leadership of any society would wish to waste such resources--and particularly in societies where skilled and highly educated workers are in great demand. During revolutionary periods, such policies are still unlikely but possible. Extreme examples of such practices are provided by the cultural revolution in China and the mass murders of intellectuals in Kampuchea under the Pol Pot regime. The costs of such policies help explain their rarity and brief duration.

This third constraint is of greatest relevance with regard to changes requiring downward intragenerational social mobility. Upward mobility, while it involves costs, does not require throwing away existing human resources. Similar though perhaps weaker constraints are involved in changes in intergenerational social mobility. While the state may be heavily involved in education, unless children are removed from their families it is difficult to prevent parents with skills from passing them on to their offspring. Thus, changes requiring downward intergenerational mobility also waste prior investments in human resources which cannot be redistributed.

As we have observed, the importance of this third constraint is a negative function of the degree of social mobility involved. All forms of career shifts discouraged by the costs of investing in or discarding human resources will be most constrained when they involve extreme, rather than small, shifts in social status. Since social status in modern societies is highly associated with differences in training and education, the costs associated with such training covary with the magnitude of career changes in status.

Finally, in the case of the East European socialist states such as Hungary, a fourth constraint has also limited the amount of social change brought about through within-career mobility. In these countries, the state has taken on responsibility for guaranteeing full employment. During the post-Stalinist period, this responsibility has involved guaranteeing not only the right to a job, but also protection from forced job changes. This policy has limited downward social mobility and the use of forced intragenerational mobility in promoting structural change.

All of these constraints made it unlikely that great changes in the distribution of social statuses in Hungary would occur through within-cohort shifts, rather than through cross-cohort differences. All three of the changes in status distributions which I have discussed are directly related to social inequalities: inequalities in the availability of better positions, inequalities in access to these positions based on gender, and inequalities in access based on social backgrounds. The fact that changes in these distributions are constrained to take place primarily through cross-cohort differences rather than through within-cohort career changes has important implications for cohort and age-based social stratification in states such as Hungary.

If increases in the preponderance of positions associated with high levels of skill, education, and productivity are monotonic, the young will always be relatively privileged in comparison with the old. The question of the degree to which differentials in skill and productivity ought to be rewarded by wage differentials has been, and remains, one of the more important political questions in the East European socialist states. The process of structural change through cross-cohort differences results in the conflict over egalitarianism being expressed partly across age and cohort lines. It is in the interest of the young that skill, education, and productivity be rewarded highly. Increases in equality, or increases in inequalities based on authority or seniority, are in the interest of the old.

In capitalist societies, the advantages of the young are counterbalanced by the fact that the old are more likely to benefit from a disproportionate hold on the distribution of property and property-based incomes. In socialist states, the absence of large-scale private ownership of property and the means of production rules out this advantage for the old--except perhaps in the sphere of private housing. In these states the primary protection for the old may rest with the political leadership. After the seizure of power the leadership, as a group, tends to age and remain old. Through their control over the system of centralized redistribution, this leadership can play a key role in the protection of those whose stage in the life-cycle they share.

References

Andorka, Rudolf
　　1970　A Tarsadalmi Atretegzodes es Demografiai Hatasai. II. Magyarorszagon. Publications of the Demographic Research Institute of the Central Statistical Office. No. 30, 394 pp.

　　1975　"Tendencies of social mobility in Hungary: Comparisons of historical periods and cohorts." Paper prepared for the Conference of the Committee on Social Stratification of the International Sociological Association. Geneva, December.

Andorka, Rudolf and Istvan Harcsa
　　1981　Results of the 1973 Hungarian Social Mobility Survey. Forthcoming in Hungarian. Budapest: Central Statistical Office.

Andorka, Rudolf and Janos Illes
　　1978　"Changes in intergenerational social mobility." Pp. 195-222 in Tibor Huszar, Kalman Kulcsar, and Sandor Szalai, eds., Hungarian Society and Marxist Sociology in the Nineteen-Seventies. Budapest: Corvina Press.

Andorka, Rudolf and Krysztof Zagorski
    1979   A Tarsadalmi Mobilitas Magyarorszagon es
            Lengyelorszagban. Budapest: Central Statistical
            Office.

Baltes, Paul B. and Sherry L. Willis
    1979   "Life-span developmental psychology, cognitive
            functioning and social policy," in Matilda White
            Riley, ed., Aging from Birth to Death:
            Interdisciplinary Perspectives. Washington:
            American Association for the Advancement of
            Science, pp. 15-46.

MSZMP KB   Tarsadalomtudomanyi Intezete
    1979   Tarsadalmunk Szerkezetenek Fejlodesi Tendenciai.
            Budapest.

Simkus, Albert A.
    1980   Social Change and Social Mobility: The Case of
            Hungary. Unpublished Ph.D. thesis, The University
            of Wisconsin.

    1981a   "Historical changes in occupational inheritance
            under socialism: Hungary 1930-1973," in Donald
            Treiman and Robert Robinson, eds., Research in
            Social Stratification and Mobility, JAI Press,
            1981.

    1981b   "Socialist structural transformation and social
            mobility: Hungary 1938-1973." Paper presented
            at the annual meeting of the Population Associa-
            tion of America, March 30, 1981, Washington, D.C.

Singelman, Joachim
    1978   From Agriculture to Services: The Transformation
            of Industrial Employment. Beverly Hills: Sage
            Publications.

9. The Lengthening of Retirement

The ability to retire is a relatively recent luxury. Only in the last forty years have most Americans considered retirement an economic right earned from a lifetime of work. Yet almost no one has considered how much of our adult lives should be devoted to work versus retirement and whether that ratio should change as the length of adult life itself changes. This paper addresses this question first by summarizing how the retired life has lengthened over time. It then describes the present situation and speculates on what may happen in the future.

The Historical Relationship of Retirement to Adult Life

In subsistence and agrarian societies the concept of a formal retirement does not exist, except perhaps for a small elite who were retired most of their lives. In addition, in many subsistence societies life expectancy is not long enough to make retirement planning necessary. And for the relatively few who become old, their extended families provide the social institution to support them as they become less productive (U.S. Congress). There may be an increasing shift in the division of labor as a family member ages, but adults with no work responsibilities are a luxury most subsistence societies cannot afford.

The industrialization of society, however, has shifted the relationship of work and retirement. Over a hundred years ago, some countries such as the U.S. began to pay pensions to their disabled veterans in recognition of their sacrifice to their countries. But it was not until 1885 when Chancellor Bismarck established a public retirement system for Germany that the concept of rewarding work with retirement was formally established.

Although the establishment of a public retirement system
in Germany is generally considered to be a major development
in social policy, Bismarck's generosity was tempered by his
retirement age of 70 years old (Meier, 1979). Life
expectancy in the U.S. and presumably in Germany was then
approximately 42 years. Today a retirement age that bears
the same proportionate relationship to life expectancy (now
73 for the United States) would be 122 years of age (Norwood,
1977). Even if an equivalent retirement age is calculated
based on the ratio of life expectancy at age 20, then and
now, the equivalent present retirement age of Bismarck's age
70 would be approximately 93. (The remaining life expectancy
at age 20 in 1890 was 41.4 years (Bureau of the Census, 1972)
and in 1977 was 54.9 years). Therefore, Bismarck's
retirement promise was more of a reward to people who had
lived beyond their life expectancy than a realistic
expectation for the average worker. In general, the few
people who received Bismarck's pension received it for only a
small fraction of their adult lives.

By 1935 when the Social Security Act was passed there
were already 28 States that had retirement plans for public
employees; 14 had a retirement age of 70, 1 had an age limit
of 68, and the rest had a retirement age of 65. The Social
Security original retirement age (65) was only five years
less than Bismarck's, but the adult remaining life expectancy
of adults (at age 20) had increased considerably from 41 to
almost 49 years. That meant that every 20-year-old adult
could plan to have almost four years at the end of their life
in retirement. These few years represented approximately 7%
of the adult life in 1940 if the adult life is defined as
beginning at age 20. Those adults who actually reached age
65 would, of course, live considerably longer (over 12 more
years). But the 20-year-old always faces a different life
expectancy than the 65-year-old person who has survived the
traumas of middle age. By 1950, the substantial increases in
life expectancy for a 20-year-old had increased the promised
retirement life as a proportion of the adult life to 12%.
Between 1950 and 1960 life expectancy for the 20-year-old
increased 1.4 years at the same time that the minimum
retirement age under Social Security was reduced from 65 to
62 years old. These two changes together increased the
expected retired life to 20% of the adult life for a 20-year-
old. Today a 20-year-old can plan on an average retirement
that is 23% of his or her adult life. This striking increase
in the share of our adult life that is devoted to retirement
is perhaps one of the largest benefit liberalizations under
Social Security. Yet it is not generally acknowledged and is
rarely discussed.

Table 1 summarizes the average proportion of adult life

that a 20-year-old could expect to be retired at different
times in the past. Of course, as people age their life
expectancy changes so that the proportions would also change.
But the change would always be in the direction of increasing
the ratio for those people still alive at any given age.
Therefore, the percentages in Table 1 are actually the
minimum proportion of the adult life the 20-year-old could
expect to be retired given average life expectancies.

The near doubling of the proportion of retired to adult
life between 1950 and 1977 raises serious questions about
what is likely to happen in the future. If the increases in
life expectancy continue then the proportion of retired to
adult life will also increase. But it is difficult to
imagine an indefinite growth in either life expectancy or in
proportion of life spent in retirement. The recent increases
in life expectancy suggest that most of the relative gains in
the future will be for people 65 and over, but other studies
suggest that these gains will be predictably limited. The
following section briefly discusses the implications of
future changes in life expectancy for the lengthening of the
retired life.

Possible Increases in Life Expectancy

Until World War II, the decrease in mortality primarily
affected the young and middle-aged. However, once people
reached old age they did not live much longer than elderly
people had lived in previous generations. Recently this has
changed as can be seen in Table 2.

Since World War II, the life expectancy of the aged has
grown at a faster rate than life expectancy at birth, and the
older the age the faster the rate of increase has been. The
biggest increases in life expectancy for people 75 and over
have come since 1965, at the time that the gains in life
expectancy for the rest of the population were slowing.

The Social Security actuaries predict under their
intermediate assumptions that life expectancy will increase
4.5 years for males by the year 2040, and 6.6 years for
females (U.S. Population Projections for OASDI Cost
Estimates). But historically life expectancies have been
consistently underestimated because past experience gives no
hint of future medical breakthroughs. In fact, there have
been several recent medical studies that suggest that the
present predictions of future life expectancies may be too
conservative and therefore misleading for purposes of
long-term planning of retirement programs.

A study by Dr. Gio Gori (Gori and Richter) published in

Table 1. The Calculation of the Average Proportion of Adult
Life That Could Be Spent in Retirement.

	1940	1950	1960	1970	1977
Life Expectancy at Age 20[1]	48.5	51.2	52.6	53.0	54.9
Social Security Eligible Retirement Age	65	65	62[2]	62	62
Expected Number of Years in Retirement	3.5	6.2	10.6	11.0	12.9
Average Proportion of Adult Life (20 Years Old +) That Could be Spent in Retirement	7%	12%	20%	20%	23%

1/ Vital Statistics of the United States, 1977, Life Tables,
   Volume II, Section 5, HEW, PHS.

2/ The retirement age was lowered from 65 to 62 for women in
   1956 and for men in 1961.

Table 2. Life Expectancy At Selected Ages.

	Birth	65 Years	75 Years
1900-02	49.2	11.9	7.1
1939-41	63.6	12.8	7.6
1965	69.5	14.2	8.7
1976	72.8	16.0	10.1
Percent Change: 1900-1940 ..	+29.3	+7.6	+7.0
Percent Change: 1940-1976 ..	+14.5	+25.0	+32.9

Source: Life table published by the National Center for
Health Statistics, U.S. Public Health Service, and the U.S.
Bureau of Census. Reprinted in Current Population Report
Special Studies Series, P-23, No. 59, May 1976.

Science in 1978 compared the U.S. mortality rate from five preventable causes of death--cardiovascular renal disease, malignant neoplasma, accidents, respiratory diseases, and diabetes mellitus--with the rates in other industrialized countries. The mortality rate from these causes can all be modified by different life styles and behavior. Therefore, international comparisons are useful to determine the range of possible improvements that can be made in mortality rates. The purpose of the study was to measure what proportion of the mortality rates from these causes could in fact be preventable in the U.S. Dr. Gori argued that comparing the mortality rate of the U.S. to the lowest rate in other industrial countries may, in fact, be misleading. Unique conditions that are not easily reproducible may account for the lowest rate. However, the second lowest mortality rate in an industrial country may be a more realistic estimate of what the U.S. could obtain.

If the second lowest mortality rate for the industrial countries is used as a comparison, it suggests that the U.S. mortality rate from these five causes of death could be reduced by at least one-third. (If comparison is made with the lowest mortality rates, it suggests that the U.S. mortality rate could be reduced approximately 70%.) This would increase the population significantly, and the average life expectancy would increase considerably from 3-1/2 years at birth to just over 3 years at 20. This would increase longevity by 5% at birth and by 12% at age 80. Actual population increases that would result from reducing preventable deaths are significant, as seen in Table 3.

There would have been 7.6 million more people in the U.S. by the year 2000 if the U.S. could reasonably reduce its preventable deaths starting in 1975. And approximately five million more people would be 65 years old and over, an increase of 15% over present estimates. Not only would there be many more people in their retirement years, but they would be living longer in retirement. Twenty-year-olds could expect their retired life to increase to 28% of their adult life.

One of the most interesting questions the Gori study poses is whether there is a predictable limit to the increase in our life expectancy and indirectly to the length of our retired life. A recent article in the New England Journal of Medicine by Dr. James Fries explores the question of life-span limits by attempting to define the biological limits of the human aging process (Fries, 1980). He discusses the the measurement of the assumed linear decline in organ researve after the age of 30, which would lead to a decrease in the ability of the organism to restore homeostasis, the

Table 3.   Estimates of Population Increases if Preventable
           Deaths Were Reduced[a] (thousands)

Ages	1980	1990	2000
10-49	238.8	654.9	967.4
50-59	351.8	575.4	864.4
60-69	607.3	1,439.9	1,534.8
70-79	504.6	1,538.9	2,206.8
80+	430.1	1,279.5	2,060.6
Total	2,121.6	5,488.6	7,634.0

a) Age-specific population increases over current census
    projections if the minimum preventable rate of five major
    causes of death had been achieved in 1975 and sustained
    thereafter.

Source: Gio Gori and Brian Richter, "Macro-Economics of
Disease Prevention in the U.S." Science. June 9, 1978, Vol.
200, pp. 1124-1130. Copyright 1978 by the American Association for the Advancement of Science.

internal balance within the organism that is requried for
life. There is, in fact, an exponential increase in the
mortality rate after the age of 30, which implies that the
increases in life expectancy and, indirectly the retirement
life, are limited. In an attempt to define those limits Dr.
Fries extended the historical average increases in life
expectancy at birth and at age 65 and found that they
intersect in the year 2018 at a mean age of death of 85.6
years. This, of course, gives only an approximation of our
biological limits based on past data. But his conclusions
have implications for the society in general and retirement
in particular.

Fries concludes that as medicine focuses increasingly on
the postponement of morbidity from chronic diseases, the span
of chronic diseases will be compressed closer to the time of
death. This could imply that there might be a decrease in
the long-term disabilities and the need for long-term care,
but that "death and disability occurring later become
increasingly unavoidable."

For retirement programs the implications of a limited
life span 85 are profound. Some retirement planners will
undoubtedly be relieved to know that the increases in life
expectancy may not go on forever. But the implications of
medical science increasingly eliminating premature deaths
before the age of 85 means that:

● there could be considerably more people who are
  65 and over than are now estimated, and

● people could expect to spend approximately 35%
  of their adult lives in retirement.

If about one-third of the adult life is spent in
retirement, this also means that the length of retired life
would be over 50% of the working life (assuming a person
works from age 20 to the retirement age of 62)! Table 4
summarizes the implication for the length of retirement of
the Gori study and the Fries' estimate of the life-span limit
of 85.

One of the major unanswered questions about the future
increases in life expectancies is how much of the present sex
differences in longevity will persist. Table 5 shows that
the difference in male and female life expectancy has been
increasing since the turn of the century. As noted above,
the Social Security actuaries are expecting the differences
to continue increasing over the next 60 years. But there is
no unanimity about these expectations.

Table 4.   Potential Increases in the Proportion of the Adult
           Life Spent in Retirement

	Life Expectancy At Age 20	Social Security Eligible Retirement Age	Potential Retired Life as a Proportion of Adult Life
If possible Disease Prevention rates are achieved	56.4[1]	62	28%
If Biological Limit of 85 is reached	65.0[2]	62	35%

[1]   Gori, Gio B., Richter, Brian J.: "Macro Economics of
      Disease Prevention in the United States," Science, June
      1978, Vol. 200, pp. 1124-1130.

[2]   Fries, James F., M.D.: "Aging, Natural Death and the
      Compression of Morbidity," The New England Journal of
      Medicine, Vol. 303, No. 3, July 17, 1980.

Table 5.   Life Expectancy at Birth

Category	1900-02	1940	1955	1965	1976
White:					
Male	48.2	62.1	67.4	67.6	69.7
Female	51.1	66.6	73.7	74.7	77.3
Difference	2.9	4.5	6.3	7.1	7.6
Black and Other:					
Male	32.5	51.5	61.4	61.1	64.1
Female	35.0	54.9	66.1	67.4	72.6
Difference	2.5	3.4	4.7	6.3	8.5

Source: Life Table published by the National Center for
Health Statistics, U.S. Public Health Service, and the U.S.
Bureau of the Census, Reprinted in Current Population
Reports, Special Studies Series p. 23, No. 59, May 1976 and
Statistical Abstract of the United States 1978.

The answer, of course, depends on how much of the
present sex difference is due to environmental, cultural, or
biological causes. One study of religious orders suggested
that a group of brothers and nuns both lived longer than the
general population, but that the nuns' life expectancy from
1900 on was considerably longer than the brothers'. The
author of the study speculated that women have a higher
constitutional resistance to degenerative diseases than men.

But there is a considerable amount of other evidence
that the differences in life expectancy may be due less to
biological factors than to environmental and social factors.
The difference in longevity between men and women has varied
so much over time, races, and countries that conclusions are
difficult to draw. An exhaustive summary of research with
over 50 types of animals to determine whether there is a
consistent pattern of increased female longevity was
published in 1948 (Hamilton). It concluded that the male has
a higher mortality rate in almost all forms of animal life.

If in fact some of the differences in life expectancy
between the sexes is due to factors that can be controlled,
then future increases in life expectancy may accrue more to
men than to women who are already presumably not as far from
their natural life span. In addition, if male and female
life expectancies converge and retirement planners have not
forecast it, their programs could be seriously underfunded.
Therefore, it may be a more prudent assumption for retirement
programs to assume that male life expectancies can approach
female than to assume that they cannot.

Implications of Future Increases in Life Expectancies

The appropriate balance between adult life and retired
life has to be addressed, given the possibility in the future
of people spending half as much time in retirement as they do
working. One question is whether there are good reasons to
insist that people work even if the society could afford to
support very long retirements. The answer to this question
presumably would be based on what is considered the basic
intrinsic value of work and its role in a society. For
instance, there is some evidence that suggests that people
who retire die sooner than those who don't. The correlation
between retirement and death, however, is confounded by the
fact that many people who retire do so because of illness.

The question of whether the promise of retirement for a
third of an adult life is affordable is more susceptible to
quantitative analysis. In 1940 when Social Security started,
the population that was 65 and over was 9% of the potential

working population that paid for their benefits; today they
are over 18%. By 2040, the Bureau of the Census conserva-
tively estimates that the people 65 and over could be between
30.6% and 39.0% of the potential working population
(Sullivan, 1980).

A substantial increase in the elderly population,
however, can be supported if there is substantial economic
growth. Or if there is a significant increase in fertility
and immigration, which would increase the labor force, the
burden of increased retirement costs could be spread more
broadly. Therefore, projections of people of working age are
as important as the projections of people of retirement age.
However, between now and the year 2040 the population of
18-64 year olds, from which the bulk of the potential labor
force would be drawn, is estimated to increase by only
between 8-32% at the same time as the 65+ population
increases 120%. It is this relative difference in the growth
of the aged and the potential labor force that is of most
concern for the public retirement systems such as Social
Security that pay the present benefits out of present
contributions. If the labor force does not increase at the
same rate as the retired population, then the costs to the
labor force of supporting the retired will increase. Under
such circumstances the length of the retirement period may
become crucial.

Conclusion and a Proposal

How should the gains in life expectancy be divided
between the potential working life and the retired life? A
fixed, immutable retirement age results in most of the gains
in life expectancy lengthening the retired life rather than
the potential working life. If a different division of these
gains was desired, then the retirement age would have to move
in some relationship to the changes in life expectancy.

There is, of course, no a priori appropriate ratio of
the retired to the adult life. The decision of what this
ratio should be is essentially a social-economic decision.
But if it was possible to decide on an acceptable ratio of
retired to adult life, then a simple formula could be
constructed based on the Decennial Census estimates of life
expectancy.

Present estimates of life expectancy could be used to
calculate future retirement ages. Presumably, people would
have to be given substantial warning about what their
retirement ages would be so that life cycle plans could be
rationally made. Each Decennial Census could be used to

calculate the retirement age that would be effective, for example, 25 years hence. If the society decided to provide a retirement that was 25% of the adult life, then the normal retirement age could be determined by selecting the age at which the life expectancy is equal to 25% of the life expectancy at age 20. If this formula had been in existence since 1940 the original Social Security age of 65 would have increased to 66 in 1965, 67 in 1975 and 68 in 1995. (The calculations are in the Appendix.)

There are, however, several problems with this kind of formula. Specific groups such as black males who have shorter life expectancies than the average for the population would be disadvantaged. Increasing the retirement age also is not an unqualified panacea for solving some of the financial and social problems of future retirement plans. Disabilities are directly related to age; therefore, if the retirement age is raised, the number of disabled who would have previously been considered retired will rise. Consequently, the number of the adult dependent population would not be reduced as much as might have been expected.

In addition, people might object to using a proportion of retired to adult life because it does not take into account the quality of life of the retired. If the last 25% of our adult life is spent when we are very old, people could object that it does them little good to be retired when they are too old to enjoy it. But the health of the elderly has been increasing at the same time as options for continued independence within the society have increased. And there is now substantial evidence that the lowering of the mortality rate will be accompanied by the lowering of the morbidity rate as well.

A number of proposals have already been made to increase the retirement age. The last two Social Security Advisory Councils and the President's Commission on Pension Policy have all recommended that the age of retirement be raised in general terms varying from 67 to 68. None, however, have suggested relating the length of retirement to the length of the adult life. Yet to replace one fixed retirement age with another runs the risk of having the new age not flexible enough to respond to the constantly changing factors, such as increases in longevity, that influence the ability of a society to pay for the retirement of its workers. There is no single formula that is correct, nor is there any single justification for a fixed ratio between adult life and retired life. But the issue should be addressed before the burdens of increasingly long retirements become severe.

There has been an explicit social contract in society that the working population support the dependent population, both young and old. Originally this was done entirely in the private sector. But in this century the public sector has assumed more of the responsibility of this support. However, if the relative size of the retired population changes significantly with respect to the working population because of both increases in life expectancy and past high fertility rates, then what is now a vaguely understood social contract may have to be reexamined. Fairness alone suggests that any changes made to the retirement system such as changes in the retirement age should be announced many years in advance of a person's retirement so that the workers who are affected can make whatever accommodations are needed. Since the baby boom will begin to retire in 30 years, the social contract between the generations for their mutual support and dependence should be reopened and examined now while we have both the time and the perspective. And one of the most important topics that should be discussed is what proportion of our adult lives should we expect to spend in retirement.

Appendix A

Illustrative Example of How to Calculate

Social Security Retirement Age[1]

1. The normal retirement age for Social Security Primary Insurance Amount, currently age 65, will be redetermined every tenth year based upon the results of the U.S. Census.

2. The redetermined Normal Retirement Age will become effective gradually beginning 25 years after the year of the Census.

3. The Normal Retirement Age will be increased by one month every six months until the redetermined Retirement Age is reached.

4. The Normal Retirement Age (NRA) will be that age at which the expectation of life after that age is equal to 1/4 of the expectation of life after the age of 20. The NRA will be the closest whole age.

5. Based upon prior census the NRAs would have been as follows:

1939-41 Census

Age	Expectation of Life
20	48.54 years
64	13.27 years
65	12.74 years
66	12.22 years

One-fourth of the 48.54 is 12.13. Therefore, the NRA would be set at age 66 to be effective in 1965.

---

[1]/A similar example was developed by Preston Bassett, actuary for Towes, Perrin, Forster & Crosby, Inc., and consultant to the President's Commission on Pension Policy.

1949-51 Census	
Age	Expectation of Life
20	51.20 years
65	13.83 years
66	13.22 years
67	12.62 years

One-fourth of 51.20 is 12.8. Therefore, the NRA would be set to age 67 to be effective in 1975.

1959-61 Census	
Age	Expectation of Life
20	52.58 years
65	14.39 years
66	13.76 years
67	13.15 years

One-fourth of 52.58 is 13.1. Therefore, the NRA would remain at age 67 following the 1960 Census.

1969-71 Census	
Age	Expectation of Life
20	53.00 years
66	14.38 years
67	13.76 years
68	13.16 years

One-fourth of 53.00 is 13.25. Therefore, the NRA would be set to age 68 to be effective in 1995.

AVERAGE ADDITIONAL YEARS OF LIFE EXPECTANCY
(Census Data, in years)

Age	1939-41	1949-51	1959-61	1969-71	1977
18	50.34	53.07	54.46	54.86	56.8
19	49.44	52.14	53.52	53.93	55.9
20	48.54	51.20	52.58	53.00	54.9
21	47.64	50.27	51.64	52.07	54.0
22	46.75	49.34	50.70	51.15	53.1
23	45.86	48.41	49.76	50.22	52.1
24	44.98	47.49	48.83	49.30	51.2
25	44.09	46.56	47.84	48.37	50.3
64	13.27	14.45	15.03	15.65	16.9
65	12.74	13.83	14.39	15.00	16.3
66	12.22	13.22	13.76	14.38	15.6
67	11.71	12.62	13.15	13.76	15.0
68	11.21	12.04	12.55	13.16	14.3
69	10.72	11.47	11.96	12.57	13.7
70	10.25	10.92	11.38	12.00	13.1

1. U.S. Department of Commerce, Bureau of the Census, U.S. Life Tables and Actuarial Tables, 16th Census 1940. Washington, D.C.: U.S. Government Printing Office, 1946.

2. U.S. Department of Health, Education, and Welfare, Public Health Service. U.S. Life Tables for 1949-51. Vital Statistics Special Report, Vol. 41. Washington, D.C.: U.S. Government Printing Office, November 1954.

3. U.S. Department of Health, Education, and Welfare, Public Health Service. U.S. Life Tables, 1959-61. Vol. 1, No. 9, Washington, D.C.: U.S. Government Printing Office, December 1964.

4. U.S. Department of Health, Education, and Welfare. Public Health Service. U.S. Life Tables, 1969-71. Vol. 1, No. 1. Washington, D.C.: U.S. Government Printing Office, May 1975.

5. U.S. Department of Health, Education, and Welfare. Public Health Service. U.S. Life Tables, 1977. Preprint. Vol. 2, Section 5.

References

Fries, James F., M.D., "Aging, Natural Death and the Compression of Morbidity," The New England Journal of Medicine, Vol. 303, No. 3, July 17, 1980.

Gori, Gio B. and Brian J. Richter, "Macro Economics of Disease Prevention in the United States," Science, June 1978, Vol. 200, pp. 1124-1130.

Hamilton, James B., "The Role of Testicular Secretions as Indicated by the Effects of Castration in Man and by Studies of Pathological Conditions and the Short Lifespan Associated with Maleness," Recent Progress in Hormone Research, Vol. 3. NY: Academic Press, 1948.

Madigan, Francis C., "Age Sex Mortality Differentials: Biologically Caused?" The Milbank Memorial Fund Quarterly.

Meier, Elizabeth and Cynthia Dittmar, "Varieties of Retirement Ages," Staff Working Paper, President's Commission on Pension Policy, November 1979.

Norwood, Douglas, Retirement Age, Office of Management and Budget Staff Paper, Washington, D.C., 1977.

Sullivan, Teresa, A., "Sex Discrimination in Employee-Sponsored Insurance Plans: A Legal and Demographic Analysis," The University of Chicago Law Review, Vol 47, No. 3, Spring 1980.

U.S. Congress, Senate Committee on Finance, Economic Security Act. Hearing 74th Congress, January and February 1935, U.S. Government Printing Office, Washington, D.C., 1935.

U.S. Population Projections for OASDI Cost Estimates, Actuarial Study No. 82, U.S. Department of Health and Human Services, June 1980, SSA Pub. No. 11-11529.

Denis F. Johnston, Sally L. Hoover

10. Social Indicators of Aging

The gradual but steady increase in both the number and proportion of the total population that is age 65 and over is commonly known, as is the anticipated rapid increase in both quantities during the second decade of the next century (30 to 40 years hence) when the large postwar "baby-boom" cohorts begin to advance into the 65-and-over age group (Table 1). Yet certain internal dynamics of this demographic process are equally significant though less often noticed. Three features are especially influential: First, the aging of the older population itself; second, the growing proportion of women in that population; and finally, the changing social attributes of elders. The purpose of this paper is to describe selected characteristics and living conditions of current elders, impending changes in these conditions and characteristics, and to discuss some of the implications of these trends. It is important for society as a whole and the older population in particular to illuminate some of the social implications of slowing population growth.

To illustrate the first point, the proportion of the population (65 and over) that is 75 and over increased from 31.5 percent in 1950 to 37.8 percent in 1980. In another 30 years (by 2010), that percent will be about 43.2, according to current mortality projections. In regard to the second point, the proportion of women in the population 65 and over increased from 52.8 to 59.4 percent from 1950 to 1980 and is projected to be 59.9 percent by the year 2010. Additionally, the average annual rate of increase in the older population

---

The views expressed are the authors' and do not necessarily reflect the policies or position of the Bureau of the Census.

Table 1. Estimates and projections of the elderly population
of the United States, by age and sex: selected years, 1950
to 2040 (numbers in thousands).

Year	Males					
	Total, 65 and over	65-69 years	70-74 years	75-79 years	80-84 years	85 and over
1950	5,857	2,447	1,644	1,005	518	243
1960	7,542	2,936	2,197	1,370	673	366
1970	8,405	3,137	2,321	1,568	882	497
1980	10,108	3,859	2,853	1,698	989	709
1990	11,999	4,471	3,281	2,148	1,264	836
2000	12,717	4,152	3,521	2,509	1,472	1,062
2010	13,978	5,251	3,487	2,355	1,605	1,280
2020	18,468	7,254	5,243	3,023	1,620	1,327
2030	22,399	7,740	6,378	4,215	2,474	1,592
2040	21,816	6,412	5,556	4,530	3,057	2,261

	Average Annual Rate of Change (Percent)					
1950-1970	1.80	1.24	1.72	2.22	2.66	3.58
1970-1990	1.78	1.77	1.73	1.57	1.80	2.60
1990-2010	0.76	0.80	0.30	0.46	1.19	2.13
2010-2030	2.36	1.94	3.02	2.91	2.16	1.09

Table 1, continued

			Females		
Year	Total, 65 and over	65-69 years	70-74 years	75-79 years	80-84 years	85 and over
-------	-------	-------	-------	-------	-------	-------
1950	6,541	2,602	1,800	1,150	642	347
1960	9,133	3,344	2,577	1,711	928	574
1970	11,680	3,885	3,143	2,290	1,427	935
1980	14,819	4,841	3,940	2,626	1,827	1,585
1990	17,824	5,551	4,501	3,353	2,375	2,045
2000	19,105	5,039	4,723	3,884	2,764	2,693
2010	20,858	6,375	4,664	3,563	2,962	3,295
2020	26,634	8,722	6,907	4,570	2,986	3,449
2030	32,624	9,347	8,388	6,297	4,504	4,089
2040	33,108	7,739	7,311	6,780	5,560	5,719

		Average Annual Rate of Change (Percent)				
1950-1970	2.90	2.00	2.79	3.44	3.99	4.96
1970-1990	2.11	1.78	1.80	1.91	2.55	3.91
1990-2010	0.78	0.69	0.18	0.30	1.10	2.38
2010-2030	2.24	1.91	2.93	2.85	2.10	1.08

Source: U.S. Department of Commerce, Bureau of the Census. Current Population Reports, Series P-25, Nos. 311 (for 1950); 519 (for 1960); 721 (for 1970); and 704 (for 1980 and onwards). The numbers shown above are identical for all series of projections until beyond the year 2040.

will continue· to be considerably higher than that of the population as a whole, at least until sometime in the 1990's
when the smaller birth cohorts of the 1920's and 1930's begin
moving into the ranks of the elderly. Illustrative of the
third change, the educational level of the average older person has risen, and will continue to do so. The societal implications of a more highly educated older population are
just beginning to be realized. These projections, it should
be noted, are insensitive to assumptions about future fertility; all persons 65 and over in 2040 have already been born.
However, they are highly sensitive to assumptions about future mortality and future patterns of migration into and out
of the country. Unfortunately, alternative assumptions about
future mortality and net migration are not available.

Several noteworthy consequences follow from these relatively predictable demographic changes. First, unless unanticipated breakthroughs should occur with respect to degenerative diseases, the most rapid period of growth in the
number of elders, especially the "old-old" (75 and over), is
largely behind us, at least until the second decade of the
next century. Second, the demand for housing, nursing, and
other health care facilities and services required by the
oldest of the population will continue to rise at least for
the next half century, but not at the rapid pace experienced
during the 1950 to 1970 period. This demand, in part, may be
influenced by the future reduced proportion of older persons
with one or more living children, siblings, or grandchildren.
Third, dramatic improvements in the health condition of the
"young-old" (persons 65 to 74 years old) presage a substantial increase in demands for active and productive roles in
the society--whether or not these roles can be played within
the framework of the market economy. Fourth, continuing
changes are anticipated in the marital status and living
arrangements of older persons, in response to both the growing disparity in number between the sexes and the economic
exigencies of prolonged retirement. Fifth, there will be a
rise in the familial dependency ratio, that is the potential
number of extreme aged to their older children (number of
persons 80 and over to persons 60-64). Finally, the rising
educational attainment of the older population is already
generating a rapidly expanding pool of highly educated persons, mostly out of the labor force, whose ability to continue to make important contributions to the society is un-
questionable. With respect to educational attainment, there
were some 650,000 college graduates in the population aged
65 years and over in 1959, of whom some 240,000 were still in
the labor force, leaving an "economically inactive" group of
about 410,000 persons. Twenty years later (1979), the number

of older college graduates had risen to nearly two million persons (1,966,000), of whom 420,000 were in the labor force, leaving a "retired" component of over 1.5 million persons. Thus the number of economically inactive college graduates in the older population has nearly quadrupled in the past 20 years. If it is assumed, further, that past trends in educational attainment and labor force participation continue during the 1980 decade, the number of older college graduates in the population of 1990 will climb to nearly 3.2 million, of whom only 500,000 are expected to be economically active (i.e., in the labor force), leaving a "retired" component of nearly 2.7 million persons (Table 2). Furthermore, this figure does not include those older persons who may return to college in their later years.

Aging, Work and Education

Differential changes in rates of economic activity (labor force participation) among persons 45 years old and over, by age, sex, and selected years of school completed, show that among males under 65 years old, the declines in labor force participation rates are inversely related to their educational attainment; that is, males age 45 to 54 and 55 to 64 with the lowest educational level are more likely than their highly educated (16 years or more) counterparts to have retired between 1959 and 1979. It is expected that this trend will continue through 1990. Of additional interest here are the dramatic declines since 1959 in the labor force participation rates for the highly educated men 65 and over. Regardless of whether less educated male workers are being pushed or pulled out of the labor force, there will be a greater proportion of that shrinking population leaving the work force at a relatively young age. This phenomenon will coincide with an upward shift in the proportion of well educated male workers also leaving the labor force. Because of various factors including types of jobs available, access to skill training and uninterrupted length of time in the labor force, the labor force participation rates of mature women differ greatly from those of men. In particular, women 55 to 64 years old experienced substantial increases in labor force participation (at all levels of education) between 1959 and 1969. Since 1969, however, the participation rates of all women 55 and over have been declining, with the sharpest declines among the most educated.

Living Arrangements of Older Persons

With respect to marital status and living arrangements, a considerable disparity is evident between males and females (Table 3). In 1979, about three-fourths of the men 65 and over were married with spouse present. In contrast, less

Table 2. Years of school completed by the civilian noninstitutional population (CNIP) and the civilian labor force (CLF) 65 years old and over, by sex: March 1959, 1969, 1979 and projected to 1990

Age group	Total		Percent distribution				
	Number in thousands	Percent	0 to 8 years	9 to 11 years	12 years	13 to 15 years	16 years or more
March 1959							
MALES							
CNIP: 65 years and over	6,699	100.0	71.2	10.0	8.6	4.5	5.6
CLF: 65 years and over	2,235	100.0	63.4	11.4	10.0	6.5	8.7
PERCENT OF CNIP IN CLF: 65 years and over	33.4	---	29.7	37.9	38.8	48.3	51.5
FEMALES							
CNIP: 65 years and over	8,039	100.0	65.4	13.4	12.2	5.6	3.4
CLF: 65 years and over	815	100.0	54.2	16.1	16.6	7.5	5.6
PERCENT OF CNIP IN CLF: 65 years and over	10.1	---	8.4	12.2	13.7	13.6	16.6

Table 2, continued

Age group	Total		Percent distribution				
	Number in thousands	Percent	0 to 8 years	9 to 11 years	12 years	13 to 15 years	16 years or more
March 1969							
MALES							
CNIP: 65 years and over	8,251	100.0	61.5	12.4	14.0	5.2	6.8
CLF: 65 years and over	2,160	100.0	50.6	14.7	16.3	7.2	11.2
PERCENT OF CNIP IN CLF: 65 years and over	26.2	---	21.5	30.9	30.5	36.3	42.8
FEMALES							
CNIP: 65 years and over	11,094	100.0	56.7	13.9	17.6	6.8	5.1
CLF: 65 years and over	1,106	100.0	44.6	13.6	22.5	10.8	8.6
PERCENT OF CNIP IN CLF: 65 years and over	10.0	---	7.8	9.8	12.7	15.9	16.9
March 1979							
MALES							
CNIP: 65 years and over	9,548	100.0	46.6	15.3	20.6	7.9	9.6
CLF: 65 years and over	1,900	100.0	32.5	15.3	26.8	10.3	15.1
PERCENT OF CNIP IN CLF: 65 years and over	19.9	---	13.9	19.9	25.8	26.1	31.4

Table 2, continued

Age group	Total		Percent distribution				
	Number in thousands	Percent	0 to 8 years	9 to 11 years	12 years	13 to 15 years	16 years or more
March 1979							
<u>FEMALES</u>							
CNIP: 65 years and over	13,627	100.0	42.4	16.1	25.1	8.6	7.7
CLF: 65 years and over	1,184	100.0	26.5	15.2	35.3	11.7	11.3
PERCENT OF CNIP IN CLF:							
65 years and over	8.7	---	5.4	8.2	12.2	11.8	12.7
1990[1]							
<u>MALES</u>							
CNIP: 65 years and over	11,547	100.0	29.8	13.9	31.0	11.5	13.8
CLF: 65 years and over	1,826	100.0	16.4	11.6	39.7	12.9	19.5
PERCENT OF CNIP IN CLF:							
65 years and over	15.8	---	8.7	13.1	20.3	17.7	22.3

Table 2, continued

Age group	Total		Percent distribution				
	Number in thousands	Percent	0 to 8 years	9 to 11 years	12 years	13 to 15 years	16 years or more
1990[1]							
FEMALES							
CNIP: 65 years and over	16,764	100.0	27.2	17.0	35.1	11.4	9.3
CLF: 65 years and over	1,225	100.0	13.6	13.6	47.5	13.9	11.4
PERCENT OF CNIP IN CLF: 65 years and over	7.3	---	3.7	5.8	9.9	8.9	9.0

NOTE: The above are projections prepared by the authors solely for illustrative purposes and are designed to reflect the continuation of observed trends in both educational attainment of population and labor force participation rates by years of school completed among persons 45 years old and over. These trends were extrapolated and adjusted judgementally from observed values for March 1959, 1969, and 1979, as presented in Table 2. March 1959 excludes persons not reporting years of school completed.

[1] Howard N. Fullerton, Jr., "The 1995 Labor Force: A First Look," Monthly Labor Review, Vol. 103, No. 12 (December 1980). Labor force reflects the "middle growth" assumption.

Source: U.S. Department of Commerce, Bureau of the Census, Current Population Reports, Series P-20, Nos. 99, Table 1; 194, Table 1; 356, Table 1, and U.S. Department of Labor, Bureau of Labor Statistics, Special Labor Force Report Nos. 1, Table D; 125, Table D and tabulations to be published.

Table 3. Marital status and living arrangements of the elderly; by age and sex: March 1979

Marital status and living arrangements	MALES			FEMALES		
	65 and over	65-74 years	75 years and over	65 and over	65-74 years	75 years and over
A. Marital status						
Total (1,000's)	9,548	6,385	3,163	13,627	8,382	5,245
Percent	100.0	100.0	100.0	100.0	100.0	100.0
Single	5.4	5.6	4.9	6.1	6.0	6.2
Married, spouse present	74.6	78.4	66.9	36.9	46.9	20.9
Married, spouse absent	2.6	2.9	2.0	1.6	1.9	1.0
Widowed	14.1	9.3	24.0	52.2	41.2	69.7
Divorced	3.3	3.9	2.2	3.3	4.0	2.2

Table 3, continued

Marital status and living arrangements	MALES			FEMALES		
	65 and over	65-74 years	75 years and over	65 and over	65-74 years	75 years and over
B. Living arrangements						
Total (1,000's)	9,548	6,385	3,163	13,627	8,382	5,245
Percent	100.0	100.0	100.0	100.0	100.0	100.0
Head of a household	92.6	93.4	90.8	51.1	45.2	60.5
Head of a primary family	76.6	80.2	69.3	8.8	8.5	9.2
Primary individual	16.0	13.2	21.5	42.3	36.7	51.3
Living alone	15.4	12.7	20.8	41.0	35.4	50.1
Other	0.6	0.5	0.7	1.2	1.3	1.2
Not head of a household	7.4	6.6	9.2	48.9	54.8	39.5
In families	5.7	4.7	7.7	47.8	53.6	38.5
Secondary individual	1.8	1.9	1.6	1.1	1.2	1.0

Source: Bureau of the Census. Current Population Reports, Series P-60, No. 349, "Marital Status and Living Arrangements: March 1979" (issued February 1980), Tables 1 and 6.

than 40 percent of the women 65 and over were in that status.
Furthermore, this disparity increases with advancing age.
Among persons 75 and over, two-thirds of the men, as compared
with only one-fifth of the women are still living with their
spouses. In the future, it will be increasingly important to
seek and implement ways of adjusting social institutions to
provide for this imbalance.

Living arrangements naturally reflect prevalent differences in marital status. In 1979, the proportion of persons
65 and over who were living as primary individuals (nearly
all of whom were living alone as single-person householders)
amounted to 16 percent of the men and 42 percent of the women.
The corresponding proportions among persons 75 and over were
22 and 51 percent, respectively.

The Income of Older Persons

An additional set of data concerning the objective circumstances affecting the quality of life of the elderly population must be mentioned, trends in their poverty status.
In 1959, about 35 percent of all persons 65 and over (some
5.5 million persons), were classified as poor according to
the official government criteria. Twenty years later (1979),
their number had been reduced to 3.6 million, or 15 percent
of the population 65 and over. The corresponding decline
among the population under 65 years old was from 21 to 11
percent. Hence, by this index at least, the elderly have
experienced a more rapid decline in the proportion of poor
among their number than has the remainder of the population[1],
but proportionate parity has not been achieved yet.

Also relevant here is the fact that a substantial proportion of the elderly population is near the poverty level
of income without actually falling below that level. Nearly
10 percent of the elderly have incomes that fall between
official poverty level and 1¼ times that level, as compared
with only 4 percent of the nonaged. Thus one-fourth of the
elderly, as compared with 15 percent of the nonaged, were
living in or near the poverty level in 1979.

Social Characteristics of Older Persons

Further clues as to the general living conditions and
quality of life of the elderly can be gleaned from the wealth

----

[1]Data from U.S. Department of Commerce, Bureau of the
Census, Consumer Income, Series P-60, No. 125 (October 1980),
Table 18.

of descriptive statistics that has been assembled by Herman B. Brotman.[2]

The following are a few of the salient facts contained in this compilation: During the early 1970's, households headed by elderly persons had about half the income, on average, as those headed by persons under 65 years of age. Among the former group, retirement income accounted for about 40 percent of total household income, earnings for 31 percent, and assets or investments for 18 percent. The remaining 11 percent of their income stemmed from welfare, contributions and all other sources. Turning to expenditures, the older group of households spent proportionately over twice as much as the nonaged on gifts and contributions, 20 percent more on food, 10 percent more on housing and over 50 percent more on health and personal care.

The health condition of the elderly is generally quite good; over 80 percent do not require any assistance in performing their normal daily activities and a similar proportion reported no hospitalization during the preceding year. However, the proportion of the elderly who do require assistance in connection with normal daily activities rises rapidly with advancing age, from about 10 percent among those 65 to 74 years old to over 70 percent of those aged 85 and over.

A general indicator of improvements in health among the elderly is life expectancy--i.e., average years of life remaining to persons who have already survived to, say, age 65 or age 75 (Table 4). Of course, these measures fail to take into account the actual physical condition of these survivors and should therefore be supplemented by information relating to the incidence of illness and the prevalence of disability. Nevertheless, the gains in average life expectancy clearly indicate major improvements during the course of the 20th century. Furthermore, these data show that these gains have been even faster during the past two decades than during the previous 60 years.

Housing costs are a large element in the budgets of many households headed by elderly persons; over 40 percent of these households spend more than one-fourth of their total income on housing, as compared with less than 20 percent of the "nonaged" households. Furthermore, the housing of the elderly population tends to be older than that of the nonaged

---

[2]Herman B. Brotman, "Every Ninth American." Prepared for the Special Committee on Aging, United States Senate (revised version dated January 8, 1981).

Table 4. Average years of life remaining to persons 65 years old and over, by sex and race: 1900-02 to 1978

Age, sex and race	1900-1902	1929-1931	1959-1961	1978	Average annual rate of change, in percent			
					1901-1978	1901-1930	1930-1960	1960-1978
WHITE MALE								
65 and over	11.5	11.8	13.0	14.0	0.26	0.08	0.32	0.41
75 and over	6.8	7.0	7.9	8.6	.30	.09	.40	.47
OTHER MALE								
65 and over	10.4	10.9	12.8	14.1	.40	.16	.55	.54
75 and over	6.6	7.0	8.9	9.8	.51	.20	.82	.54
WHITE FEMALE								
65 and over	12.2	12.8	15.9	18.4	.53	.16	.72	.81
75 and over	7.3	7.6	9.3	11.5	.45	.11	.68	1.18
OTHER FEMALE								
65 and over	11.4	12.2	15.1	18.0	.59	.25	.70	.98
75 and over	7.9	8.6	10.1	12.5	.60	.30	.53	1.18

Source: Public Health Service, U.S. Department of Health and Human Services, Vital Statistics of the United States, 1978, Volume II - Section 5, Life Tables, Table 5-4.

--nearly half of the housing of the former group was constructed before World War II, as compared with 30 percent of
the housing of the latter. Households with older heads also
occupy nearly half (46 percent) of all low-income public
housing, or 552,000 out of 1.2 million units.

Persons 65 and over are somewhat less likely than those
under 65 to be living in metropolitan areas, but those who do
are about 10 percent more likely to be living in the central
city portions of those metropolitan areas. In 1979, 63 percent of persons 65 and over were in metropolitan areas, with
30 percent in central cities. The 37 percent of the older
population living in nonmetropolitan areas compares with
about 32 percent for persons under 65.

Migration Patterns

As would be expected, the elderly are considerably less
mobile than those under 65. Between 1975 and 1979, 83 percent of those aged 65 and over were nonmovers (i.e., living
in the same house the entire period), as compared with only
55 percent of those under 65. Among persons 65 and over who
moved across state boundaries between 1975 and 1979, only 29
percent of those whose initial place of residence was in the
Northeast remained in a Northeastern state, while about two-
thirds moved to the South or the West. Among the corresponding group whose initial residence was in the North Central
states, only 19 percent moved to another state in the North
Central region, while nearly four-fifths moved to the South
or West. By contrast, 56 percent of the elderly trans-state
movers whose initial state of residence was in the South remained in the South after moving, and only 30 percent moved
to the Northeast or North Central regions. Finally, two-
thirds of the elderly interstate movers whose initial state
of residence was in the West remained in some other Western
state, with only 11 percent moving to the Northeast or North
Central regions. These patterns of interstate migration are
of course reflected in the initial findings of the 1980 Census of Population and Housing, which show a dramatic shift in
residential patterns toward the South and the West.

One final characteristic relates to the male population
65 and over and has an important bearing on that population's
need and eligibility for medical care and other public assistance: Veteran status. Between 1980 and 1990, the proportion
of males 65 and over who are veterans is expected to increase
from 29 to 60 percent (a rise from about 3 to about 7.2 million veterans). This precipitous rise is attributable of
course to the movement of large numbers of World War II and
Korean War veterans into the 65-and-over age group during
this decade. The increase will be concentrated in the age

Table 5. Selected domain satisfaction, measures, by age and sex: 1972 to 1980 consolidated samples

	Age Group					
	18 to 29	30 to 39	40 to 49	50 to 64	65 to 89	Total
PERCENT "FAVORABLE"[1]						
General Happiness						
Males	24.3	31.4	33.4	34.4	42.2	32.3
Females	33.9	37.0	37.0	37.2	34.6	35.8
Satisfaction with—						
Own Health						
Males	72.2	70.4	64.7	57.9	49.5	63.7
Females	66.0	57.8	56.5	52.1	43.1	57.9
Family Life						
Males	69.4	79.4	76.9	76.1	74.7	74.9
Females	77.2	80.9	78.7	76.8	70.9	77.0
Hobbies, etc.						
Males	60.8	63.8	58.2	59.6	52.9	59.4
Females	52.3	54.8	51.9	57.4	58.3	54.9
Friendships						
Males	67.3	68.1	66.0	70.2	70.2	68.4
Females	69.7	71.5	71.3	75.8	75.8	72.7
Place of Residence						
Males	30.7	43.7	45.9	57.9	63.9	47.2
Females	34.6	44.7	52.6	59.6	65.8	50.2

Table 5, continued

				Age Group			
		18 to 29	30 to 39	40 to 49	50 to 64	65 to 89	Total
PERCENT "UNFAVORABLE"[2]							
General Happiness							
	Males	14.8	11.0	12.8	13.9	13.2	13.3
	Females	12.9	10.3	10.9	13.2	15.3	12.5
Satisfaction with—							
Own Health							
	Males	4.0	6.2	7.8	13.0	19.4	9.5
	Females	6.5	6.9	9.5	14.7	19.3	11.0
Family Life							
	Males	8.3	6.0	6.9	7.5	9.1	7.6
	Females	4.7	2.6	3.4	5.5	10.0	5.2
Hobbies, etc.							
	Males	11.6	10.7	11.7	13.2	18.6	12.9
	Females	15.0	13.3	14.7	13.1	13.7	14.0
Friendships							
	Males	5.6	6.0	4.9	5.2	6.7	5.6
	Females	5.9	4.5	5.1	4.4	5.0	5.0
Place of Residence							
	Males	22.3	15.1	12.6	8.6	7.0	13.8
	Females	20.4	12.8	12.2	9.6	7.7	13.1

[1]For general happiness, "VERY HAPPY" versus "Pretty happy" or "Not too happy." For other items, "A VERY GREAT DEAL" or "A GREAT DEAL" of satisfaction versus "Quite a bit," "A fair amount," "Some," "A little," or "None."

[2]For general happiness, "NOT TOO HAPPY" versus "Very Happy" or "Pretty happy." For other items, "SOME" or "LITTLE or NONE" versus "A fair amount," "Quite a bit," "A great deal," or "A very great deal" of satisfaction.

Source: Special tabulations from the General Social Surveys of 1972 to 1980, National Opinion Reserach Center, University of Chicago, courtesy of Dr. Tom W. Smith.

group 65 to 74, where the proportion of veterans is expected
to increase from 33 to 76 percent (up from 2.2 million in
1980 to 5.9 million in 1990).

Perceptions of the Quality of Life

To summarize, our older population is growing older,
healthier, better educated and more independent with respect
to its marital status and living arrangements. It is also
becoming less poor and less active economically. A final set
of data seeks to provide at least a hint of an answer to the
ultimate "quality of life" question: Are elders becoming
happier or more content with life?

Unfortunately, it is not possible to compare today's
older adults with those of earlier times except by means of
impressionistic conjectures. The data available do suggest
that men tend, overall, to grow happier as they grow older,
whereas women appear to remain about constant in general
happiness until reaching age 65, when they seem to grow somewhat less happy with advancing age.[3] With regard to the five
"domains" of life for which satisfaction measures were obtained, it is noteworthy that only personal health or physical condition is a source of consistently diminishing satisfaction as persons grow older, and that women of all ages
are less satisfied than men with this sphere (Table 5).
Women appear to be more satisfied with family life until the
immediate pre-retirement years. Only after age 65 are men
likely to be slightly more satisfied than women with family
life. This cross-over effect appears to have less to do with
an increase in male satisfaction, than a greater decrease in
female satisfaction. More information is needed on the impact of widowhood in the decline of family satisfaction in
older women.

Conversely, the male level of satisfaction with nonwork-
ing activities or hobbies decreases after age 65, giving the
appearance that for the first time older women are more satisfied with this activity. For both sexes alike, satisfaction with friendships remains constant with advancing age,
while satisfaction with one's place of residence increases.

---

[3]The reader is warned that these inferences and ones
that follow assume that differences observed during the early
1970's among persons in different age groups reflect the differences that would emerge in the same cohort of persons as
it grows older. These assumptions are plausible at best, but
are not proven.

Given the higher general happiness of older men as compared to older women, it is possible to speculate about the relative importance of both health and family relationships in the older years. Generalizations based on these rather flimsy data are hazardous, but the aging process does not appear to entail a drastic loss of satisfaction with what life has to offer, except of course for the common annoyances that accompany the aging process. Whether the stability in expressed satisfaction and happiness is in turn attributable to diminished aspirations and expectations or to actual achievement of one's life goals and realization of expectations must remain a matter for further research.

One major trend that may pose significant problems in the future, however, is the previously mentioned rapid growth in the number of well educated and obviously experienced older adults who are no longer economically active. The point is not that these persons are necessarily poor, frustrated, or unhappy, but rather that their talents and experience may be dissipated among a variety of daily routines that do not offer opportunities for their productive use. In raising this issue, attention was focused on the growing minority of college graduates among the older population in order to highlight the potential of a group whose skill and experience could most readily be utilized. The alleged loss of status that accompanies withdrawal from economic activity[4] is not expressed in available information relating to general happiness or satisfaction. It is possible that retirement, at least for most working men and women, still represents a long sought-after release from onerous duties and stresses, rather than a painful surrender of status and prestige. It is also possible that growing numbers of healthy and vigorous elders are finding considerable challenge and satisfaction in a wide variety of volunteer activities in community services or in mutual aid, most of which simply escape the conventional definition of "work." If so, more appropriate concepts and measurements need to be developed before either the style or the quality of life among this segment of the population can be gauged properly.

----

[4]On this point, see Richard M. Cohn, "Economic Development and the Status of the Aged," Center for Demography and Ecology, University of Wisconsin-Madison, CDE Working Paper 80-8, July 1980.

11. Perspectives on Changing Age Systems

Scholarly discourse on age and aging may not speak of changing age systems as such, but scholars have documented many historical age-related changes: for example, that older people in Colonial America were treated with more deference than older people today (Fischer, 1978); that life stages we now take for granted--like adolescence and the "empty nest"-- were not socially recognized in previous centuries (Kett, 1977; Uhlenberg, 1969); that cohorts of males born around 1940 have made the transition to adulthood more rapidly than male cohorts born earlier (Winsborough, 1979). Often scholars studying such changes focus on a particular period, or a particular society, or a particular type of change. This paper seeks to put such specific changes in broader perspective by considering the general nature and sources of change in age systems. It discusses two sets of questions: What is meant by changing age systems? How do changes in age systems come about?

The Nature of Change in Age Systems

To understand change in age systems, let us start off, paradoxical though it may seem, with a view of the age structure at a given time. For if we are to appreciate the nature of change in age systems, it is important to identify what is subject to change. First of all, the term "age structure" refers to a social structure, a fairly stable arrangement of two or more age strata--in our society, childhood, adolescence, middle age, and old age, for example. Members of each age stratum are governed by socially defined age norms (Riley et al., 1972; Riley, 1976). They are expected to fill certain roles and not to occupy others--in our society, for example, sixteen-year-olds are expected to go to school, but they are considered too young to marry. Members of the various strata are expected to act and think in a manner appropriate to their age and the age-related

roles they fill. Older people are thought to be wise from
experience (Harris, 1975); young people are often forgiven
the follies attributed to inexperience. Although definitions
of age-appropriate roles and behaviors may be influenced by
biological capacities, these definitions are in large part
socially determined. Thus an eight-year-old girl cannot give
birth; but in some societies in the not-too-distant past, and
perhaps still today, eight-year-old girls could marry. (For
other examples, see Kertzer in this volume.)

The capsulized description of the age structure I have
put forth does not mean that the age structure itself is
simple. Actually, the age structure includes many different
elements: the number of socially recognized age strata; the
proportion of the population in each stratum; the location
and distinctiveness of the boundaries between the strata; the
social definitions of roles, behavior, and appropriate age of
role partners of members of each age stratum, and the
characteristic relations among the different strata--whether
conflict or cooperation, or dependence or independence is
emphasized, for example. Each of these elements is subject
to change; but rarely is change confined to just one element.
Rather, as part of a system of age stratification, a change
in one element is likely to trigger change in other elements.
Further, as these changes take place, the nature of aging
over the life course is transformed.

Viewed in these terms, the age system of our own society
has changed dramatically from colonial times to the present.
First, the number of socially recognized age strata has
increased. There has been the discovery of adolescence with
its characteristic roles and age-related attitudes and
behaviors. And some scholars have suggested that we are now
witnessing the bifurcation of the old age stratum into the
young-old and the old-old (Neugarten, 1974; see Fry and Keith
in this volume for the several categories of the old
recognized in non-industrial societies). Second, the
absolute and relative size of the old age stratum has
increased, as it has in most industrial countries. Third,
boundaries between age strata have become more distinct as
primary and high schools have become more strictly age graded
and as age of entry into and exit from the labor force and
assumption of marital and parental roles have become more
standardized (Kett, 1977; Modell et al., 1978). However,
there is some speculation that these recent patterns are now
being reversed and that age grading is becoming less rigid
(Neugarten, 1980).

Fourth, age norms governing attitudes and behavior have
varied in myriad ways. Think of the shifting age norms for

children. In the early 19th century it was acceptable to
teach very young children to read and to send these young
children to infant schools. Later on this early instruction
was considered too strenuous a regimen for children under
five or six. These latter attitudes persisted until the
recent developments of middle-class nursery schools and the
Head Start program (Kaestle and Vinovskis, 1978). When
children reached their preteen and teen years in early
America, many of them were sent out of the parental homes as
boarders, apprentices, or servants. By the late 19th
century, residence patterns of young people had changed.
Many young people remained in the parental home during the
first years of employment and often until they married (Katz
and Davey, 1978; see also chapter by Katz in this volume).
As for the old, according to several historians of old age,
in the colonial period the position of the old was quite
favorable; the old were respected and many of them held
positions of authority. But at least since the post-Civil
War period and possibly before, the prestige and influence of
the old have declined. And, unlike early periods when old
people were expected to remain economically active as long as
possible, today, at least in the decade of the 1970s, old
people are expected to leave the labor force to make room for
the young (Achenbaum, 1978; Fischer, 1978). Many of these
changing age norms have resulted in the moving up or down of
transition points over the life course. As the age at
entering and leaving school, age at marriage, and age at
entering and leaving the labor force, for example, have
changed, so has the experience of growing up and growing
older.

Changing age norms and transition points have, in turn,
affected relations among the age strata. As young people
remained in school longer, they became increasingly dependent
on parents; as mature women resumed education and careers,
they had less time for teen-age children and household
chores. In short, the shape and character of the whole age
system today looks different from that of even a century ago.

Sources of Change

Portraying transformations in the age system constitutes
but one part of the analysis of change. To take off from
Marx's well-known aphorism: scholars have described change;
the point is to interpret it. What then accounts for changes
in age systems? Those who have sought to shed light on this
issue have tended to emphasize forces external to the age
system as the major fount of change. Certainly these sources
of change should be explored fully and I shall comment on
them. But we must also consider a relatively neglected

theme: that is, sources of change inherent in the age
structure itself and the way the internal and external
influences on the age system interact. Let us turn first to
external forces for change.

External Sources of Changing Age Systems

A major issue in discussions about the forces leading to
change in age systems is the role of "modernization." In
particular, much of the debate concerns the view that the
decline in the position of the old and concomitant changes in
the status of the young in the United States and other
Western societies can be attributed to the complex processes
subsumed under the rubric "modernization." Fischer (1978),
for one, challenges this theory. He claims that in the
United States many age-related changes in the status of the
old occurred before the period of industrialization,
urbanization, and growth of mass education (see also,
Achenbaum, 1978: Kett, 1977). These issues deserve further
examination. But here I want to suggest that as
all-encompassing as the term modernization may be—after all,
it has been used to refer to such processes as
industrialization, urbanization, educational upgrading,
growth of large-scale and bureaucratic organizations, and the
emergence of a distinctive set of values—the modernization
model of change in age systems is actually limited. It does
not account adequately for the differential impact of
modernizational processes within a society or across
societies. As the Katz chapter in this volume shows, for
example, industrialization in the second half of the 19th
century affected the family cycle of middle class and working
class North American families differently (see also, Hogan in
this volume for class and other subgroup variations in the
timing of early life transitions). Moreover, the
modernization model does not deal with changes in societies
in premodern periods or in societies that have reached the
pinnacle of modernization—a point to which I will return.

This is not to say that modernization processes have
played no part in changing age systems. We know that
colonialism, contact with industrial countries, the
introduction of mass education, and political development
have impinged on and helped to shape the age systems of many
premodern and relatively undifferentiated societal groups. A
few specific examples from recent ethnographies are cases in
point. In an urban Hausa community in Nigeria, women in
purdah (that is, who are spatially segregated and restricted)
were able to carry on trading activities from their homes
because their children did errands and engaged in street
trading for them. But, as primary education expanded, the

time that children had to help their mothers was curtailed. An indirect effect was to cut off these women from communication with the outside world and to limit their independent economic activities. Thus not only were children's roles affected, but also their relations with their mothers (Schildkrout, 1978). Among the Sidamo of Ethiopia, the formalized judicial structure in the larger society competed with and encroached upon important functions of older men (Hamer, 1970). In a number of societies, new wage-earning opportunities for young men have helped to promote a degree of economic independence from elders (Bledsoe, 1980; Schapera [1940] 1971).

Important as such influences are, age systems in premodern groups have changed as a result of forces not linked to modernization per se. Several societal groups with highly structured and formalized age set systems apparently "borrowed" these systems from other premodern, nonindustrial societal groups (Foner and Kertzer, 1978). Age set systems may also change as a result of environmental forces. If the membership of a given age grade is reduced by epidemics or natural disasters, for example, openings are created which, in turn, can hasten the timing of the transition into that age grade.

In modern, industrial societies age systems have also responded to external forces that are not directly related to modernization. Wars have had both long-term and short-term impact. World War I depleted a cohort of young men in several European countries and thus affected the relative size of the age strata. A French sociologist suggests that members of the immediate post World War I cohort had access to jobs that had become vacant as a result of the massacre of young men in the preceding cohort. According to this scholar, this shift to a youthful establishment contributed to the decade of the roaring 20's (Kriegel, 1978). In the United States there was an interruption of the secular trend toward declining labor force participation of older men during the period of World War II (Riley and Foner, 1968). And, the peace time draft in the period following World War II seems to have motivated many young men to complete their higher education without interruption, thus affecting the timing of subsequent transitions into marriage and parenthood (Winsborough, 1979).

Or, consider the impact of a change in legislation. Changes in Social Security regulations in the United States lowering the age when retirement benefits could be claimed played an important part in the unanticipated trend toward early retirement, in effect helping to redefine the

appropriate age of exit from the labor force. The spread of
social welfare entitlements has underwritten norms of
independent residence among older people. A century ago few
widows lived by themselves; in 1978 more than a third of
women 65 and over lived alone (U.S. Bureau of the Census,
1979). Hess and Waring (1978) suggest that with increasing
societal rather than private responsibility for the economic
welfare and health of older people, relations between
middle-aged adults and their elderly parents have come to
rest increasingly on a voluntaristic rather than an
obligatory basis. That such developments in the lives of old
people are not directly associated with important indicators
of modernization is suggested by a study which finds that in
Japan--a highly industrialized and urbanized society--
residential patterns and roles of older people are unlike
those in the United States. A majority of older people live
with their children, and older men in Japan are more likely
to be in the labor force than older men in the United States
(Palmore, 1975).

Changes in other systems of stratification can also
affect the age stratification system. Changes in women's
roles--increased labor force participation and higher
educational attainments--have helped to reverse a long-term
trend toward declining age at marriage. In addition, the
phenomenon of the "older parent" is receiving attention as
more and more women, having first established themselves in
their careers, venture to have their first child in their
thirties.

My general point is that age systems in all periods and
in all types of societies are subject to change. To focus
only on the impact of modernization is to pass over important
stimuli to change. Further, whatever the nature of external
forces of change, these forces do not have the same impact on
all sectors of the society. Nor are the consequences for the
age system of such external pressures automatic or even
predictable. That brings me to what I have called internal
sources of change in age systems.

Internal Sources of Change in Age Systems

By internal source of change I refer to factors related
to the operation of the age system itself. These processes
provide the motive power and the agencies of change, whether
or not the processes themselves are activated by economic,
political, social, or demographic trends external to the age
system.

One impetus to change stems from age conflicts which are
endemic to age systems. Like other stratification systems,

the age stratification system is characterized by structured
social inequality. The young, middle-aged, and the old do
not have equal access to the social goods of a society--to
material benefits and positions of great power and prestige.
These inequalities may be legitimated by beliefs that the
young will get "theirs" one day or that the old had their
turn. But often the young feel that they are not getting
theirs as rapidly as they want or need, while the old do not
want to give up privileges (See Chapter by N. Foner in this
volume, for example). The result is a tug of war--sometimes
open, sometimes muted--between age strata in the family, at
work, and occasionally throughout the whole society (A.
Foner, 1974; Foner and Kertzer, 1978).

Conflicts over the distribution of social rewards are
especially likely to lead to change when another source of
age conflict is brought into play. For age conflicts are
also kindled by the different collective histories of
successive cohorts. (By cohort, I refer to a group of people
born in the same time period). These dissimilar experiences
often engender conflicting values and world views and clashes
over life styles, cultural tastes, life goals, and political
policies. Without institutionalized power to impose their
views, the powerless--typically the young with fresh
viewpoints--have at times resorted to militant struggles to
press their case. Resolutions of such open clashes can lead
to change in the age system. Although the youthful militancy
of the 1960s and early 1970s seems far behind, the student
rebels did leave a legacy: a degree of pluralism about
appropriate behavior and appearance for young people and
greater youth representation in the governance of
institutions in which young people are involved. And young
people's actions played a part in lowering the voting age in
the United States.

Whether or not the succession of cohorts gives rise to
age conflicts, <u>cohort succession</u> generates change in age
systems in another way. As a cohort proceeds through
childhood, adolescence, adulthood, and old age, its members
are guided and molded by age-related social expectations and
constrained by the roles open or closed to them in each age
stratum. But the membership of the different age strata is
constantly shifting as people grow out of childhood,
adolescence and so on and are replaced by members of new
cohorts. Thus no two cohorts experience their youth,
adulthood, or old age under the exact same historical
circumstances (Riley, 1978; for some specific examples, see
chapter by Vinovskis in this volume on changes in the
experiences of successive cohorts of ministers in early
America and chapter by Simkus in this volume on changing
occupational patterns among successive cohorts in post-World

War II Hungary). As members of each new cohort deal with the unique social environment that only they face at a given age--only one cohort faced World War II in their twenties, only one cohort retired in the early years after the establishment of the Social Security system in the United States--they leave their mark, often creating new age norms. Cohorts just assuming adult roles tend to have a special impact. Not having had time to firmly internalize established ways, they are open to new modes of thinking and acting. As we know, the responses of important sectors of young people have been inscribed in the names given to their cohorts--the "lost", the "silent", and the "me" generations. Members of given cohorts can also help to redefine age norms at later ages, as have the mature women who pioneered the return to formal education in the person's middle years and the large number of older people who chose to retire before age 65. Although sectors of these different cohorts were reacting to changes in the whole society, their responses were not inevitable; nor had they been predicted.

A third, related basis of change inherent in the operation of the age system can be traced to the <u>tension</u> that frequently arises <u>between the structure of the age system and the continual flow of new cohorts</u> into that system. Societies must deal with the constant infusion of new members and the death of the old. An important function of age norms is to regulate this shifting stream by establishing the ages at which it is appropriate to undertake certain tasks and assume certain roles. There is a time to marry, to have children, to retire. But age norms may not take into account shifts in the size and composition of successive cohorts. In the United States, for example, there has been a boom and bust cycle of births over the past forty years that has produced successive cohorts of vastly different size (Easterlin, 1980). Under such conditions, it is difficult to assure conformity to societal age norms for assuming or leaving given roles. There are either too many or too few school openings, jobs, marriage partners for the number of candidates of the prescribed age. As Waring (1975) points out, one solution to these imbalances is to change the age norms. Too few job openings? Keep students in school longer. Too few potential husbands the right age? Marry younger men or stay single. Not enough openings for middle and top management? Devise incentives for older people to retire earlier.

Currently much of the talk about the "problems" of social security in the United States involves just such a change. As is well known, when the baby boom cohorts start to retire in about thirty years or so, there will be relatively fewer workers per each retiree than there are today. Since the social security system is on a pay-as-you-go basis, with current workers paying for current retirees, there is concern about how to keep the social security system--which underwrites an important share of retirees' income--viable. One of the proposed solutions is to find ways to raise the average age of retirement--by direct regulations, by incentives to stay in the labor force, or by disincentives to retire (Foner and Schwab, 1981). If such solutions are implemented, they will ramify through the whole age system, affecting job openings for young people, promotion opportunities for adults, decisions about when to marry and have children, and relations among young, middle aged, and old.

Conclusion

What, then, about the future? Is there some decisive underlying direction of change? Some have suggested that a dominant historical pattern in the United States has been the increasing differentiation of the age structure into more and more clearly defined age strata (Smelser and Halpern, 1978). Can we predict that such a process of increasing differentiation will continue? Or are we becoming an age irrelevant society--that is, will age norms be loosened so that chronological age will become less and less important in the assignment of roles and the definitions of appropriate behavior (Neugarten 1980)? Looking forward to the turn of the century, perhaps we can make a few specific predictions with some confidence, as, for example, that the proportion of older people in the society will be greater than it is today or that old age will be healthier (see chapters by Johnston and Hoover, and Torrey in this volume). But the direction of large-scale political, economic, and social trends is uncertain. And given the interplay between these external forces which impinge on the age system and the operation of processes internal to the age system, forecasts about master trends are risky. In dealing with societal changes, new cohorts will help fashion future age systems and some of the outcomes will not have been anticipated. People may not make history as they please, but--to reverse Marx again--they do make history, often with unintended consequences.

References

Achenbaum, W. Andrew. 1978. Old Age in the New Land. Baltimore: The John Hopkins Press.

Bledsoe, Caroline H. 1980. Women and Marriage in Kpelle Society. Stanford, California: Stanford University Press.

Easterlin, Richard A. 1980. <u>Birth and Fortune</u>. New York:
    Basic Books.

Fischer, David Hackett. 1978. <u>Growing Old in America</u>. New
    York: Oxford University Press. Expanded Edition.

Foner, Anne. 1974. "Age Stratification and Age Conflict in
    Political Life." <u>American Sociological Review</u> 39: 187-96.

Foner, Anne and David I. Kertzer. 1978. "Transitions over
    the Life Course: Lessons From Age-Set Societies."
    <u>American Journal of Sociology</u>, 83: 1081-1104.

Foner, Anne and Karen Schwab. 1981. <u>Aging and Retirement</u>.
    Monterey, California: Brooks/Cole.

Hamer, John H. 1970. "Sidamo Generational Class Cycles: A
    Political Gerontocracy." <u>Africa</u> 40 (1); 50-70.

Harris, Louis and Associates. 1975. <u>The Myth and Reality of
    Aging in America</u>. Washington, D.C.: National Council
    on the Aging.

Hess, Beth B. and Joan M. Waring. 1978. "Parent and Child
    in Later Life: Rethinking the Relationship." In <u>Child
    Influences on Marital and Family Interaction</u>, edited by
    Richard M. Lerner and Graham B. Spanier, pp. 241-273.
    New York: Academic Press.

Kaestle, Carl F. and Maris A. Vinovskis. 1978. "From Apron
    Strings to ABCs: Parents, Children, and Schooling in
    Nineteenth-Century Massachusetts." In <u>Turning Points</u>:
    <u>Historical and Sociological Essays on the Family</u>, edited
    by John Demos and Sarane S. Boocock, pp. 39-80.
    Chicago: University of Chicago Press.

Katz, Michael B. and Ian E. Davey. 1978. "Youth and Early
    Industrialization in a Canadian City. In <u>Turning
    Points: Historical and Sociological Essays on the
    Family</u>, edited by John Demos and Sarane S. Boocock, pp.
    81-119. Chicago: University of Chicago Press.

Kett, Joseph F. 1977. <u>Rites of Passage</u>. New York: Basic
    Books.

Kriegel, Annie. 1978. "Generational Difference: The
    History of an Idea." <u>Daedalus</u>, 107: 23-38.

Modell, John, Frank F. Furstenberg, Jr., and Douglas Strong.
    1978. The Timing of Marriage in the Transition to

Adulthood: Continuity and Change, 1860-1975." In Turning Points: Historical and Sociological Essays on the Family, edited by John Demos and Sarane S. Boocock, pp. 120-150. Chicago: University of Chicago Press.

Neugarten, Bernice L. 1974. "Age Groups in American Society and the Rise of the Young-Old." Annals of the American Academy of Political and Social Science. 415: 187-198.

Neugarten, Bernice L. 1980. "Acting One's Age: New Rules for Old." Psychology Today, 13: 66-80.

Palmore, Erdman. 1975. "The Status and Integration of the Aged in Japanese Society." Journal of Gerontology, 30: 199-208.

Riley, Matilda White. 1976. "Age Strata in Social Systems." In Handbook of Aging and the Social Sciences, edited by Robert H. Binstock and Ethel Shanas, pp. 189-217. New York: Van Nostrand Reinhold.

Riley, Matilda White. 1978. "Aging, Social Change, and the Power of Ideas." Daedalus, 107: 39-52.

Riley, Matilda White and Anne Foner. 1968. Aging and Society. Volume 1. An Inventory of Research Findings. New York: Russell Sage.

Riley, Matilda White, Marilyn Johnson, and Anne Foner. 1972. Aging and Society. Volume 3. A Sociology of Age Stratification. New York: Russell Sage.

Schapera, Isaac. (1940) 1971. Married Life in an African Tribe. Harmondsworth: Penguin Press.

Schildkrout, Enid. 1978. "Age and Gender in Hausa Society: Socio-economic Roles of Children in Urban Kano." In Sex and Age as Principles of Social Differentiation, edited by J.S. La Fontaine, pp. 109-137. New York: Academic Press.

Smelser, Neil J. and Sidney Halpern. 1978. "The Historical Triangulation of Family, Economy, and Education," in Turning Points: Historical and Sociological Essays on the Family, edited by John Demos and Sarane S. Boocock, pp. 288-315. Chicago: University of Chicago Press.

Uhlenberg, Peter. 1969. "A Study of Cohort Life Cycles: Cohorts of Native Born Massachusetts Women, 1830-1920." Population Studies, 23: 407-420.

U.S. Bureau of the Census. 1979. <u>Statistical Abstract of</u>
<u>the United States</u> Washington, D.C.: Government Printing
Office.

Waring, Joan M. 1975. "Social Replenishment and Social
Change: The Problem of Disordered Cohort Flow."
<u>American Behavioral Scientist</u> 19: 237-256.

Winsborough, Halliman H. 1979. "Changes in the Transition
to Adulthood." In <u>Aging from Birth to Death</u>, edited by
Matilda W. Riley, pp. 137-152. Boulder, Colorado:
Westview Press.